Also by Richard R. Niebuhr

RESURRECTION AND HISTORICAL REASON

THIS BOOK IS
THE GIFT OF
Rev. R. REES, C.M.
TO THE LIBRARY
OF KENRICK

SCHLEIERMACHER
ON CHRIST AND RELIGION

SCHLEIERMACHER

ON CHRIST AND RELIGION

A New Introduction

RICHARD R. NIEBUHR

CHARLES SCRIBNER'S SONS, NEW YORK

Quotations from the authorized English translation of
Schleiermacher's "The Christian Faith" are given with
the permission of the publishers, T. & T. Clark, Edinburgh

A-10.65[M]

PRINTED IN THE UNITED STATES OF AMERICA

Library of Congress Catalog Card Number 64-22393

ACKNOWLEDGMENTS

My particular thanks are due to the United States Government for the Fulbright research grant in 1958 that made my study of Schleiermacher possible; to the American Association of Theological Schools for supplementary funds, which helped my family to accompany me to Germany; to Harvard University for the leave of absence it gives to its Assistant Professors; and to the Ruprecht-Karl-Universität in Heidelberg for its hospitality and the use of its library. I wish also to thank the *Harvard Theological Review* for its consent to my publishing again the article, "Schleiermacher: Theology as Human Reflection," which appears here in somewhat altered form as Chapter III.

I apologize for the large number of footnotes, but the present state of affairs in Schleiermacher interpretation makes it advisable to refer constantly to the original sources, in order that the reader may easily judge for himself the meaning of Schleiermacher's own words and the plausibility of my exposition. I should also explain that I do not carry on a controversy with other books about Schleiermacher, save on isolated occasions, for such a procedure would have doubled the volume of the following pages. What I have to say about Schleiermacher must stand, not strictly on its own, but in more or less silent conversation with other expositors and interpreters of Schleiermacher's thinking. I am nearly equally indebted to the authors with whom I disagree and to those from whom I have more directly learned: to Emil Brunner and Karl Barth, and to Wilhelm Dilthey from whose prodigious biography as well as essays I have taken much information. The careful editing, exposition and explanation on the part of August Twesten, Hermann Mulert, Hermann Süskind, Rudolf Odebrecht, Otto Braun and Prof. Redeker have been indispensable to me; and many students in the Schleiermacher seminars at Harvard Divinity School have put me in their debt for their fresh criticism of the theologian.

R. R. N.

CAMBRIDGE, MASSACHUSETTS

CONTENTS

CONTENTS

LIST OF ABBREVIATIONS

Braun II — *Fr. D. E. Schleiermacher, Werke: Auswahl in vier Bänden,* ed. O. Braun and D. J. Bauer, Leipzig (1913), Vol. II. The second volume of these four is a critical edition of Schleiermacher's philosophical ethics, containing both essays and lecture notes.

Br. I-IV — *Aus Schleiermachers Leben, in Briefen,* Vols. I and II, 2nd edition, Berlin (1860); Vols. III and IV, Berlin (1861, 1863).
E.T.: *The Life of Schleiermacher as unfolded in his Autobiography and Letters,* trans. F. Rowan, London (1860). A translation of Vols. I and II of the German, with some letters omitted.

Dial. — *Dialektik, aus Schleiermachers handschriftlichem Nachlasse,* ed. L. Jonas; *Friedrich Schleiermachers sämmtliche Werke,* Division III, Vol. 4, part 2, Berlin (1839). This, the first edition of the material, includes Schleiermacher's own lecture notes and those of students from several different years. The lectures of 1814 form the basis. The introduction Schleiermacher wrote for the book that he did not live to work on is also included.

Dial. (O) — *Friedrich Schleiermachers Dialektik,* ed. Rudolf Odebrecht, Leipzig (1942). This volume includes the introduction Schleiermacher prepared for the press himself, the lecture notes for 1822, and a reconstitution of the lectures based on student notebooks, which is distinguished from Schleiermacher's own notes.

"Erwählung" — "Ueber die Lehre von der Erwählung, besonders in Beziehung auf Herrn Dr. Bretschneiders Aphorismen"; *sämmtliche Werke,* Division I, Vol. 2, Berlin (1836).

Gl. *Der Christliche Glaube nach den Grundsätzen der evangelischen Kirche im Zusammenhange dargestellt,* 7th ed., 2 vols., ed. Martin Redeker, Berlin (1960). A critical edition with appendices and Schleiermacher's own marginal notations.

E.T.: *The Christian Faith,* trans. H. R. Mackintosh and J. S. Stewart, Edinburgh (1948, 2nd impression); also New York (1963), 2 vols. A translation of the 2nd, revised edition.

All references are to the proposition and text following, indicated by the proposition number, e.g., Gl., §3, or to a particular paragraph within the text following a proposition, e.g., Gl., §3,2.

Herm. *Fr. D. E. Schleiermacher, Hermeneutik: Nach den Handschriften,* ed. H. Kimmerle, Heidelberg (1959). A new edition that omits all student notes. Some references are to the first edition edited by F. Lücke, *sämmtliche Werke,* Division I, Vol. 7, Berlin (1838), and are so marked.

KD[1] and KD[2] *Schleiermachers Kurze Darstellung des theologischen Studiums,* ed. Heinrich Scholz, Leipzig (1910). A critical edition containing the materials of the first (1811) and the second, revised edition (1830). The superscript (1) refers to that of 1811, and (2) to 1830, in which the system of numbering the propositions was altered. All references to the 2nd edition may be found also in the

E.T.: *Brief Outline of the Study of Theology,* trans. W. Farrer, Edinburgh (1850), under the corresponding §.

Leben Jesu *Das Leben Jesu, Vorlesungen an der Universität zu Berlin im Jahr 1832 gehalten von Dr. Friedrich Schleiermacher,* ed. K. A. Rütenik; *sämmtliche Werke,* Division I, Vol. 6, Berlin (1864). This volume contains Schleiermacher's notes and student notebook materials.

LS[1] — *Leben Schleiermachers,* by Wilhelm Dilthey, Berlin (1870). This first edition contains an appendix of early fragments and essays, etc., entitled "Denkmale."

LS[2] — *Leben Schleiermachers,* by Wilhelm Dilthey, ed. Hermann Mulert, Berlin (1922). Mulert has included more material from Dilthey's literary remains and omitted the "Denkmale."

Redeker — Material to be found in the 7th German edition of Gl. listed above but not in the English translation.

Reden — *Reden über die Religion,* ed. G. Ch. B. Pünjer, Braunschweig (1879). Critical edition.
E.T.: *On Religion: Speeches to its Cultured Despisers,* trans. John Oman, London (1893). A translation of Schleiermacher's third, revised edition. The pagination of the Harper Torchbook edition (New York, 1958) is the same.

SW — *Friedrich Schleiermachers sämmtliche Werke,* Berlin (1835–1864). The only edition of Schleiermacher's collected works. It falls into three divisions: I, theological subjects; II, sermons; III, philosophical and related subjects. Citations give the division in Roman numerals and the volume in Arabic numerals, e.g., SW III/3.

Send. — *Schleiermachers Sendschreiben über seine Glaubenslehre an Lücke,* ed. Hermann Mulert; *Studien zur Geschichte des neueren Protestantismus,* ed. H. Hoffmann and L. Zscharnack, Giessen (1908). The page numbers in parentheses refer to the Sendschreiben as they appear in the *sämmtliche Werke,* I/2.

Wf. — *Schleiermachers Weihnachtsfeier,* ed. Hermann Mulert; *Philosophische Bibliothek,* Vol. 117, Leipzig (1908). A critical edition. All page numbers cited in the footnotes below are of the first edition of 1806, as given by Mulert. An English translation, entitled *Christmas Eve: A Dialogue on the Celebration of Christmas,* Edinburgh (1890), was made by W. Hastie. It is, however, all but unknown in the United States and extant in such a limited number that I have not included page references to it, in distinction from the practice followed for other works that do have an English translation and that requite citation by page number rather than by §.

NOTE ON TRANSLATIONS:

I have used the English language translations of the *Speeches on Religion* and the *Soliloquies,* although I refer the reader on occasion to the German critical edition of the first work. In most instances I have employed the English translation of the *Der Christliche Glaube* or *The Christian Faith* by Mackintosh and Stewart but in some cases I have preferred to give my own translation from the German. All quotations from other works and lectures by Schleiermacher are rendered in my own translation.

SCHLEIERMACHER
ON CHRIST AND RELIGION

INTRODUCTION

§1.

My intention in this book is to describe the most critical and characteristic features of Friedrich Schleiermacher's theological thinking. The art of photography affords the most suitable analogy to my purpose, for the photographer who focuses his camera upon a fellowman seeks to capture one instantaneous glance that expresses and conveys the infinite mobility of his subject. I have tried to focus my own mind upon a series of moments in Schleiermacher's thinking that are revelatory of the man's theological style. Accordingly, the following chapters are not an intellectual biography, and I have not set out to reduplicate what Wilhelm Dilthey accomplished nearly one hundred years ago in his inestimable life of the young Schleiermacher. Nor does this book constitute my version of its subject's "real" or "ultimate" importance for the history of Protestant theology. Those who are looking for a summary of Schleiermacher's theology and philosophy—for the results, so to speak—may consult other works. It is Schleiermacher's thinking in motion that has aroused my interest, that I have attempted to represent here, and that I hope will prove to be instructive to others, as I believe it has been to me.

Each of the "moments" in Schleiermacher's thinking that I have chosen for description and analysis displays the formulation of an important material consideration, principle or conviction. Each of them reveals a significant characteristic of Schleiermacher's theology. In the first part of the book, I have dealt with a small and little known writing by Schleiermacher, *Die Weihnachtsfeier: Ein Gespräch,* or *The Christmas Eve: A Dialogue,* and with his lectures on hermeneutics and ethics. *The Christmas Eve* is important for a number of reasons which I set out in Chapter I. Here it is enough, perhaps, to say that Schleiermacher composed the dialogue during a time when the external circumstances of his life were changing in a drastic way and when the intellectual interests were crystallizing that were to occupy him for the remainder of his career. Consequently, while the first publication, *On Religion: Speeches to its Cultured Despisers* (1799), is far better known, *The Christmas Eve* exhibits a more mature Schleiermacher, a chastened Schleiermacher, and a Schleiermacher already engaged in intense systematic thinking and in teaching theology. In particular, it gives the reader a much more critical discussion of human religion than does the *Speeches;* it represents Schleiermacher's thinking about the specific nature of Christianity and shows how his increased grasp of the social and historical character of human existence and of Christianity has carried him far beyond the standpoint of 1799. Furthermore, whoever would understand the greatest of Schleiermacher's works, *The Christian Faith,* can never appreciate the idea of theology his magnum opus embodies unless he acquaints himself with the notion of religious and Christian affective states that *The Christmas Eve* portrays.

The second "moment" described here is Schleiermacher's lectures on hermeneutics. These lectures are of interest to the historian of ideas, because they are the inspiration for Wilhelm Dilthey's idea of a historical reason and because they are the point of departure for so much of contemporary hermeneutical theory. But they are of importance for understanding Schleiermacher's theological thinking, because we perceive in them the development of his conception of speech (*Rede*) and understanding (*Verstehen*), a conception that is implicit in his employment of the device of dialogue in *The Christmas Eve* and that is fundamental to the theory of communication and preaching upon which *The Christian Faith* depends. The hermeneutics illustrates the intensity of Schleiermacher's preoccupation with man as a historical being and with the historical character of human understanding.

The historical character of human reason in general is more broadly delineated in the third "moment" of Part I, the description and analysis of Schleiermacher's philosophical ethics. The ethics is Schleiermacher's philosophy of history and culture. In it the ideas of human society and individuality emerge, and the reader realizes that these two ideas are of major import for the whole range of Schleiermacher's thought. It also becomes evident that he attends closely to man as a feeling being, not simply because feeling offers a convenient haven to a theology no longer allied to metaphysics, but because human history and ethical agency demand of the philosopher and theologian that he consider human nature under this aspect. At the same time, the ethics makes it impossible to stereotype Schleiermacher as a theologian of mere feeling; his theology obviously involves long and careful reflection on human nature as such and particularly on human reason and history.

These two chapters of Part I are meant to furnish an introduction to the most influential elements at work in Schleiermacher's highly individual style of thinking. Together they provide the reader with a view of the moral, historical and religious world as it appeared to this theologian.

Part II of this book concentrates on a fourth "moment," *The Christian Faith. The Christian Faith* is, to be sure, a systematic theology that encompasses all of the doctrines of Protestant Christianity, but I have directed my discussion of the work toward the answering of three related questions: What is the nature of Christianity, according to Schleiermacher, and how is it related to other human religions and to human religiousness as such? What is theology and what place does it have in Christianity? How is the redeemer, Jesus of Nazareth, related to human nature, to human religion and to theology? These questions are fundamental to the particular procedure of the author of *The Christian Faith*, and they are also, I believe, fundamental to present-day Protestant theology. This book about Schleiermacher is, then, a study of religion, Christ and theology.

§2.

The reader is probably aware that contemporary Protestant theologians and students of the history of Christian thought are, for the most part, uncomfortable in the presence of Friedrich Schleiermacher. The cause of this discomfort is the fact that Schleiermacher is mainly responsible for the redirecting of Protestant theology at the beginning of the nineteenth century. He broke the stalemate of rationalism and orthodoxy, and set the mind of the Protestant church free once more. As such, he holds an undeniable position as a reformer inside Protestantism, the most influential thinker since Calvin. But while there is no gainsaying that Schleiermacher was a gigantic revolutionary figure, many men today deeply deplore the motives, the methods and the results of his revolutionary activities. Honesty to the reader constrains me to state here at the outset that I am not one of these men. Having made my confession, however, I must immediately add that the attitude of reverence toward Schleiermacher's theology—an attitude which I admit I have not detected abroad in the world—will do no more to further the cause that theologians serve than has the prevailing prejudice against him and his mind, in the recent past.

What is needful is that his theological thinking be recognized for what it is, criticized and used to whatever advantage it may lend itself. But there has been relatively little disposition to adopt such an attitude toward Schleiermacher in recent times, especially since the advent of crisis theology immediately after World War I. The most violently adverse interpretation of the theology of this father of modern Protestantism appeared in the book entitled *Die Mystik und das Wort,*[1] by Emil Brunner. *Die Mystik und das Wort* is in fact not so much a stringent critique of Schleiermacher as it is a manifesto of the new continental orthodoxy, and an onslaught upon all that Brunner found vexatious in the "liberalism" of the nineteenth century and upon Schleiermacher because, as one who stood at its beginning, he personified the milieu. The value of Brunner's book today lies in its position as an early specimen of neo-orthodox polemics. The most brilliant spirit of the new theology of the twenties was Karl Barth, and he also gave to the public his opinions of Schleiermacher, in several articles now collected in a volume of essays, *Die Theologie und die Kirche.*[2] Barth said, at the conclusion of one essay, that he regarded this theologian as one with whom he could not suppose that he had finished upon the "first felling of the trees," or the second or even the third, and he would with his friend Brunner have to conduct a battle against the man that permitted plenty of room for maneuvering. Despite this rather guarded profession of respect for Schleiermacher, Barth at this point was not above treating his thinking in a lofty fashion, indiscriminately mixing together materials gathered from a period covering thirty years or more of Schleiermacher's authorship and preaching, and offering as his distillate of this brew the doctrine: peace is truth.[3]

The trend, set by these two pioneers of the theological movement that has passed through the mood of judgment upon the nineteenth century to the constructive plateau of so-called neo-orthodoxy, has continued into the present. One need only select

[1] Tübingen (1924, 1st ed.).
[2] Zürich (no date).
[3] *Ibid.*, pp. 149f.

at random today a book touching upon developments of one kind or another in the Protestant theological world since the Enlightenment, locate Schleiermacher in the entries of the index, and quite likely one will find in the corresponding text either a criticism that is offered as self-evident or a denunciation of the man, but there is rarely any documentation or independent assessment of the tradition so firmly proclaimed by Emil Brunner and Karl Barth long ago. Among the books lying at hand this moment of writing, I read a warning against Schleiermacher's "philosophical mysticism," in a recent volume dealing with the theological idea of history.[4] The author is a staunch representative of the general view which we associate principally with Rudolph Bultmann and Friedrich Gogarten and which we customarily refer to, in a loose way, as existentialism. He offers, as warrant for this warning, Emil Brunner's "devastating criticism" of Schleiermacher in *Die Mystik und das Wort.* Yet the intellectual tradition Bultmann embodies draws many of its insights ultimately from Schleiermacher, although that fact has not been much acknowledged. However, existentialists have precedence for their disapproval of Schleiermacher since Kierkegaard himself was critical, while at the same time borrowing important elements from the doctrine of sin in Schleiermacher's principal work, *The Christian Faith.*[5] Another, more recent chapter, which surveys the nineteenth century, gratuitously repeats the old remonstrance against Schleiermacher's Spinozism, saying: "Schleiermacher requires little more than that the universe as a whole be understood as a living and infinite unity on which each of its parts must be seen as absolutely dependent. Specifically, Schleiermacher finds fully acceptable the philosophy of Spinoza."[6] And a study of hermeneutics asserts that in Schleier-

[4] Carl Michalson, *The Hinge of History: An Existential Approach to the Christian Faith,* New York (1959), p. 106.

[5] *The Journals of Søren Kierkegaard,* trans. and ed. A. Dru, London (1951, 2nd printing), no. 78.

[6] John Cobb, *Living Options in Protestant Theology,* Philadelphia (1962), p. 131.

macher's dogmatic theology we have another example of the philosophy that treats the history of the human race as a self-evolving history of the development of human subjectivity, and that the fact that in Schleiermacher's theology the end point of this evolution is the "self-understanding of Christian faith" does not affect the idealistic presuppositions operative therein.[7] None of these judgments is accurate. But these are examples of no more than passing references to Schleiermacher in strictly contemporary theological writing, occupying a single sentence or a few pages. And one cannot reasonably demand that each and every soul who contributes to the public conversation on current theological issues should make himself a specialist in Schleiermacher scholarship and interpretation. However, they do serve to illustrate the state of affairs.

What is far more serious and discouraging is the survival of real misunderstanding and misinterpretation of Schleiermacher in books that are devoted exclusively to his thought. So, for example, Holger Samson's *Die Kirche als Grundbegriff der theologischen Ethik Schleiermachers*—a book that offers much of value concerning a side of Schleiermacher otherwise virtually neglected—informs the reader that Christ, as a person, is a man just like every other man, according to Schleiermacher, and nothing can be said, therefore, about a relation between God and Christ but only about the influence of a divine spiritual principle in the man Jesus Christ.[8] Nor is it astonishing, Samson writes in another place, that Schleiermacher begins his *Glaubenslehre* with propositions borrowed from philosophy, and derives his principal dogmatic concept of the God-consciousness and of the church from philosophy.[9] These observations are clearly tendentious.

By no means is every allusion to or study of Schleiermacher

[7] Lothar Steiger, *Die Hermeneutik als dogmatisches Problem,* Gütersloh (1961), p. 19.

[8] Basel (1958), p. 48.

[9] *Ibid.,* p. 72, n. 92.

that has appeared in recent years informed by a hostile spirit. The most detailed book on Schleiermacher in English, Richard Brandt's *The Philosophy of Schleiermacher*—now more than twenty years old, to be sure—is quite free of theological bias, although Brandt is critical of his subject on other grounds. More recently there seems to have been something of a renascence of serious interest in Schleiermacher. The book by Samson is one example of this phenomenon, and there are also Felix Flückiger's *Philosophie und Theologie bei Schleiermacher,* Werner Schultz's *Schleiermacher und der Protestantismus, Die Theologie des jungen Schleiermacher* by Paul Seifert, and P. H. Joergensen's independent and valuable study, *Die Ethik Schleiermachers,* to attest it further. I attribute this renascence in part to the towering authority of Karl Barth. Barth's later book on the theology of the nineteenth century has done much to stimulate reading in the original materials, more than has any other secondary source.[10] And though Barth is generally understood as the author of the break with the spirit of nineteenth-century theology, his more mature critique nevertheless served to intrigue many readers with the period. For while he never approved of the era, he has indicated that he could not dismiss it as merely shallow. But of more significance is the fact that Barth has concentrated his attention particularly on Schleiermacher over the years, so that the pages of his manifold publications from the early twenties to the present are filled by colloquies with this theologian who has become one of Barth's chief friendly adversaries. Barth enjoys the larger part of the credit, therefore, for having kept Schleiermacher in the eye of the theological public. Or, if we choose to adopt a less personal interpretation of the history of ideas, we may say that history has selected Barth to be the most audible voice in our times through which the theology of Schleiermacher continues to speak.

[10] *Die protestantische Theologie im 19. Jahrhundert,* Zürich (1946) E.T. *From Rousseau to Ritschl,* London (1959), includes eleven chapters from the original.

But the natural concomitant of this development is the dominance that Barth's interpretation of the history of theology has exercised and still exerts today. Something very nearly approaching a Barthian captivity of the history of modern Christian thought reigns in theology outside of ultra-orthodox circles. It manifests itself in the efforts, sometimes rather strained, to interpret the theology of the Reformation in conformity to the canons of Barth's *Church Dogmatics,* and it also appears in the evident preconceptions with which the nineteenth century and Schleiermacher are interpreted by those who have fallen under the sway of this captivity. I suspect the time to be not far away, when the Barthian reading of the history of Christian thought will be corrected in a fashion comparable to that in which the last generation veered away from the theological presuppositions of Adolf von Harnack's history of dogma. In any case, it is this phenomenon, I believe, that does much to explain the character of Schleiermacher research, in the present, and the general lack of esteem for his theology. Schleiermacher provokes disapproval now on so wide a front, not only because many of his theological positions seemingly ill agree with our prevailing temperament today, but also because he entertained questions that we are inclined to regard as settled and even inappropriate to Christian theology. He drew distinctions where the majority of theologians do not want to have them drawn and refused to separate what the majority believe to be irreconcilable. So much of the present-day distaste for Schleiermacher is basically a suspicion of him as a theologian who fraternizes with philosophy, for example, that one can only suppose his critics assume the divorce of these two disciplines to be an absolutely self-evident axiom, and while Karl Barth himself is not single handedly responsible for this dogma, we can scarcely deny that the ethos of neo-orthodoxy has fostered it vigorously. What is regrettable in this state of affairs is not merely that Schleiermacher may be less wrong-headed and his opponents less profoundly right than they believe but that so few of his critics have troubled, before drawing up a list of his errors, to try on his manner of thinking in order to lend their refutations of his theology a greater semblance of authority. This Barthian captivity severely restricts the freedom of serious study of Schleiermacher, as Samson's book indicates, and also Flückiger's in a more conspicuous fashion.

However, not only the change of fashions in theology but also modern political history has affected Schleiermacher's reputation. Schleiermacher associated in his youth with many Romantic writers, and he lived out his days during the epoch of German idealism. Because he learned much from his early friend, Friedrich von Schlegel, and addressed his first book, the *Speeches,* to such men as Schlegel, he has been identified as the theologian of Romanticism. Romanticism is surely as amorphous an intellectual movement as any that has appeared in the West, and there were as many varieties as participants. But the name is now used largely as a term of reprobation, and those to whom the label is historically applicable are suspect. The German Romantics have been blamed for a share in creating the Third Reich. Schleiermacher has suffered as a consequence of these associations in the eyes of those who read history in what Herbert Butterfield has called the Whig fashion. Moreover, Schleiermacher believed that the Christian church has a responsibility to culture, although he fought for the independence of the church from the state. He also became a nationalist of sorts, during the German struggle with Napoleon. All of these elements of his history have helped to shape the resentment of our times against him as one who espoused a culturally conditioned Protestantism and the German *Volkgeist.* But above all, the fate that put Schleiermacher into the midst of the halcyon days of philosophical idealism has tarnished his name in this post-World War I and World War II era, when idealism is the scapegoat for so many misfortunes and new difficulties that Europe has had to face and endure. Schleiermacher was deeply interested in and influenced by the philosophy of his contemporaries, yet his criticisms of it are not taken as seriously as is his indebtedness to it.

These circumstances have combined to create the habit of inveighing against the author of *The Christian Faith.*

§3.

As I have already stated, much of the impatience with Schleiermacher that one meets today is due to the fact that he wrestles with issues that are no longer regarded as issues, and, on the other hand, he appears to be oblivious of the self-evident character of much that is now taken as absolutely self-evident. Hence, the criticism of Schleiermacher is so often nothing more than the noise of "schools" and parties clashing, rather than an intelligent consideration of the issues and the first principles involved or of the real intentions motivating the other's thinking and molding his style. There is, for example, the Kierkegaardian-Kantian dictum of the infinite abyss between God and man. Although this dictum actually entails a virtual metaphysical dualism, so far as Christian theology is concerned, it is, nevertheless, accepted as a maxim in several quarters of the Protestant theological world today and with particular ardency among the existentialists. The grip of this maxim or convention on the existentialist mind prevents the existentialist theologian from seeing anything but pantheism or "mysticism" in a theology of Schleiermacher's brand. Schleiermacher conceives of the doctrine of creation as an important doctrine. He begins with the absolute dependence of the creature on the creator, not with the infinite abyss between the two. But any theology that takes creation and divine government of the world as seriously as it takes the doctrine of original sin is bound to appear mystical in the eyes of the existentialists.

One among the conclusions to which I have come in the course of my preoccupation with Schleiermacher is, consequently, that the study of the man's mind is eminently worthwhile, if only because it forces the imagination out of the provincialism and parochialism of the present and requires us to think the perennial problems and affirmations of Christianity from a standpoint other than that from which we are accustomed to proceed in our problem-solving for the present and in our assessment of the meaning of the theologians of the past. This I regard as a positive result of engagement with Schleiermacher's theological and philosophical thinking.

A second, more specific benefit is the fact that Schleiermacher finally demands of the reader who does not put him down too quickly that he ask himself what indeed is the proper relation between theology and philosophy. Is theology any less a human enterprise than philosophy? If it is not, ought two human disciplines to be segregated? The tone in which many a commentator informs us that Schleiermacher "deduced" his theology from his philosophy conveys the impression that the man was a rascal performing sleight-of-hand tricks. But even though I do not believe that Schleiermacher did deduce his theology from his philosophy, I wish to point out that he employed his philosophy in the course of his theological thinking in full view of the reader, and sought to conceal nothing. When one encounters a spirit such as this, the shape of the theology of our own times begins to appear differently; and one wonders whether the Platonism, Kantianism and Hegelianism that so deeply inform the theologians of these decades would not profit their work far more, if the presence of these shades was acknowledged. On this score, the existentialist theologians stand up much better when compared to Schleiermacher than do the dogmaticians.

In the third place, I have come to appreciate greatly the fashion in which Schleiermacher connects preaching and theological thinking. Schleiermacher presents theology as the servant of the church's preaching, but he does not worship the church, although his ecclesiology is technically a "high doctrine of the church." The result is that theology is very much a human enterprise, as *The Christian Faith* exemplifies it, and while it is related genetically and linguistically and institutionally to preaching, it is not the same thing as preaching. The mode of theological discourse is recognizably different in Schleiermacher from the mode of homiletics. Theology is an instrument of criticism, not of conversion. Concomitantly, *The Christian Faith* is a tightly knit piece of writing that is not given to animadversions and digressions, on the whole. A stringent consistency or passion for consistency governs the book and imposes upon it a rigorous style of exposition and systematic exclusion of all that is not immediately pertinent. Schleiermacher saved his "aphorisms" and "unscientific postscripts" for publication in other forms.

Whether this tightly plaited character of *The Christian Faith* is a pure virtue, I hesitate to say. I prefer to speak of it simply as a distinguishing feature that has both advantages and disadvantages. The work brings the architectonic impulse to its highest pitch in the history of Protestant theology. So far as I am aware, nothing matches it in this respect either before or after its publication. Schleiermacher contributed heavily to the authority of such a form, and he is doubtlessly the theological prototype for the Tillich of *Systematic Theology* as well as for Barth whose *Church Dogmatics* is actually far looser in its structure because of its encyclopedic and often homiletical nature, although it presents the same external appearance of progressing by stating theses which are explicated in numbered paragraphs, organized around one or two basic principles. This appearance is partly responsible for encouraging the interpretation of *The Christian Faith* as speculative, reminiscent as it is of such a classical philosophical treatise, *more geometrico,* as Spinoza's *Ethics.* To that extent, it contradicts Schleiermacher's own intentions, for he did not believe that theology has only one principium or that it is a deductive, a priori science. When one places it alongside *The Institutes of the Christian Religion,* it suffers by comparison because of its intensely systematic aspect, just as it quite possibly suffers because of the too scrupulous suppression of all that is personal or faintly autobiographical.

I would offer my critical comments on a number of material defects of Schleiermacher's theology, but so much has been said and written by others about these, that further entries on this side of the ledger are hardly necessary. Schleiermacher patently fell short of the insight of the greatest theologians on many a score. If one looks at his theology in the perspective of the long continuum of Christian thought about God, his doctrine of God seems poor indeed and his fear of anthropomorphism misplaced. A man of Schleiermacher's intellectual gifts ought to have seen that anthropomorphism is inevitable in any case, and is not necessarily a blemish in Christian theological thinking. The question is what kind of anthropomorphism one chooses to permit and how one controls it. To vacillate, as Schleiermacher did, by allowing the attributes of love and wisdom to stand as the two properties that represent the essence of the Godhead but by refusing to speak of God as personal is a worse error than to take the risk of personalism and attempt to govern it. Furthermore, the a-personalism of Schleiermacher's doctrine of God does not comport with his intense interest in the constitution of human selfhood, with his insistence that reason appears at its highest in personal, individualized existence, and with his conviction that the human spirit stands nearest to God in the order of creation.

Perhaps it is a more serious defect that his conception of the task of Christian "dogmatics" is not realized with the complete success that it deserved at his own hands. He defined the task of "dogmatics" to be the describing and systematizing of the contents of the Christian religious affections. The definition is an excellent one, in my opinion. But Schleiermacher neglected the hard work of examining the Christian affective life with the critical acumen that such a definition demands. Perhaps his temperament did not fit him for what his intelligence perceived as the right way in which to help theology and preaching forward. I have said something about this default in the chapters that follow. In any case, Schleiermacher falls below the standard set by Jonathan Edwards in his sensitivity and perspicacity in the realm of the Christian and religious affections, and since Edwards had easily a philosophical aptitude equal, if not superior, to Schleiermacher's, the latter cannot match the American theologian precisely at one of the material points where he has the most to contribute still to theological progress. But Schleiermacher was a modern man, in a sense that Edwards never was, and his influence on theology has been far more fateful.

Moreover, none of these faults is sufficient to obscure the lasting significance of the man. Schleiermacher's statement of the function of theology remains unexcelled. That is one of his undisputed contributions. The other that is chief, at least in my own mind, is a contribution especially apparent to a generation raised on Kierkegaard and Barth. Whoever reads Schleiermacher will find himself instructed not only in the doctrines of Christianity but also upon the meaning of Christ and Christianity for man as a religious being.

PART ONE

The Elements of Schleiermacher's Style

Chapter One

THE CHRISTMAS DIALOGUE

§1 HALLE, 1805

Die Weihnachtsfeier: Ein Gespräch,[1] hurriedly composed in the closing weeks of the year 1805, preserves a moment of transition in the life and thinking of its author, Friedrich Daniel Ernst Schleiermacher. In the fall of that year Schleiermacher firmly believed that the promise of his personal happiness had been permanently eclipsed. Eleonore Grunow had once again, but this time with unmistakable finality, withdrawn from their proposed marriage. In so doing she put an end both to her own long vacillation on the moral licitness of divorce from her husband and to Schleiermacher's waiting. Her decision re-created in the preacher and recently appointed professor the old despondency in which he had first accepted the call to the university in Halle and to the vocation from which he had hoped to gain the sense of purpose that his life seemed to lack.[2] Once in an earlier and more confident mood, Schleiermacher had written to his sister, Charlotte, that he could

[1] Hereafter, in the text I refer to the work as *The Christmas Eve* but in the footnotes use the abbreviation, Wf.

[2] LS², p. 702. For an account of the relation between Schleiermacher and Eleonore Grunow, see LS², pp. 523ff. Schleiermacher described Eleonore's final break with himself in a letter to Joachim Christian Gass; *cf. Schleiermachers Briefwechsel mit J. Chr. Gass,* ed. W. Gass, Berlin (1852), p. 38.

easily foresee the time when he would be numbered among those men whose words carry a certain weight, but however agreeable this would be, "nevertheless it would vanish from sight and I should count it as nothing compared to the prospect of a quiet, happy family life. . . . Except in family life all that we enjoy and all that we can do in the world is vain and a deception."[3] Now the future appeared all the more daunting, since, at Halle, Schleiermacher was virtually surrounded by friends whose domestic bliss emphasized the shadow lying over his own prospect. One of these friends was his colleague, Henrich Steffens, whose father-in-law presided nearby over a sophisticated and lively household into which Schleiermacher had been warmly welcomed. Two others were the young pastor, Ehrenfried von Willich, and his wife, with whom Schleiermacher maintained a fatherly correspondence. In October of the same fall, he was hearing from Henriette von Willich about her own joy in the God-given harmony of the life that she and her husband shared. The world, she wrote, had grown more lucid to her.[4] But Schleiermacher was not the man to feed upon his disappointment, and in the same breath that he despaired of the meaning of his life he affirmed his will to build again from the wreckage whatever he could.[5]

Two supports in particular strengthened him, his joy in his friends and his love for his work. Schleiermacher wrote to the von Willichs who had a new child: "With such a daughter and with such friends as all of you are to me, it is simply not possible that I should be defeated by any kind of grief; it must leave room for joy."[6] The motifs of friendship, joy and sorrow often combined themselves in his mind during these days, and more than once Schleiermacher was evidently struck by the peculiar capacity of these moods to arise, apart from any special circumstance, and to

[3] Br. I, pp. 284f. (E.T. I, pp. 272f.).
[4] *Ibid.*, II, p. 32 (E.T. II, p. 32).
[5] *Ibid.*, p. 39 (E.T. II, p. 38).
[6] *Ibid.*, p. 45 (E.T. II, p. 43).

exercise a transforming power upon his whole subjectivity. "Grief has a life of its own that fluctuates in itself and has an ebb and flood; I know of nothing external that can have excited it more especially [now]," he explained several months after Eleonore Grunow's decision. "Certainly joy does not displace sorrow, but both overspread one's entire being."[7] However, joy displayed this power even more apparently to his mind, largely because of its intimate connection with his relations to his friends. "I know right well that the joy emanates only from you and from everything fair that shines upon me from the world; in myself alone I cannot keep it fresh and living, but I am quite content to live through and in you all."[8] He told Ehrenfried von Willich that as a consequence of his loss of Eleonore his friendship with Henrich Steffens had deepened and that he now felt himself to be "the focal point" in which the joy and suffering of his friends were concentrated and reflected back upon them; "and for this I live. Therefore I must also endeavor not to allow the twofold vocation to which I belong to be disturbed by the feelings that still reach out from my own life to sadden it."[9] As *The Christmas Eve* testifies, Schleiermacher attributed not only a personal but also a religious import to these moods; indeed, he had already described Christian piety as excitatory of pain, "the sweet pain of melancholy, so well calculated to sooth other pains. Surely, if there was any good in Saul's soul, it must have been an adagio that exorcised the evil."[10]

The "twofold vocation" that was Schleiermacher's second support consisted of his duties as preacher to the university and of the several courses of lectures he was offering his students. In the fall of this year, 1805, he was still engaged in only the preparation for the university services of worship, but the contemplation of the imminent necessity of expressing his thoughts in an evangelical as

[7] *Ibid.*, p. 53 (E.T. II, p. 47).
[8] *Ibid.*, p. 45 (E.T. II, pp. 43f.).
[9] *Ibid.*, p. 43 (E.T. II, p. 42).
[10] *Ibid.*, I, pp. 330f. (E.T. I, p. 320).

well as academic form gave him some anxiety. Nevertheless, the pulpit had been his first profession, and he could see the advantage of this dual role. At the same time, moreover, Schleiermacher felt no doubts in his liking for the academic society. His letters to his friends, and especially to his lifelong correspondent, Joachim Christian Gass, are filled with accounts of his colleagues and enthusiastic descriptions of details concerning his present and projected lectures. The winter before, he had occupied himself with his first sketch of a theological encyclopedia (the nature and interrelation of the theological disciplines), the published version of which appeared in 1811 as *Kurze Darstellung des theologischen Studiums* (*Brief Outline of the Study of Theology*). In the summer semester of 1805, he had begun his lectures on hermeneutics, drawing upon his long practical experience in the translation of Plato, and now, the following semester, he was further developing his conception of critical interpretation in his lectures on the exegesis of Galatians.[11] Simultaneously, he entered upon the teaching of dogmatic theology and believed he was thereby substantially clarifying his view of Christianity, although he predicted that what he published in a few years would be received as "an offence to the Jews and foolishness to the Greeks."[12] On the other hand, he was repeating his philosophical ethics for the second time, and he saw himself as making real progress in the discipline that he defined as "the science [of the principles] of history" and that he regarded as coördinate in ultimate importance only with "physics," the general science of nature.[13] And finally—and of equal importance with all of these curricular activities and of decisive significance for our understanding of Schleiermacher's mind and spirit—there was the arduous labor that he was still expending upon the translation of Plato, a task which he had first set about in 1799 in coöperation

[11] *Ibid.*, II, p. 40 (E.T. II, p. 39).

[12] *Ibid.*, p. 44 (E.T. II, p. 43).

[13] Braun II, "Brouillon 1805/06," p. 80; *cf.* also KD², §29; also SW III/5, *Sittenlehre*, §55, p. 32.

with Friedrich von Schlegel but now carried on alone. This continuing work on Plato and the parting with Eleonore Grunow were undoubtedly the two most potently shaping events in Schleiermacher's early personal history.

However, the immediately personal was not the only kind of history to claim its due from Schleiermacher at this time. The political fortunes of the German peoples were also affecting the course of his life and thinking. It seemed that no sooner had he adjusted himself to the university environment and its routine than the new mode of existence was threatened by Napoleon. The following year this threat became a reality, and Schleiermacher together with the whole of Halle had to suffer through the violent seizure of the city and the dissolution of the university by order of the French conqueror. Since his brief two years of teaching had been enough to convince him that the academic lecture was to be his métier, this second disruption of plans and hopes was nearly as painful as the first, and he chafed under the restrictions imposed by his involuntary retirement to the "paltry, inactive life" of a private scholar.[14] The same catastrophe also sharply reduced his opportunities to preach. But in the midst of these events, the breadth of Schleiermacher's spirit was revealing something of its true measure.[15] Two sermons delivered in 1806 bespeak this spirit. In the first ("That there is always peace in the Kingdom of God"), Schleiermacher admonished his congregation that peace is born out of strife and the fundamental strife is with ourselves. In the second ("On the Useful Employment of Public Disasters"), he added that it is only in a general crisis, when all external supports are torn away, that we come to know ourselves and God's love. As he carefully watched the progress of Napoleon's ambitions in the German lands and waited for some decisive sign of resistance by Prussia, he crystallized his ideas on the nature of Protestantism, on the signifi-

[14] Br. II, p. 80 (E.T. II, p. 74).
[15] *Cf.* LS², pp. 799ff. for an account of these events.

cance of German culture whose destiny he believed to depend upon Prussia, and on the connection between these two. These emerging convictions were finally to lead him into a position of central importance for the German church and nation. The relationship in which Schleiermacher saw the German spirit and the Protestant idea has since become for many people one of the most objectionable features of his thought and work, closely bound up with his supposed failure to distinguish sharply enough between man's religion and God's revealing of himself, between human creativity and the will of the Creator. But this reputed vice was unquestionably of the splendid kind, inspired by the great virtue of Schleiermacher's growing conviction that an ultimate unity undergirds and expresses itself through the multiform flowering of life in unrepeatable personalities on the individual and corporate levels of existence. Nation as well as church constitute such manifestations of individuality, and the destruction of any one of these forms would mean a loss to the private citizen, the people and the culture. Furthermore, religion, Schleiermacher had already written, is the primary agent for the intuition of this cosmic-historical order of individuality in unity.[16] The course of German history in 1806 gave new meaning to these reflections. Schleiermacher became increasingly fearful of Napoleon as the embodiment of a Roman Catholic desire to extinguish Protestantism and of the imperial French design to unite Europe into a single cultural entity unleavened by the marks of national and religious differences. Living daily with these wider concerns did not wholly obliterate Schleiermacher's sense of personal loss, but the latter remained present more as an impetus than a distraction in the thoughts, forebodings and hopes that held his attention, as Protestantism and the church drew more and more into the foreground. In December of 1806, he wrote to Ehrenfried von Willich that he was certain Germany, the heart of Europe, would reconstitute itself in noble form; "concerning the smallest, the personal, and concerning the greatest, the na-

[16] Reden, *cf.* 2nd speech, *passim.*

tion, I am entirely calm, evil as it looks for them both—but that which lies in between, the means by which the individual can work upon the whole, the entire scientific and ecclesiastical organization, fills me with anxiety. Especially the last! For Napoleon hates Protestantism, as he hates speculation; my prophecy in the *Speeches*, I believe, is not wrong.[17] If that happens, then let us only stand by our posts and shun nothing. I would that I had a wife and child, that I should be second to none in this crisis."[18]

Not long after these events Schleiermacher left Halle to settle in Berlin once again, there to become a notable preacher and to participate in the founding of the university, to assume active membership in the Royal Academy of the Sciences and to enter into a leading rôle in the union of the Reformed and Lutheran communions in Prussia. In the capital he also emerged as an outspoken defender of the rights of the church against the state, and—what is of most immediate interest—he deepened and increased the scope of his critical and systematic powers through his lectures in the university on hermeneutics, ethics, philosophy and theology, as well as on a wide variety of other subjects. *The Christian Faith presented systematically according to the basic propositions of the Evangelical Church,* published in 1821/22 and again in revised form in 1830/31, stands as the intellectual and spiritual monument of this later period of Schleiermacher's life and as the principal nineteenth-century work with which Protestant theology has still to reckon.[19] To be sure, the years at Halle give us a Schleiermacher who is still nearly a decade and a half from his greatest achieve-

[17] In 1806 Schleiermacher revised the *Speeches* and added an epilogue, in which he prophesied that Napoleon would fail, should he try to destroy the Protestant character of Germany. *Cf.* also explanatory note no. 4 to the epilogue in the English translation.

[18] Br. II, p. 79; *cf.* also pp. 63f. (E.T. II, p. 73, pp. 57f.).

[19] For a brief account of Schleiermacher's whole life, see Wilhelm Dilthey, "Friedrich Daniel Ernst Schleiermacher," *Gesammelte Schriften,* Vol. IV, Stuttgart (1959). The same author's essay, "Schleiermachers politische Gesinnung und Wirksamkeit," covers an important side of the subject's maturity and is one of the most illuminating descriptions of Schleiermacher to be found. *Gesammelte Schriften,* Vol. XII, Stuttgart (1960).

ment, but at this time the future author of *The Christian Faith* had already disclosed a mark of his genius that was to stamp his later work in a most conspicuous fashion: the unmistakable relevance of his own thought and activity to the dominant intellectual, cultural and political as well as ecclesiastical issues of the day. Schleiermacher stated the principle of this relevance in its most encompassing form in his lectures on ethics and philosophical thinking, both of which teach the indissoluble relation between internal and external history and seek to expose the roots of thought in the native dialogue of the thinker with his community and with himself.[20] In theology itself, more narrowly conceived, he reiterated the conviction by placing practical theology at the apex of the curriculum and defining it as "thoughtful activity" by those in whom the interests of the living church and "the scientific spirit" are united.[21] During this period, 1804–1806, we see Schleiermacher consciously resolving to embody this polarity more consistently in his own life and turning from preoccupation with personal matters to the service of the educational and ecclesiastical institutions of whose importance he had become acutely aware. The Christmas dialogue portrays many of the decisive moments in this movement. Against the background of the tranquil, provincial life its author was about to leave, it exhibits the themes that molded Schleiermacher's future thinking, themes, to be sure, that were not entirely new to him at that time but that were fraught now with hints of fresh significance.

§2 NEW ACCENTS

The Christmas Eve: A Dialogue is, in the true sense, an occasional writing. In view of the large part that music played in

[20] *Cf.* Dial. (O), pp. 47-56; also *ibid.*, "Einleitung in die Dialektik," pp. 5-44.

[21] KD[2], §257, §258.

Schleiermacher's life at Halle, it is not entirely surprising to hear him say shortly after publication that the original inspiration for the dialogue had come to him as he was leaving a flute concert.[22] He finished the writing in three weeks' time, hoping to show it to his friends on the festival for which the piece was named in 1805, but publishing complications delayed its appearance until the next month.

As the title indicates, Schleiermacher consciously drew upon Plato's example in the composition.[23] Since 1799 he had been occupied not only with the translation of Plato but also with all of the critical problems entailed in such an enterprise. First in company with Friedrich von Schlegel and then singly, Schleiermacher had had to settle to his own satisfaction the problem of the chronological order of the dialogues and the questions of authenticity. The resolution of these difficulties required, in his mind, a definite theory of the dialogic form. Three points which he made in the exposition of his theory of the form merit particular attention, because of their bearing on *The Christmas Eve* and its author's own thinking. To begin with, Schleiermacher believed that the dialogue form is a reflection of Plato's own idea of the nature of philosophical communication and that in the literary form we see a basic and distinctive characteristic of the author himself. Secondly, he reasoned, we fail to take the dialogue seriously as a form, if we attempt to identify Plato's own thought unequivocally with a particular member of the colloquy. The dialogue is not a collection of discrete views; it is a living whole. It is a reproduction of thought in motion. The dialogue as a dramatic form shows thinking as self-activity in the presence of others, and the purpose of its employment by an author is to reenact the original thought processes by which a discovery or conviction was achieved and to arouse in the readers a similar activity. In the third place, then, the unfinished

[22] Br. IV, p. 122.
[23] *Ibid.*, II, p. 50.

appearance of the dialogues is not an imperfection or accidental idiosyncrasy but an essential feature of the form itself.[24] One need only read Schleiermacher's lectures on hermeneutics and dialectic to see that his analysis of the Platonic style made to his own manner of thinking a contribution, the importance of which we can hardly overestimate. "Speech," Schleiermacher was to say later, "is the means for the communality of thinking . . . [it] is to be sure also the means of thinking for the individual. Thinking becomes complete through inner speaking and to that degree speech is only completed thought."[25] Again, thinking never begins with absolute, self-evident axioms but in a situation of conflict with other thinkers; nor does it issue in an absolute knowledge—at least not in history.[26] And by *style*, he added, we are ordinarily accustomed to understand "only the way in which the language is handled. But thoughts and language always inform each other, and the distinctive way in which the object is grasped informs the arrangement and thereby also the treatment of the language. Since the individual is always in the midst of a multiplicity of conceptions, every style is engendered out of an activity of adopting and excluding. But if this or anything else does not arise out of the genuine personality of the individual, but is rather learned or borrowed, or cultivated for its effect, then we have mannerism, and what is mannered is always bad style."[27] These ideas, basic to the later lectures on hermeneutics and dialectic, were already being explicitly formulated in the ethics of 1805/06.[28] We may surmise, therefore, that when Schleiermacher yielded to the impulse to write on the meaning of Christmas, he employed the dialogic form not only because it promised to heighten dramatically the impact of his

[24] *Platons Werke*, trans. Friedrich Schleiermacher, Division 1/Vol. 1, Berlin (1804), Introduction, pp. 10f., 19f., 40.

[25] Herm., §4, p. 80.

[26] Dial. (O), "Einleitung in die Dialektik," pp. 28f., 32, 37, 41f.

[27] Herm., §3, p. 108.

[28] Braun II, "Brouillon, 1805/06," pp. 161-169.

ideas but also because it now seemed the most proper way of setting forth the full intention of his reflections.

In distinction from the principle it embodies, however, the actual execution of the dialogic form in *The Christmas Eve* is not its main attraction. On the contrary, Schleiermacher himself recognized its weaknesses, regretted the haste in which he had produced the work, and, in any case, doubted that it did much honor to the name of Plato. He referred to it as a precursor of the *novella* rather than of the philosophical dialogues he hoped to write. But whatever may be one's judgment on its literary merit, much of the importance of the composition lies in the vividness with which it portrays Schleiermacher's spirit and temper at that time along with the intellectual motifs that were then forming and re-forming in his mind in interaction with the history of Germany and of his personal circle. *The Christmas Eve* enables us, as Schleiermacher himself liked to say, to seize the chain of thought of a man as an integral moment of his life.[29] At this juncture, Schleiermacher's thinking was quite obviously seeking a new direction. A number of contrasts appear between the professor of 1805/06 and the young author of the well-known books, *On Religion* (1799) and the *Soliloquies* (1800). These contrasts are closely related to the form and content of *The Christmas Eve* and help the reader to interpret the intentions expressed in this dialogue.

First of all, Schleiermacher was now manifesting his propensity towards systematic thought more insistently than before, particularly in his preoccupation with problems in ethical theory and with philosophical ethics as such. To be sure, even in his most youthful writings, especially in the essays on Kantian themes, Schleiermacher had displayed a keen critical sense. Moreover, in 1802, after leaving Berlin for Stolpe, he had worked upon a critique of some of the great, historical systems of ethics, but the long labor

[29] SW III/3, "Ueber den Begriff der Hermeneutik," p. 353 (Herm., p. 131); *cf.* also SW I/7, p. 148 (student notebook).

with Plato more than any other experience tempered and sharpened the systematic bent of his mind. He had, as Dilthey has said of him, "a Plato-kindred nature."[30] Throughout the remainder of his life, he strove in every discipline to combine the most careful analysis and drawing of distinctions with his philosophical faith in the ultimate unity of knowing and being, of appearance and power. These systematic inclinations were expressing themselves at Halle in his work on the theological curriculum and also in the growing interest in dogmatic theology as well as in philosophical ethics.

In the second place, Schleiermacher was becoming more closely allied in his own thinking with institutional Christianity. The original edition of the *Speeches* contained notoriously little orthodox sentiment concerning the organized church and the institutional nature of Christianity, but in 1806, as he worked on the second edition, he made significant modifications and additions, though apparently he was restrained from incorporating more, lest the book lose its character.[31] We cannot pretend to discover here a sudden revolution in the course of Schleiermacher's development, for he had thought of himself in the rôle of preacher from his student days in his university, and he had occupied the office of preacher even as he wrote the *Speeches* and the *Soliloquies*. Furthermore, Schleiermacher issued both of these earliest publications anonymously and counseled his friend Brinkmann to regard them as impromptu pieces, preliminary to the "regular concert."[32] Nevertheless, the man whose fears in the Napoleonic invasion were chiefly for the church and the university was not entirely the same person who in the *Speeches* advocated free and unstructured religious association founded upon little more than psychological affinities between individuals.[33]

A third characteristic gaining increasing ascendency was

[30] LS², p. 652.
[31] Br. II, p. 57.
[32] *Ibid.*, IV, p. 60.
[33] *Cf.* the 4th and 5th speeches.

Schleiermacher's interest in the historical unity of human nature, in the manner in which the universally human qualities and the unrepeatable individuality of the person are united. Once more, we must note in the *Speeches* and to an even greater extent in the *Soliloquies* the vigorous exposition of the significance of individuality, a problem with which Romanticism was much occupied. Writing in the confessional style affected in the second of these works, he said, "I was not satisfied to view humanity in rough unshapen masses, inwardly altogether alike, and taking transient shape externally only by reason of mutual contact and friction . . . each man is meant to represent humanity in his own way, combining its elements uniquely, so that it may reveal itself in every mode."[34] Behind these words lie Schleiermacher's study and reflection of several years upon Immanuel Kant's *Critique of Practical Reason*, and there is here an obvious thrust against the latter's ethic of the categorical imperative and its correlative anthropology. According to Kant, radical freedom and hence human dignity are truly manifested in the feeling of obligation and reverence for the one, universal law of moral action. But Schleiermacher was then coming to regard the moral agent, and so the individual, as something more than a particular example of an unvarying rational principle. Instead, he professed to find genuinely moral freedom and the essence of the specifically human as such in the realization of individuality. The individual is constituted a person not simply by his participation in Reason but also by his standing forth as a peculiar embodiment of Reason in a community of other persons likewise constituted. In the year of the *Soliloquies*, Schleiermacher had also published a review of Johann Gottlieb Fichte's *Vocation of Man* in which the same reservation is obviously present. The reviewer expressed doubt concerning Fichte's idea of the relation of the finite ego to the infinite Reason or Will. Insofar as Fichte

[34] *Schleiermacher's Soliloquies*, trans. Horace L. Friess, Chicago (1926), p. 31.

writes to refute the determinism of nature and to make room for freedom, has he really won his point, Schleiermacher asked, by subsuming the finite self into an infinite now conceived as Spirit rather than as Nature? Or is not the finite ego reduced once more to a mere instrumentality of infinite Reason?[35] He was also puzzled by the form of the book which begins as a monologue of the "I" and then resorts to the device of a dialogue between the "I" and a nameless "Spirit," in order to advance the former in its pursuit of self-knowledge, only to relapse into the monological again. Schleiermacher confessed that he himself always required a social context, a company of friends, even for solitary acts of contemplation and for the "assimilation of anything new." Although it was only later that he provided the theoretical justification of this preference, we see that already in 1800 he lacked confidence in the ability of the single, finite consciousness to relate itself immediately to absolute Reason. Moreover, he possessed a sense for the particular and for the integrity of the given, which set him off from the thoroughgoing idealism of his philosophical contemporaries.[36] Nevertheless, the heroic style of the *Soliloquies* also gives evidence of a broad sympathy with Fichte and betrays a man who faces the future with very few fears, a man who is confident: "What the external life really contributes . . . is thus only a confirmation and test of an inner life which is prior and richer." With Fichte, he rejoiced in the dominion of Freedom over the raw material of the world. Six years later, however, after the dissolution of the university, Schleiermacher confided to Charlotte von Kathen, "what a pair of birthdays have I experienced, one after the other! Before the first, the bloom of life fell from me, and before the second, the fruit was thrown down by the storm. What shall we do with the barren trunk?"[37] In these latter times, the enthusiastic appreciation

[35] SW III/1, p. 534.

[36] "The principium individui is the mystical in the realm of philosophy." Letter to Brinkmann, 22 March 1800. Br. IV, p. 59.

[37] Br. II, p. 80 (E.T. II, p. 75).

of individuality has not been destroyed, but it has been integrated into a more sober understanding of the limitations of human freedom and a more realistic appraisal of the interdependence of inner and outer personal history. The professor at Halle had already gone far toward fulfilling his promise to himself that he would enter by his imagination into the many types of humanity and of science that were still strange to him in 1800.[38] But his interest in other persons, times and modes of thought has lost some of its aesthetic curiosity, and we now see in Schleiermacher a starker realization of the fatefulness for the individual of the unity as well as of the diversity of human nature. Furthermore, he no longer seeks the source of religion primarily in individual piety, nor suggests that piety is merely immature without social cultivation; now he recognizes the original rôle of community in the molding of religious feeling and intuition.[39] The picture of Jesus in the *Speeches*, as one whose primacy depends upon his unique grasp of the Idea of mediation rather than upon his person, is redrawn in *The Christmas Eve* with greater emphasis on the historical necessity of his person as the embodiment of original and true humanity. Jesus is now presented as more firmly rooted in history. Even Leonhardt, the historical skeptic in *The Christmas Eve*, values the Christmas myth because of its mysterious power to bind families and men together. It is, then, not only the infinite possibilities lying within the grasp of the individual that Schleiermacher now sees but also the web of human relatedness and the involvement of the individual in a common destiny.[40] Significantly, the author of the

[38] *Soliloquies*, pp. 76f.

[39] In the *Brief Outline of the Study of Theology*, Schleiermacher was saying that the idea of religious community is an indispensable critical tool for understanding the distinctive nature of Christianity. The development of this idea is the task of the philosophy of religion, which is a special department of ethics. *Cf.* §23.

[40] *Cf.* the sermon, "On the Useful Employment of Public Disasters," for a forceful illustration of this conviction. *Predigten von F. Schleiermacher, Zweite Sammlung*, Berlin (1808).

Soliloquies could grow impatient with the public language as too crude a vehicle for the expression of his inner self, while the lecturer on ethics and hermeneutics was coming to believe that thought becomes real only on the ground of an historically given tongue.[41]

These characteristics, as they assume increasing dominance, indicate the changes in Schleiermacher's character between his first notable appearances in print and the publication of *The Christmas Eve*. The analogy of biological growth is clearly preferable to that of political revolution in describing the sequence of those six or seven years, although the question of the true relationship between the Romantic apologist for religion in Berlin and the professor at Halle will undoubtedly remain a tantalizing literary mystery for many, much as the reconciliation of Augustine's *Confessions* with the evolution of his thought as suggested in the Cassiciacum dialogues continues to baffle students of the mind of the Bishop of Hippo. Later on in life, Schleiermacher himself adopted the principle of psychological unity as one of the cardinal tenets to be employed in the interpretation of individual works within a single authorship, a principle that reflects its author's own strong personality and that expresses the continuity he intuited in his own career.[42] One would be ill-advised, therefore, to attempt to excerpt *The Christmas Eve* from the preceding history of its author or to argue that here we find Schleiermacher making a radically new departure. What the dialogue does offer is a glimpse into the formation of Schleiermacher's final theological perspective. Or, to change the metaphor, it provides us with an audition of certain dominant motifs seeking their proper contrapuntal relationships; here the reader familiar with the magnum opus can already dis-

[41] *Cf. Soliloquies*, pp. 64f. and Herm., §4, §5, pp. 80f., which belong to the lectures of 1819. However, the same idea is present earlier, especially clearly in the ethics; *cf.* Braun II, "Brouillon 1805/06," pp. 166-169.

[42] *Cf.* Friedrich Lücke's "Reminiscences of Schleiermacher," *Brief Outline of the Study of Theology*, p. 33. *Cf.* also Br. I, pp. 329f. (E.T. I, p. 319).

tinguish in the sound of voices in dialogue the logic and the spirit of *The Christian Faith*.

§3 SCHLEIERMACHER AND THE VOICES OF THE DIALOGUE

When turning to *The Christmas Eve* itself, the reader familiar with the circumstances recognizes the theme, the setting and the personalities of the dialogue as deriving directly from Schleiermacher's own life. One can hardly be surprised, therefore, when he finds Schleiermacher disclosing to a correspondent that he published the work anonymously in Berlin and Halle, in order that his friends would have to surmise the identity of the author.[43] They should have had no difficulty in doing so. Indeed, many of them found themselves, or incidents out of their own lives, only thinly disguised in one or another of the "voices" of the evening's conversation.[44] We shall reserve a discussion of the complex of ideas of the dialogue for the following sections, but a brief introduction to the personalities of the conversation is appropriate here, because of their bearing upon the interpretation of Schleiermacher's intention in the book as a whole.

No doubt Schleiermacher should have drawn the ideas of the dialogue, and the characters personifying them, with equal skill, but only three or four of the dramatis personae emerge as definite individuals and as moving forces in the plot, a fact that betrays Schleiermacher's lack of any special aptitude for such literary effort. First of all there is Ernestine, the hostess and wife of Eduard. She is the embodiment of confident motherhood and, in antithesis to her speculatively inclined husband, the personification of well-educated, optimistic, unreflective immediacy for whom the immanence of the supranatural in the natural is no problem at all; she

[43] Br. II, pp. 62f. (E.T. II, p. 57).

[44] *Ibid.*, p. 63, p. 50 (E.T. II, p. 57, second reference omitted).

does not blush to think of herself as another Mary. The daughter, Sofie, represents this same kind of unnatural "naturalness" on the child's level. Her unaffected surrender to her moods, her passion for music, and the concern that she arouses in Leonhardt for her religious nurture make occasion for much of the conversation. She is the least convincingly delineated of all the characters, being overly self-conscious, as one friend told Schleiermacher.[45] Together with her mother, Sofie fairly well indicates the limits of Schleiermacher's dramatic art. Leonhardt, on the other hand, is the genuinely dialectical spirit whose skepticism and outspoken criticism of orthodoxy and idealism are the negative impetus for the whole evening. He is the only one through whom Schleiermacher allows his own wit and irony to show, and, although at the end Josef names him the "evil principle" of the company, Leonhardt represents in an outsized fashion an authentic side of Schleiermacher's temperament. It is his sense for the concrete, his awareness both of the tide of political events menacing Germany and of the growth of historical science, that leavens the lofty and oftentimes complacent idealism of the small circle of friends. The remaining characters all stand somewhere between Ernestine and Leonhardt: Eduard, who together with Leonhardt is the most articulate and who offers a speculative view of human nature that is heavily tinged with a Schelling-like idealism;[46] Ernst, the most nearly orthodox member of the group and the mediator between the various extremes; Karoline, the young woman who is the keenest of her sex in the give-and-take of the evening and who possesses a more realistic sense of the pain as well as the joy of life; and, finally, the betrothed Friederike and the matron, Agnes, with her two young sons. Josef, the fatherly friend beloved by the entire company, makes his enigmatic appearance only at the close, so that one can-

[45] Br. II, p. 50.

[46] Schelling's mixed reaction to Eduard's discourse is to be found in his review of *Die Weihnachtsfeier*. *Cf.* F.W.J. von Schelling's *sämmtliche Werke*, Stuttgart (1860), I/VII, pp. 498ff.

not easily identify his position on the spectrum of life-philosophies that the evening has yielded. Although he hints at his opposition to Leonhardt, it is apparently directed more against the latter's forensic aggressiveness than against the content of his views. The true function of Josef is not to negate or to affirm the various conceptions of the human spirit expounded but to represent the common spirit uniting and inspiring the assembly.

Commentators on *The Christmas Eve* have inevitably attempted to correlate certain of the members of this company with Schleiermacher himself or with specific theological tendencies of the day. Both procedures are justifiable. When we are mindful of the variety of Schleiermacher's own activities, as philologist, philosopher, educator, theologian and preacher, and of the range of his personal associations beginning with his membership in the Berlin circle, we would expect to find the opinions, philosophical climate and scientific progress of the day mirrored in the conversation of his characters. But into this opinion and philosophical climate the author breathed so much of his own personality, that it is doubtful that *The Christmas Eve* contains any judgment or idea wholly foreign to Schleiermacher's nature at that time. It would, of course, be highly unrealistic to attribute the entire contents to the author without distinguishing degrees of importance and centrality, but the image of the inner man lies in the work as a whole. So much becomes even more evident when we apply a principle of interpretation borrowed from Schleiermacher himself, the principle of style, which dictates that the reader pay attention not only to what the writer has included in his work but also to what he has omitted.[47] This hermeneutical rule is important for us aside from its intrinsic value, because it is the kind of rule that is devised by a man with an exceptionally strong systematic bent and a highly developed sense of identity. Even in such a casual piece of literature as this Christmas dialogue, it is significant that we do not find

[47] *Cf.* above, p. 30.

Schleiermacher incorporating material that did not suit his own tastes as well as immediate purpose, and no reader can overlook the silence of all voices that might represent a consistent biblicism or a really speculative idealism or a sterner moralism. *The Christmas Eve* is, therefore, much less a reflection of the times as such than of Schleiermacher's interests in the times and of the circle of friends and acquaintances in which he was so much admired.

If it is then with the work as a whole that we must identify Schleiermacher's personal thoughts, and if we remember the import of the dialogic form, it follows that we must resist the temptation of equating Schleiermacher's thinking with only one or two of its personalities. Dilthey has pointed out that the mysterious Josef speaks sentiments that could only be the author's, for the latter's Moravian youth is obviously recalled in Josef's preference for music above theological speculation; and Schleiermacher's pain over the loss of Eleonore Grunow, combined with his heightened sense of oneness with his friends, lies near the surface, when Josef compares himself to a child who chokes back his sighs at the sight of a childish joy.[48] Indeed, Josef's transparency becomes almost tasteless, as he draws an analogy between the solitariness of Christ and of himself. But these unmistakable traits are to some extent shared by other participants in the evening. Josef is not the only one for whom music has such significance, or who rises above his careworn self on the influx of a nobler stream of life. Eduard, Karoline and Ernst all dwell upon the affinity of music and religion, and the precise relationship between the two is actually left undecided. Again the idealization of childhood and the yearning to be reborn into its innocent serenity run through the converse of all. Hence, it is evident that Schleiermacher endowed all of his literary progeny with at least some of himself. And, in fact, it is possible to find

[48] LS², p. 780. David Friedrich Strauss has seen most clearly the connection between Schleiermacher and the major speakers in the dialogue. *Cf. Charakteristiken und Kritiken,* Leipzig (1844, 2nd ed.), p. 43.

echoes of nearly every one of the company in the letters written by Schleiermacher during that fall and Christmas season. Of course, present-day readers, having the advantage of a hindsight lacking in his contemporaries, will naturally identify Schleiermacher more closely with some of the views espoused in *The Christmas Eve* than with others. It would perhaps be possible to defend such an interpretation with Schleiermacher's own conviction that it is feasible and even necessary for the interpreter to know an author better than the author knew himself, but the danger of oversimplifying the relation between the writer and his composition is that we shall thereby miss the complexity of his personality and a most distinctive feature of his manner of thinking here, namely, his employment of unresolved antitheses. *The Christmas Eve* is not a finished essay and comes to no explicit conclusion, but like its Platonic prototype is designed to involve its readers in the movement of thought and—something more—to awaken in them a deep feeling of the irresistible, humanizing stream of life that breaks forth in the Christ child and elicits from every sentient being an irrepressible rejoicing.

Despite the fact, however, that *The Christmas Eve* is obviously not a completely successful literary creation, the reader is carried forward by a definite movement within the narrative and dialogue. The successive phases of this movement may be broadly sketched in the following manner. First of all, Schleiermacher sets out to evoke the basic mood and life-feeling in which the members of the Christmas assembly are caught up, each in a manner differentiated by his or her personality.[49] He strives to this end by combining description of the setting with episodes of whimsical and serious conversation and of music, and gives an account of the crèche, arranged by Sofie, in which the Holy Family is symbolically lost to view in the profusion of other scenes from the history of Christianity. The crèche thus foreshadows the theme of the ulti-

[49] Wf., pp. 3-21.

mate dialogue. Schleiermacher then offers a multifaceted development of the central theological motif of *The Christmas Eve.*[50] Through the devices of the exchange of gifts and of repartee and increasingly serious conversation, he subjects to examination the mother-child relation, the polarity of the masculine and feminine natures, the religious nurture of the child, the affinity of music and piety, the mode of transition from childish innocence to a true godly joy, and, finally, the capacity of Christmas itself to re-create the childlike nature. All of these topics are so handled as to exhibit the completion of human nature by grace. This central portion of the work naturally culminates, therefore, in the allegorically intended reminiscences of three of the women, in three tableaux, as it were, that repeat the nativity theme in various forms. These personal narratives, drawn in actuality from the history of Schleiermacher's own friends, provide the impetus for the final phase of the work, three discourses by the men on the meaning of the celebration of Christmas.[51] While the discourses all start from the common ground of the conviction that an indomitable vitality informs the whole of human nature in all of its manifestations and that this vitality issues into human consciousness through the channel of religious joy and psychical serenity, the speakers differ in their analyses of the historical and psychological, sociological origin of the humanizing power. But the differences are allowed to remain standing in the recognition that both the life symbolized in the Christmas child and the human response to its advent transcend all dialectic. "The speechless object," says Josef, whose appearance brings the evening and the analysis to an end, "demands or creates in me a speechless joy. . . . I feel myself to be at home and as born anew into the better world."[52]

The movement of the whole composition can be summarized

[50] *Ibid.*, pp. 22-96.
[51] *Ibid.*, pp. 98-135.
[52] *Ibid.*, pp. 133f.

as an evocation of mood that gradually crystallizes into poetic imagery, the whole of which is then taken up into a series of half-rhetorical, half-didactic discourses without being destroyed; and at the conclusion the basic mood again asserts itself but in and through a more explicit self-consciousness.

§4 GRACE AND NATURE

The theme of this Christmas symposium is, then, the new life released in the nativity of Christ and the inward appropriation of the same as joy and peace through the feast of Christmas.[53] The focus of the work is certainly upon something more inclusive than a pure description of Christian experience. There are far too many reflective and critical elements in it for such an oversimplification. But *The Christmas Eve* is, with equal certainty, not an essay on the theology of revelation, in which revelation is construed as the inbreaking Word of God, and the reader who approaches it in the expectation of finding a theological view that is transparent to the fifth-century terminology of Chalcedon or to the paradox-christology of early neo-orthodoxy will be disappointed.[54] Schleiermacher's interest in 1805 centered upon Christmas as a historical, social and psychological fact whose significance must be gauged with every apperceptive faculty and critical discipline that modern man possesses. This apparent concentration on the festival itself does not mean, however, that the christological content of Christmas has been impetuously discarded in favor of an examination of

[53] Dilthey has written an excellent account of *Die Weihnachtsfeier*, although he tends to overemphasize the element of feeling at the expense of the genuinely critical, theological content of the dialogue. *Cf.* LS², pp. 765ff.

[54] Karl Barth, who constantly uses Schleiermacher as a foil for his own thinking, finds the absence of a post-Kierkegaardian concept of revelation and Christ to be the chief fault of *Die Weihnachtsfeier*. It is impossible to take seriously Barth's other objections, namely, that music and feminine nature are the foci of Schleiermacher's idea of Christianity at this time. *Cf. Die Theologie und die Kirche,* Munich (1928), pp. 106-135.

the folk customs that it has nurtured and by which it has been sustained. On the contrary, the end that the whole dialogue has in view and towards which the entire work strives is the discernment of the relationship between the festival as a social event and the redeemer who is the author of Christian faith and life.

Actually the structure of *The Christmas Eve* seems to have been determined by a series of related theoretical considerations. Among these is the conviction that the central figure of Christmas can be approached, if there is any access to him at all, only through the experience of his benefits or of his life as it is mediated in the historical continuity of such human fellowship as is represented here by the circle of family members and friends. The small assembly gathered in the home of Eduard and Ernestine on the occasion of Christmas eve represents in a microcosm the interpenetration of Christianity and the basic forms of historical life. The reader does not encounter in the dialogue an obviously articulated doctrine of the church, because piety, friendship, familial relations, etc., are still mingled, in what Schleiermacher regarded as a realistic fashion, and therefore they are not distinguished with the aid of any explicit doctrine of nature and grace. It is evident, for example, that the new life, mediated as a heightened and harmonized self-consciousness, is a restored and perfected instance of human life as such, and it is not, therefore, a creation *de novo*. Nevertheless, insofar as this new humanity presupposes the appropriation of Christ, "the absolute son of man," it is further clear that the church is presented by Schleiermacher as the final form of historical human existence, which is already implicit in these other social forms. Under these circumstances, it is not surprising, but rather in keeping with the whole spirit of the dialogue, that there is no hint of an immediate, mystical relationship to Christ himself as that which constitutes the inner meaning of Christmas. There is no trace here of a Kierkegaardian notion of timeless, direct contemporaneity with the God-man. Contemporaneity in *The Christmas Eve*, to the extent one can speak of it at all, is with Christ as he is reflected and refracted in the innumerable facets of socially mediated experience. Consequently, the question, whether it is finally possible to speak confidently of an historical figure standing behind all of these festival intimations and adumbrations of an originally sinless and incorruptible human nature, is one that is reserved for the final discussion on the part of the men. It is a question that can only be raised, once the direction of the whole line of inquiry has been firmly established, and it is this direction that the opening narrative and conversation promptly make clear. The line of inquiry lies through the investigation of the content of the Christmas festival itself, on the one hand, and through the analysis of the historical, social and psychological continuity of human nature, on the other.

Therefore, Schleiermacher defers the theological discussion of the person of the redeemer and takes up first of all the examination of such issues as the nature of childhood, education, superstition, and so forth. He deliberately seeks out the redeemer and founder of the church in the midst of contemporary religious institutions and customs, for he is not in quest of a Christ who, as the absolute paradox of finite and infinite, negates the continuity of human nature and history. He takes his departure from a humanity that is already celebrating Christmas and participating in "the better world," and his goal is the aboriginal Man-in-himself from whom this human nature receives its form.[55] This procedure conforms to

[55] This was the assumption on which Schleiermacher also preached, as he explained in a sermon at Halle in 1806. "That we have all made the beginning, I presuppose. Just as through his revelations and our growing up into his community, our first life has taken the course that we understand the language of the Lord, that we know and honor the customs of his house in general, that we feel and worship the Spirit of love that reigns everywhere, that we see how everything at least intimates and aims toward the glorifying of God and the gathering of multitudes of men before God." "That we are not to be servants but friends of God," SW II/1, p. 211. See also his introduction to his first book of sermons: "I always so speak as if there were still communities of the faithful and a Christian church; as if religion were still a bond which unites Christians in a special way. To be sure, it does not seem as if this were the case, but I do

Schleiermacher's often repeated assertion that thinking, both analytical and constructive, never starts from an absolutely self-evident point but rather only at a relatively self-evident point. That is to say, thinking starts in history, *in mediis rebus,* in relation to its object as already existing in an historical context. As we shall see subsequently, *The Christian Faith* expresses this principle more systematically, but the consequences it entails are no less decisive here. One of them is that Schleiermacher reverses the usage of much of classical theology in two important respects. Instead of beginning his delineation of the redeemer with the doctrines of the Trinity and the divine nature, he begins with human nature; and, instead of suggesting the otherness and sinlessness of the redeemer's humanity by contrasting him with natural, fallen man, he speaks of the likeness, that is, the relatedness, of redeemed humanity to Christ. Such a method reflects Schleiermacher's general conviction that the inquirer cannot abstract himself from his historical situation, and it reflects his particular conviction that the

---

not see how we can avoid presupposing it. If we should give to our future religious assemblies a missionary form, in order first to make men into Christians, then we must go to work without this presupposition. But if we are not to speak at all about their relationship to Christianity, I do not see why we should talk about Christianity at all . . . there is nothing more destructive for our religious discourses than vacillation between both views, that we should speak as if to Christians, and that we should speak as if to non-Christians." *Predigten, Erste Sammlung,* Berlin (1806, 2nd. ed.), eight pages after the title page (the pages of the introduction being unnumbered). It is clear that Schleiermacher does not believe that human words have the power to create the relationship to Christ but rather he believes that the relationship is established by Christ himself or by the Spirit of Christ. But preaching is still the means by which Christianity spreads and is nourished, according to Schleiermacher, who was a preacher all of his life. On this basis and on the basis of many other elements integral to Schleiermacher's thinking we can see, and shall further see, how implausible is Emil Brunner's assertion that according to Schleiermacher word and concept are completely severed from the mystical core of religion. *Cf. Die Mystik und das Wort,* Tübingen (1928, 2nd. ed.): "Everything conceptual, every thought is alien and accidental to religion as such" (p. 34). Brunner insists that the *Speeches* is the key to the sum and substance of Schleiermacher's theology, and he repeatedly invokes Goethe's "Gefühl ist alles, Name is Schall und Rauch" as the expression of the import of Schleiermacher's thinking from 1799 to the *Glaubenslehre.*

Christian theologian or thinker on Christ and man cannot abstract himself from his relation to Christ. The theologian cannot speak first about man as he was apart from Christ and then about man in relation to Christ; neither can he describe first Christ in himself and thereafter Christ in relation to man. Rather he can speak about both only as they appear in the very relation to each other that makes each term significant for the other. In a contemporary sermon on the Johannine text, 15:15 ("for the servant does not know what his master is doing; but I have called you friends"), Schleiermacher strikes this same theme, when he says that understanding must be founded on true likeness or "friendship." The likeness of the disciple to the master, and hence his ability to understand what the master does and says, is itself founded on the self-giving of the master, on the master's act of choosing the disciple.[56] To be sure, this friendship is always an imperfectly appropriated bond, never wholly free of fear and ignorance, but Schleiermacher clearly believes that all edifying discourse about Christ must assume some friendship or likeness or being conformed to Christ on the part of the hearer, if any genuine understanding of the master is to occur. The reader familiar with the history of modern Protestant theology can see in *The Christmas Eve* the first adumbration of the characteristic theological stance developed later by Ritschl and more flamboyantly by Barth: the insistence upon participating in Christ as the precondition of knowledge of Christ. The development to which Schleiermacher himself brought this idea in *The Christian Faith* was, however, as we shall observe in the last chapter, far more complex and subtle than that to be found in either Ritschl or Barth.

The program that Schleiermacher actually carries through here, albeit in only sketchbook fashion, is formally justified in the *Brief Outline of the Study of Theology*, in which he stipulates that the true nature of Christianity can be construed in neither a one-

[56] SW II/1, pp. 214f.

sidedly deductive nor a one-sidedly empirical manner but only by a critical combination of the two methods. True Christianity—one might say, the nature of Christianity—emerges as we continually revise our initial idea in the light of empirical data and subsequently test the revised idea against the new pattern of data that has become relevant in the light of the revised idea. Thus, that in Christianity which has accrued to it accidentally is gradually distinguished from the genuinely Christian. And as we bring the idea of Christianity into relation with other major types of religious communion, the conception of human nature and the meaning of redemption entailed in it become more apparent. These two processes, the internal, critical and the external, comparative, must in fact keep pace with each other, for each presupposes the other, and the entire effort to achieve an understanding of the nature of Christianity plainly assumes a knowledge of the science of man and a knowledge of positive or historical Christianity.[57] *The Christmas Eve* embodies a roughly similar procedure, as it takes up the examination of human nature and of religion, not in the broadest scope, to be sure, but within the limited variety afforded by the personalities brought together by the Christmas festival and mood, and then subjects this total phenomenon to a many-sided critique. The true human significance of Christmas will appear only if we deal critically both with the nature of man and with the meaning of the tradition of Christmas.

Therefore, the Christmas dialogue commences with real humanity as it is actually determined by relatively natural factors, such as sex and personal temperament, and by more ethical or historical factors, specifically education, relationship to Christianity, marriage and politics. Unless there is a preliminary discussion to this end, it will be impossible to evaluate the heightened sense of life, the transformation of pain through joy, the spirit of serenity and resignation that make up the mood and much of the efficacy of

[57] KD^2, "Einleitung" and §32.

Christmas. Furthermore, the failure to develop such information would mean, in its turn, that the image of the author of this new life must remain little more than an empty symbol whose real historical, ethical significance can be neither affirmed nor denied.

As befits an occasion of the sort depicted in this Christmas dialogue, the various topics mentioned above are not discussed systematically and seriatim, but they are, rather, woven together, now interrupting each other, now echoing each other and now carrying each other forward. However, the discussion follows three major lines which can be summarized here without detailed reference to the actual sequence of the conversation itself.

1) The child Sofie is the center of attention, as she displays the crèche she has decorated and arranged, and then again as her enthusiasm for music induces in the whole company appreciation of the presence in their midst of the Christmas spirit. Critically surveying her own handiwork in the crèche, she says that she has not been able to think of a way to introduce a rainbow, for Christ is the trustworthy pledge that life and happiness will never again disappear from the world. Next, becoming aware that her mother, Ernestine, is standing directly behind her, she exclaims: "Oh mother, you could just as well be the blessed mother of the divine child, and does it not sadden you that you are not?"[58] This demonstration of childish piety and impulsiveness provokes the ensuing discussion of the question: what kind of religious education is appropriate to the child, if piety is to assume its natural and proportionate place in her adult character? Sofie's parents must defend their practices against Ernst, on the one hand, who finds in the family too little manifest attention to things Christian, and against Leonhardt, on the other, who fears that the girl is being too much exposed to patently ecclesiastical influences that can only subsequently reappear as affectations. A boy, Leonhardt wryly adds, can always study theology for a year and be healed of such eccen-

[58] Wf., p. 19.

tricities, but Sofie seems already to be well on the way to the cloistered life of nun or Herrnhuter sister. The parents then expound a philosophy of education in which confidence in the power of the natural predominates. In a family regimen in which religion is a matter of spontaneity, there being no set hours of prayer, no formal instruction in the Bible, the child's development is entrusted to her own healthy common sense. For example, Eduard finds that the discrimination between myth and history comes easily to Sofie as she reads the nativity stories of the Gospels. In a word, the girl's nurture represents the median between a too formally religious and an artificially naturalistic environment, by virtue of which she will in time pass into the inheritance of a balanced disposition, evenly watered by a constant piety rather than subjected to the alternating periods of aridity and flood that mark the lives of enthusiasts and proselytes.[59] Karoline underscores this point, when she declares that Sofie "has shown us very clearly what the temper of a child is, without which one cannot enter into the Kingdom of God: just this—to take every mood and feeling for itself and to want to have it only as unalloyed and whole."[60] These words show, furthermore, how the topic of child nurture has worked itself round to the basic theme of the evening.

2) The exchange of gifts prompts Leonhardt to observe that the women are by nature far better devisers of fitting and amusing gifts than the men, and they also are much cleverer in divining the identities of the anonymous donors. With this remark, Leonhardt introduces another facet of the discussion of human nature, one already unmistakably anticipated in the opening description of the festivities and Ernestine's rôle as the chief architect of the evening's amenities. The polarity of the feminine and masculine natures becomes the subject of light, and then increasingly significant, re-

[59] The "proselytes" here is a reference to the Romantics, among them Friedrich von Schlegel, who had recently joined the Roman Catholic Church. *Cf.* Wf., pp. 35f. and LS², pp. 783-805.

[60] Wf., pp. 60f.

marks; but what is finally at stake is the temperamental difference not only between the two sexes but also between two ways of appropriating redemption—in the terminology of William James, the difference between the "once-" and the "twice-born man." Women are the once-born. The life of woman knows no abrupt changes of direction; the transition from childhood to the "higher existence," of which the group is speaking, proceeds gradually, evenly and imperceptibly, while the majority of the best men appear, at least to Ernestine, to lead the greater part of their lives in a wasteland, estranged from both youth and this "higher existence." The games of children already contain the whole of the feminine attitude toward life. In Ernestine's eyes, the nature of woman is immediacy, both with the world and God.[61] Hence, in the execution of the all-important trust of the education of children, mothers more readily perceive and nourish the divine promise implicit in the child's being, for they themselves always seem "to live in the inner temple as vestal virgins who keep watch by the holy fires." Men, on the other hand, according to Eduard, "practice discipline and preach repentance, or lift the cross onto the back of the pilgrim and gird him with his sword, to seek out a lost holy land and to win it again."[62] Paradoxically, the observation of these differences leads to the conclusions that the preservation of the Christmas tradition is principally due to the distinctively feminine genius, but men appear to be more Christian than women, for Christianity speaks always of conversion and *metánoia*. Again, according to the feminine point of view, the fundamental chord of woman's nature, echoed repeatedly throughout *The Christmas Eve* in the image of the mother and child, is not easily diminished or distorted by the intrusion of private, personal concerns. She is essentially determined by sympathy, her sorrow is co-sorrow and her joy is a rejoicing with others.[63]

[61] *Ibid.*, p. 65.
[62] *Ibid.*, p. 27.
[63] *Ibid.*, pp. 121f.; *cf.* above, p. 23.

The immediate course of Schleiermacher's life in 1805 makes it impossible to overlook a certain personal pathos in these remarks on the differences between the sexes, particularly in view of the fact that the true destiny of women is consistently depicted as motherhood,[64] and the mother, whether it be Ernestine, Agnes, or woman in the abstract, is obviously acknowledged as the center of the family. But at the same time the reader cannot help but note that the "thinking, reflecting, dialectical, over-intelligent man," Leonhardt, makes many of the most incisive and sweeping of the above generalizations about the other sex, illustrating a truth for which the dialogic form of the work as a whole is also a warrant, namely, that each sex becomes conscious of the specific quality of its humanity only in the presence of the other. While then, the shadow of loneliness that threatened Schleiermacher undeniably must have enhanced the lustre of the feminine nature, as he worked on the dialogue, there can be no doubt that the real point of the whole discussion is not woman as such but the family.[65] The antithesis in which Leonhardt, who has no family ties, stands to Ernestine, the personification of wife and mother, underscores such an interpretation, as to a much greater degree does the structure of the whole work. Man himself can only be understood as he appears determined by the unending reciprocity of the sexes and by the unique responsibility that he has for the education of his offspring. Not only do the masculine discourses of the third part build upon and explicate the meaning of the feminine reminiscences of earlier Christmases, but Eduard's long address on the church in particular presupposes the image of the family that the first and second parts have drawn. Although an examination of Schleiermacher's idea of

[64] Br. II, pp. 44, 61f.

[65] Karl Barth professes to believe that in Schleiermacher's portrait of woman here, he intended to represent her as a being beyond the ethical dialectic, a vessel through whom the Christian spirit is immediately imparted. But Barth could not say this, even in jest, if he took the form of the work and the third part as seriously as he does the middle portion. *Cf. op. cit.*, p. 135.

the relation of church and family cannot be undertaken here, the notion of marriage and the family as "natural" facts or orders upon which the church rests is clearly already present in *The Christmas Eve.*[66] While the church is, of course, a "supernatural" community, in one sense, it stands in a clear line of continuity with the family, and the polarity between the two kinds of humanity, the "once-born" and the "twice-born," does not express a mere accident of nature, but reflects the duality of the historical condition of the Christian community, which is always, at one and the same time, the body of many members through whom the Head works and the sojourning people still in Sinai's desert, still in exodus and far from the promised land.

3) Again, the exchanging of the gifts moves both Ernst and Eduard, on two different occasions in the evening's conversation, to remind the friends of the symbolism of this custom: it is a "pure manifestation of religious joy"; "it portrays the great gift over which we all rejoice equally." "The more purely this disposition comes to the fore as a whole," says Eduard, stating the third and most fundamental theme, "so much the more is our nature engaged [by it]. And on this account, we were so delighted, my dear Ernestine, by your arrangement of the evening, because you have so well expressed our Christmas spirit: the growing young again, the return into the feeling of childhood, the serene joy in the new world, for which we have the celebrated child to thank."[67]

In the ensuing discussion, it is as though Nicodemus were present again with his question, not in haste and secrecy this time but in confidence that this urbane and genteel group with the resources of its broad variety of views can surely explain how a man is born again. Both the discussion of child nurture and of the differences between the sexes have shown that this question touches on the center of any Christian understanding of man. But the

[66] *Cf.* SW I/12, *Christliche Sitte,* pp. 336-338.
[67] Wf., pp. 46f.

assembly inquires now not so much into the possibility of rebirth, for Christmas is already an historical, social fact, as into the manner in which it is experienced.

The answer to this question is that rebirth is experienced as a "feeling of higher joy," a feeling moreover of which the individual cannot properly speak as being his own, since it is a joy by which one is "grasped," and it "is immediately grounded in that which does not pass away." Karoline describes it as blossoming in us unhindered even next to the deepest pain; it "purifies and ameliorates [the pain] without thereby being disturbed, so original is it," and Eduard even believes that this "joyful superfluity of pure serenity" could endow him with the courage to defy fate itself.[68] Music suggests itself to them as an analogy for this joy-determined life, in part because it has figured so much in the evening already, but more significantly because: "Nothing accidental, nothing individual halts either [godly feeling or music]. . . . Music never weeps or laughs over individual occurrences but always only over life itself."[69] Another virtue of music also occurs to Eduard, namely, that it is a more immediate expression of religious feeling than words can ever be, and, therefore, church music could easily dispense not with the singing voices but with the definite words. Apart from the sometimes varying and sometimes complementing opinions concerning music, however, the fundamental idea that Schleiermacher conveys through all of the "voices" at this juncture is that music images life as a sustained, flowing chord and as an inner harmony, the feeling or awareness of which constitutes the highest moment of exaltation. Nevertheless, the godly, religious or pious feeling of which the author speaks here is not indeterminate, for even if at this point we take Eduard—the most ardent champion of the kinship of religion and music—as the transparent mask of Schleiermacher himself, we find him applying the analogy of mu-

68 *Ibid.*, pp. 48f.
69 *Ibid.*, p. 52.

sic not in the interests of stressing the indeterminacy of religious feeling but for the sake of illustrating the power of character or form. "This close kinship," says Eduard, "is well implied by the fact that only in the immediate relationship to the highest, to religion, and a definite form of the same, has music enough of the given to be intelligible without being connected with a single fact. Christianity is a single theme presented in endless variations, which are united by an inner law and which fall under a definite general character."[70] Hence, a Miserere, a Gloria, a Requiem are intelligible simply through their character. These words, along with the rest of Eduard's utterances, directly reveal his idealistic orientation, although the extent to which he can be identified as a genuine idealist as such is still debatable at this point. But, that Eduard or the analogy between music and Christian existence, to which Agnes, Ernst and Karoline also subscribe, bespeaks a religious mysticism is most doubtful. For even despite the fact Eduard styles himself a mystic, his use of the term, like Schleiermacher's, is highly specialized.[71] He has clearly not given up determinacy. As for the concrete, his conviction is that life itself—life as qualified by a particular religious *Stimmung* (mood or attunement)—is able to control and unite its individual historical moments in a virtually indestructible harmony. Pattern or form, then, is prior to the particular, but the dialogue here never suggests that religious intuition and feeling as such are formless.[72] On the contrary, Christianity is the highest form of life.

Yet, notwithstanding the near unanimity of the participants in their acclaim of the musical analogy and the idea of the higher life

[70] *Ibid.*, pp. 50f.

[71] *Cf.* above, §2, p. 34, fn. 36.

[72] On his interpretation of this point Barth (*op. cit.*, p. 134) again seems to me incorrect. The idea of the whole that governs and endows its parts with a unifying meaning is paramount in *Die Weihnachtsfeier* and Schleiermacher's whole philosophy. Schleiermacher's Platonism marks him off from *Lebensphilosophie*, however, especially from the variety represented by Henri Bergson.

entailed therein, Leonhardt so eloquently protests that he is able to plant a seed of doubt. In the ensuing exchanges, we are given a direct view of the personal genius that so vigorously animated Schleiermacher's thinking, as Leonhardt, the critical, realistic Schleiermacher, scornfully attacks the whole conception of life-harmony only just so carefully articulated. The women have been quick to appropriate Eduard's heroic philosophy of life and to transmute it into a paean extolling woman's immunity to the purely personal and to suffering. Alluding to the threatening Napoleon, Leonhardt retorts: "if all that were true, certainly you would be the heroes of these times, you dear, idealistic dreamers with your contempt of the particular and the real, and one should regret that your community is not stronger and that you do not have honest, qualified, war-fit sons already able to bear arms. You must be the real Christian Spartans. But if that is not the case, then take care. . . . A great fate moves restlessly up and down in our neighborhood with strides that shake the earth . . . may reality with its proud might not revenge itself on you."[73] The heat of this rejoinder leaves little doubt that the attainment of such inner harmony appeared far less easy and matter-of-fact to Schleiermacher in 1805 than Eduard's smooth rhetoric suggests, if taken by itself. Later, in 1806, when the "restless fate" was more imminent, Schleiermacher preached on I Corinthians 14:33 ("God is not a God of disorder but of peace"), stressing that the peace of the kingdom of God is not a dead calm but a creating power of God that is born into human life through strife, and thereto "our first and last battle that never ceases . . . is against ourselves."[74] Leonhardt of the Christmas dialogue is already the spokesman of the wiser, sadder, historically conscious preacher, and he is so effective that he forces the conversation to turn from its contemplation of religious joy itself to the examination of how it is inherited. Must it begin with strife and war, with the expunging of innocence? Does the way from the

[73] Wf., pp. 55f.
[74] SW II/1, p. 249.

"first, original joy of life" to the other lie only through a state of nothingness?

From this summary of the three major lines of discussion we can certainly infer that all of the important members of this Christmas colloquy are agreed upon the fact that the observation of the festival of Christ's nativity expresses a power at work upon the humanity of the celebrants. Participation in the festival of the advent of the Christ child implies at least a tacit recognition of the actuality and hence possibility of the union of the divine with human nature in a state of true innocence. But the mere celebration as such cannot answer the practical, troublous question elicited by Leonhardt's criticism. Nor is it now sufficient merely to point to the differences between the sexes, for these differences are, after all, contained within a single humanity.

In fact, the reader may well look in vain for an unambiguous answer, a circumstance that one may attribute to the author's intention or simply to his state of mind in those days. In any case, the three stories by Ernestine, Agnes and Karoline, concerning their most vivid memories of the Christmas season from other years, are clearly designed to dramatize the possibility of finding an answer to the question at more than one level of human self-consciousness.

The first of the narrators, Ernestine, recalls a scene from her own childhood: at a Christmas eve service she accidentally notices a mother sitting with her infant son in what appears to the enthralled Ernestine to be a wholly self-contained sphere of beatitude, devotion and resignation. The mother, who is Ernestine's future sister-in-law, subsequently lost her son in war. She is one of the "thousand images" of Novalis' lines:

> Ich sehe dich in tausend Bildern
> Maria, lieblich ausgedrückt.

Agnes is the second to tell her story which relates another gathering of family and friends on a Christmas eve at the home of

Agnes' brother where a child has just been born. When the nursemaid protests because all have brought gifts only for the mother, in the belief that as yet the child has no separate identity, Agnes philosophizes: "Yes, so it is, children. He is still wholly directed on his mother, and even she can do nothing more for him today than awake in him the same feeling of contentment as on every other day. His feeling is still united with her, it dwells in her, and only in her can we nourish and rejoice over it."[75] But thereupon the guests disperse and return with presents, not for the infant but the future youth and man. The highest of these gifts is baptism which the child's father himself, as a pastor, resolves to administer. The symbolism of this scene is markedly different from the first. In place of the madonna, attention is now focused on a child's destiny ("as Christ was given gifts that hinted at a glory of which the child as yet knew nothing. Let us now also appropriate to him the highest, Christ himself, although at this moment it still can grant him neither delight nor joy"[76]); and this destiny is perceived and mediated not directly and merely by the mother but indirectly by the whole assembly who all participate in the baptism by laying hands on the child, "according to the good, old custom of that place," for "Not in the mother alone, nor in myself," says the father, "but in us all dwells the religious feeling that cannot yet be in him, and it is from us all that he must appropriate it in days to come."[77]

The last of the narrations, Karoline's, recounts the grief of a mother, well-known to the whole company, whose child lay dying in the days immediately before a previous Christmas. Gradually the mother is able to find reconciliation, even while she is in the midst of the preparations for the celebration that must go forward for the sake of the other children. On "the feast of the rebirth of the world" she awakes from a sleep of exhaustion and complete

[75] Wf., pp. 80f.
[76] *Ibid.*, p. 84.
[77] *Ibid.*

resignation to discover the child past the crisis and on the way to recovery. This scene with its combination of sorrow and joy in the Christmas mood also represents a development beyond the first story and stands in marked contrast with it and the second story.

The connection between these narratives and the foregoing conversation needs little comment. They are the pictorial counterparts of Eduard's variations on the theme of Christianity, all bound together by a common character, the common character here being the actual, effective presence of grace as exalted life, and the variations being the different relations, in which this grace is conceived to stand, to human life as such. Here we have, furthermore, the earlier discussion of human nature mirrored in a series of pictures of humanity in which the subject of grace is invariably presented as a member of the minimum "natural" society, the family; and the distinction between this society and the church as the mediator of grace is left vague, for now one and now the other community appears to be the presupposition of the bestowal of the higher life. Thus within this short space, we have encountered a self-sufficient Mary, wholly absorbed in her relation to her infant son, and an "inverted Maria" receiving her child a second time as "a gift of grace"; a Christ child hidden in the midst of the Christmas eve service, from whom, however, the true nimbus of purity radiates, and a "negative Christ child" into whom streams the divine blessing through the congregational baptism; an image of a family in which the seal of grace (baptism) is given to the child in its first days, and an image of a family in which the promise of life is given only after the death of hope. None of the earlier questions is answered in these narratives. Instead, the recollections serve to crystallize these questions and motifs in such a way that it is clear no further progress can be made through simple observations. It is now time to apply analysis, therefore, specifically to the connection between these various experiences that the Christmas season has brought with itself and the unvarying background against which all have occurred, namely, the figure of Christ.

§5 MAN-IN-HIMSELF

At Friederike's urging, the men, whose turn it now is, speak ostensibly on that which has brought them all together, the festival itself. But in fact what they discuss are its historical foundations.

Leonhardt begins, promising that he will avoid as far as possible any repetition of the thoughts that his friends will hear on the next day at church. Accordingly, he sets out to praise and analyze the power of Christmas to maintain itself without external support and to achieve so perfectly its goal as a festival. The first and positive assertion of Leonhardt's half-mocking, half-serious eulogy is that society lives by tradition mediated through stereotyped and ceremonial actions rather than by the written word. The basis of Christmas is to be sought, therefore, in the yearly observance of the customs associated with it and not in the Scriptures as historical accounts. So much can be proven by the fact that the people have no real understanding of the theological meaning of Christmas. It perpetuates itself on the unconscious level of social habit. Leonhardt cites, as corroborative evidence, the additional fact that present Christianity as such depends very little on the historical details of the life of Christ. He excepts from this generalization the doctrine of Christ's reconciling work, but even this, he says, "is grounded more upon an eternal decree than upon a definite, individual fact, and on this account cannot be spoken of in a definite moment but is rather elevated above temporal history and must be maintained mythically."[78] The obvious lesson is that the religion of the folk has little to do with any objective history, and, in reality, we have ample reason to suppose that just such festivals as this

[78] *Ibid.*, p. 104.

Christmas feast can and do create their own historical background.[79]

Readers familiar with the course of later nineteenth-century theology will recognize a similarity between Leonhardt's suggestion of the social origin of myth and David Friedrich Strauss' basic thesis in his *Life of Jesus*. Strauss himself found Leonhardt to be the most convincing character of the dialogue.[80] But Strauss evidently did not observe that Schleiermacher built Leonhardt's case on the conception of a society that generates myth necessarily, no matter what its stage of development. Strauss believed myth to be an attribute of primitive mentality, and he originally maintained that mythic religion could be replaced by rational religion. Leonhardt offers no support for this distinction between the primitive and the modern, rational man.

The anticipation of Strauss is present again in the second of Leonhardt's thrusts, as he draws the conclusion that the Christ of history is an unknown person completely obscured by the Christ of the festival and popular religion. Using a sharp, historical criticism based in part on shrewd psychological insight and also to some extent on rationalistic presuppositions, he shows, for example, that Jesus is much more nearly related to John the Baptist than to Paul and the early church—if the latter as a distinct institution lay within his horizon at all—and that the Gospels, far from being simple reports about him, are warped by partisan and polemical motives. (Despite the fact Schleiermacher later thought of Leonhardt's speech as frivolous, it is not difficult to perceive here the outline of the lecturer on the life of Jesus and of the emerging New Testament critic.) After this and other incisive verdicts, Leonhardt assures his friends that his intention is not to "impugn Christianity as a strong and powerful force in the present" but to reveal the unexcelled virtue of the festival by which it endures and

[79] *Ibid.*, p. 103.
[80] Strauss, *op. cit.*, p. 39.

molds our spirit. "To me, at least," he concludes, "even the smallest feature is full of meaning. For as a child is the central subject of the celebration, so it is also principally children who foster and support the feast and thereby also Christianity itself. And as the night is the historical cradle of Christianity, its birthday celebration is commemorated in the night, and the candles that it boasts are at the same time the stars over the hostel and the holy light without which one would not be able to find the child in the darkness of the stable and in the otherwise starless night of history."[81]

The succeeding discourse by Ernst is perhaps the most famous portion of *The Christmas Eve*, because it contains Schleiermacher's first projection of the argument to the existence of an historical founder of Christianity from present religious experience. Actually, the argument ultimately rests upon a particular idea of man, of which religious experience is only one aspect, as becomes evident when Ernst does not attack Leonhardt's conception of society and myth but only the positivism which had prevented the latter from going beyond the phenomenon of Christmas to its essence. The essence of Christmas, Ernst reasons, is to be found in the temper of joyousness that it arouses. It is a specific joyfulness, moreover, possessing its own character, as over against simple "birthday joy" or the fitful hope, subject to the rhythm of time and the seasons, that leads men to confuse the spirit of Christmas with the mood of the New Year holiday. Its distinctiveness may be defined in large part by its "thorough-going universality," by which Ernst means the capacity of this mood to endow the particular with a larger meaning and to qualify the whole world within which the newly enlivened self moves. Whatever is so universal in this sense, he continues, can never have been artificially formed, and, turning to his own advantage Leonhardt's perception of the astonishing social potency of the festival, he concludes: "Something inward must lie at its basis, otherwise it could neither be effective nor endure. This

[81] Wf., p. 109.

inner something, however, can be nothing else than the ground of all joy itself."[82] In other words, Ernst is saying, myth is not arbitrary. But he must go further in order to connect the ground or *Prinzip* of all joy with the birth of a divine child. His actual argument, however, does no more than suggest the kind of logic that a Leonhardt would demand. If we ignore the random order of his reflections, we can reduce his case to the following three points: 1) The phenomenon of Christmas itself makes us "aware of the inmost grounds and of the inexhaustible power of the new, undisturbed life." We are, furthermore, aware of this life as something in which we are already caught up. The feeling seizes everyone, and "however unconsciously it may occur in many, this wondrous feeling can result in nothing but [the] concentrated intuition of a new world . . . it is presented in a thousand images, in the most diverse ways, as the setting and rising sun, as the spring of the spirit, as the king of a better kingdom, as the most faithful messenger of God, as the most gracious prince of peace."[83] 2) Christmas simultaneously presents us with the picture of that new, undisturbed life in its genesis and in its "noblest flowering and highest perfection," namely, the Christ child. 3) The causal connection between these two features of the Christmas festival is provided by the crucial conviction that this universal joy in which we already share bespeaks an original human nature free of the antitheses between time and eternity, appearance and essence, and of every other division; but this archetypal human nature is not originally ours, for we begin "as divided selves and achieve harmony only through the redemption," which is to say, insofar as we are grafted on to a nature in whom these divisions never existed.[84]

While it is possible to read Ernst's own argument as a sidestepping rather than a meeting of the issues that Leonhardt has

[82] *Ibid.*, p. 116.
[83] *Ibid.*, p. 119.
[84] *Ibid.*, p. 118.

raised, the careful reader perceives that it also puts emphasis upon features of Christian faith and life that Leonhardt has omitted. Ernst has, for example, transposed the locus of the meaning of Christmas from innocent childhood to mature and inwardly divided selfhood. Furthermore, Leonhardt's historical skepticism is, from his point of view, founded upon considerations that we today would subsume under the discipline of lower criticism as well as upon specific, psychological, sociological dogma, while his own confidence depends on a different conception of historical knowledge. For Ernst the idea of a redeemer has been made necessary—not in a syllogistic sense but historically necessary—by virtue of the irrefutable knowledge that Christmas itself has given men, the knowledge of a human nature that is, in classic Reformation language, *simul iustus et peccator*. Hence, even the "weakest historical traces" suffice as historical evidence for such a redeemer. "The greatest crystallization requires only the smallest particle to which to fasten itself; and whatever of this joy breaks out from within needs only the slightest occasion to posit itself in a definite form."[85] Further than this, Ernst or Schleiermacher does not choose to go. Only the precarious phrase, "weakest historical traces," marks the boundary line beyond which lie the limitless regions of speculative idealism where the idea creates its own "smallest particles" and "slightest occasions" to posit itself.[86]

Actually, Eduard, the last of the speakers, reveals more of the foundations of Schleiermacher's future theology than does Ernst. While the other discourses have amply established the significance of mood (*Stimmung*) and feeling for Schleiermacher's interpretation of Christianity, it is only in Eduard's words that the anthropological, philosophical and theological themes appear in their true

[85] *Ibid.*, p. 120.

[86] Strauss commented on this argument: "As Kant called the existence of God a postulate of practical reason: so the dogma of Christ can be called by Schleiermacher a postulate of Christian experience" (*Op. cit.*, p. 41).

articulation and that the Platonic, Johannine spirit betrays its dominant position in Schleiermacher's thought.[87] Accordingly, Eduard does not stop to criticize the earlier speakers but announces that he will talk about the meaning of Christmas as it is found in the "mystical" Gospel in distinction from the "mythical" or synoptic Gospels to which Leonhardt's remarks obviously had reference. The Fourth Evangelist, Eduard declares, gives us nothing external or visible but the "spiritual and higher view of our festival."

Eduard's interpretation of the prologue of the Fourth Gospel is predicated on an idealistically modified Platonic doctrine of man. Human nature in this view must be considered in its dual aspects of the individual man and of Man-in-himself. Man-in-himself, archetypal man, is the apogee of the created order, the "Earth-spirit," the act through which the earth knows itself in "its eternal being and in its ever changing becoming." Individual man, on the other hand, insofar as he fails to recognize himself as the place in which the earth achieves self-consciousness and insofar as he seeks to find himself in other terrestrial structures and organisms, is in a state of fallenness and inner discord. The fallen individual is pure becoming. Salvation comes to him as he realizes that he himself, as an individual, is the place in which Man-in-himself is actualized. Salvation comes as he also perceives that his own finitude and all other becoming is grounded in the eternal being that has united itself with time in Man.[88]

The Johannine modification of this view of man comes to the fore as Eduard explains that this "higher life and peace of God" are present in the individual only through a moral perception, only "when the individual sees and constructs humanity as a living community of individuals, carries its spirit and consciousness in himself

[87] *Cf.* Dilthey's interpretation of Eduard's speech, LS², pp. 791ff.

[88] It is at this juncture, in the anthropology expressed by Eduard, that Paul Tillich's affinity for Schleiermacher is most easily recognizable. But this in turn is due to the common relation of Tillich and of the "Eduard side" of Schleiermacher to Schelling.

and in it loses and rediscovers his isolated being."[89] The discovery of Man in the self depends, therefore, on the discovery of Man in the other. The community in which this discovery and acknowledgment occur is the church. Only through her spirit is rebirth possible. Thus, according to Eduard, this higher life and potentiated self-consciousness is *historically* mediated. The community of self-consciousness is both already the church and always becoming the church, for it rests upon the communication of its being by its members. Hence, it is necessary to look for a point of origin in which this self-knowledge and community of feeling freely break forth. "That one," Eduard believes, "must already be born as Man-in-himself, as the God-man. . . . originally born of God. He is the absolute son of man."[90] In the Logos appearing in our finite, sensible nature we have the principle by which we are able to recognize our own humanity. Thus, he is the light of men, the dawn of the earth's self-consciousness in the individual.

With these words, Eduard lays bare the skeletal structure of *The Christmas Eve* and outlines the systematic principles operative in the ethics and theology as they are to take shape for Schleiermacher in the future with the help of a less speculative vocabulary. Christ is the presupposition of our understanding of man ("In respect to him, everything before him was intimation, was related to him, and was good and divine only on account of him"[91]), so that in Christ we celebrate ourselves collectively and also all that are to come in the church. Therefore the concomitant of perceiving and understanding Christ is the perception and "construction of humanity as a living community of individuals." The church in which the perfected humanity of Christ is mediated is itself rooted in human nature as it appears in the family and community. For this reason, the church is nothing less than the very self-conscious-

[89] Wf., pp. 127f.
[90] *Ibid.*, pp. 129f.
[91] *Ibid.*, p. 130.

ness of the race, and all who are within her already possess science, *viz.*, the ripest fruit of human culture, within themselves, and, conversely, all who live for science cannot inwardly deny the church. Therefore, when Christ's birth is celebrated in this community, there is also "a universal pulsing of joy in the entire regenerated world that only those members who are temporarily ill or lamed do not feel."[92]

In concluding this account and analysis, we need to take notice of Josef, for it is he and not Eduard who has the last word in the dialogue, and commentators have made much over this fact. However, enough has been said concerning the form of the whole work to make it plain that Josef's last word is not the final word of the author. That he represents the author himself in his then painful loneliness is hardly to be contested. But, it cannot be said that Josef is simply the embodiment of an aesthetic religiosity that would sweep away all thought in the interests of a pure enjoyment of life itself, for, notwithstanding his rebuke of the men for spending so much time in discourse, Josef himself immediately rationalizes his own "speechless joy," and more than any other member of the company gives embodiment to Eduard's declaration that only "when the individual sees and constructs humanity as a living community of individuals, carries its spirit and consciousness in himself and in it loses and rediscovers his isolated being, only then does he have in himself the higher life and the peace of God." "To me all men are children today," Josef says, "and are on that account so lovely. The serious creases are for once smoothed out, preoccupation and sorrow stand, for once, no longer written on the forehead, the eyes sparkle and are alive and there is in them an intimation of a beautiful and graceful presence. . . . I feel myself at home and as born anew into the better world."[93] Josef too echoes the polarity that imparts movement to the whole dialogue, the polarity between

[92] *Ibid.*, p. 131.
[93] *Ibid.*, pp. 133f.

the perception of the irresistible surge of new life into the human cosmos through the power of Christmas and the need to understand and to take this life up into the unity and integrity of the present.

§6 CONCLUDING OBSERVATIONS AND QUESTIONS

The specific genius of Schleiermacher discloses itself here, both in its virtue and weakness, with an imaginative force that the reader of *The Christian Faith* fain would find in its pages. Among the peculiarities revealed all the more clearly here, because they are concretely illustrated rather than systematically stated, is the steadfast retention of nature and grace in an unending dialectic. Yet whether this dialectic of nature and grace is in fact a theological weakness is itself an open question. For this refusal to divide the realm of nature from that of the supernatural is, of course, but one side of the massive thrust of Schleiermacher's thinking throughout his life. But for Eduard apparently it means that science, in the broadest sense, and Christian faith are always compatible. In order to interpret this conviction correctly, one would have to take into account the principles of Schleiermacher's *Dialektik* and *Ethik*. This is something that subsequent theologians have not always done, with the result that Schleiermacher's prestige has been used to dignify an otherwise dishonorable posture of submissiveness on the part of theology toward its sister disciplines. More serious, however, are the possible implications of the way in which Christ, church and humanity are related to each other in *Die Weihnachtsfeier*. Does Eduard leave sufficient room between Christ and the church for the absolute son of man to exercise a true criticism of his community's stewardship of humanity? This question is particularly relevant to *The Christmas Eve*, because the dialogue makes so little use of the New Testament history, of the concrete Christ over against the idea of the redeemer. Theologians of the recent Confessing Church of Germany believe that the answer to this question is a "No" and that Schleiermacher is partly responsible for the rise of so-called "culture-Protestantism," which forgets that the Head of the church is more than the apotheosis of human nature but also its judge, both within and without the church. The tendency toward accommodation to the ethos of the present—a tendency that follows in the wake of too swift a traverse of the "mythical" or synoptic Gospels—is uncomfortably present in the setting of the dialogue itself. This Christmas gathering of family and friends is too restricted, too much defined by a single social and emotional level of life, to be the Christian community as it exists historically. Consequently, the "temper" or "mood" that Schleiermacher so carefully portrays is always in danger of becoming smug. But, in the present instance at least, this defect appears to be a consequence not of the dialogue's basic idea of Christianity, but of the way in which it is realized. Ernestine, for example, represents an element in the whole that is far more significant than the actual execution of her character suggests to a present-day reader; the same is true of Leonhardt, while Josef obscures the significance of his thoughts with the effusiveness of his words.

Another distinctive feature of Schleiermacher's thinking here, which is offensive to the same theological mentality, is the liberal use of philosophical language and dialectic in the shaping of the form of theological reflection. The very lively possibility is that the influence of such dialectic reaches further than merely the form of the reflection. Schleiermacher himself would have to admit the seriousness of the charge, especially in view of the fact that he so firmly believed form and content to be virtually inseparable facets of any idea. He was, however, acutely conscious of the issue, made all the more complex for him because he believed the task of theology to be the service of preaching and at the same time regarded philosophizing as the natural business of the human understanding.[94] Eduard's discourse contains several examples of Schleiermacher's endeavors to honor both of these convictions without

[94] *Cf.* below, Ch. III.

surrendering the substance of the Christian faith. For example, Eduard speaks of the earth and the Earth-spirit, or Man-in-himself, as a synthesis of "being" and "becoming"; these are Platonic terms traditionally used in Christian metaphysics. Eduard makes no attempt to deduce the becoming from the being, and in this respect he is very much like Kierkegaard, but, unlike Kierkegaard, neither does he distance being and becoming so radically as to run the danger of dualism.[95] Again, he makes redemption to consist in the realization of human self-consciousness, a point much approved by Schelling; but he limited the dawning of this self-consciousness to the process of rebirth that occurs in the historical church, a point to which Schelling took considerable exception.[96] These examples, however, merely serve to clarify Schleiermacher's approach to the use of philosophy. The evaluation of his success requires far more extensive references to his own philosophy and theology.

But this same *daimon* that prompted Schleiermacher to reject dogmatically simplified solutions of the relationship of Christ and man, Holy Spirit and culture, and theology and philosophy, also sharpened his sense for the complexity of historical life and the real, and this particular sense is undoubtedly much of the foundation of Schleiermacher's creativity. Wherever he turned his gaze, the real appeared to him in a network of relationships. By isolating an object from its organic matrix, he implies, one can only succeed in dissipating its reality. Knowledge of an object, he was later to say, means an exhaustive knowledge of all the relationships in which it stands, and hence true knowledge is only an eschatological possibility. But this sense for the organic is already quite evident in

[95] *Cf.* Hermann Bleek, *Die Grundlagen der Christologie Schleiermachers,* Freiburg in Br. (1898), pp. 207f.

[96] Schelling, *op. cit.,* pp. 507ff. It is also to be observed that the birth of self-consciousness involves a moral act and that it leads not to the idea of Man-in-himself in the abstract, but to Man-in-himself present in a community of individuals. Schelling also disliked the way in which Schleiermacher held the individual outside of God and emphasized his relation to God rather than his unity with God (p. 504).

The Christmas Eve, where no individual comes before us as such, but always as mother or father or child or friend. It is clearly significant that when, in Eduard's speech, the Logos becomes flesh, he is described as the one in whom "the community of feeling" breaks forth. In him we celebrate humanity. Despite the difficulties that Schleiermacher offers present-day readers with his Son of Man Christology, he pricks the conscience of the modern theologian who has sought so long to find the image of God in the self-sufficient exister, whether he be the knight of infinite faith or the alone-real, alone-human Son of God. Schleiermacher challenges such romanticism and thoroughgoing idealism.

Chapter Two

HERMENEUTICS AND HISTORY

§1 DIRECT COMMUNICATION

There are few men in the history of theology whose inner histories are as accessible as Schleiermacher's. The autobiographically revealing works of his youth, together with his lifelong copious correspondence, provide us with the means for direct insight. On this score of an inner openness, Schleiermacher calls to mind the contrasting figure of his contemporary, Søren Kierkegaard, whose own ethical and religious thought was also adumbrated in the response of his spirit to his personal fate. The literary expression of that response has made Kierkegaard the poet of indirect communication and the most influential exemplar of the dialogical method in our recent history. Today, his story is not only well known; it occupies the position of an archetypal myth of the modern soul. Rejecting marriage with Regine Olsen, first of all, and subsequently nearly every other possibility of sharing immediately in the forms of public life, Kierkegaard sustained himself by his activity as an author, ostensibly disguising his personality behind an array of pseudonyms which, nevertheless, sufficed to induce a recognition of their creator in the eyes of the "single reader" for whom his authorship was intended. His style was one of indirectness, designed to conceal the ultimate religious identity of the self within the everydayness of its aesthetic and ethical-social preoccupations and at the same time to betray the presence of such an identity through the irony employed to characterize these same preoccupations. The aesthetic and the ethical spheres of life, but particularly the latter, constitute at one and the same time the barrier and the hidden way to faith. This style has given to us the "knight of faith" whose faith is wholly inward and the "disciple" whose discipleship is an aesthetic and ethical offence. Thus Kierkegaard's "openness" is founded on the conviction that the external and internal identities of the self are discontinuous. The aesthetic-ethical and Christian spheres of existence cannot be plotted with the same coördinates, and yet truth transpires only in and through the collision of selves in dialogue about the God-man.

Because of the parallelism between the two men, it would be tempting to propose that, if the break with Regine made Kierkegaard a "poet," it was his rejection at the hands of Eleonore Grunow that made Schleiermacher a preacher and an educator dedicated to the nurture of the church, the university and the nation. But, in fact, we cannot accept the absolute priority of the external over the internal, into which this parallelism might easily entice. The enlightening point of comparison between the two lies at the level of their differing conceptions of the moral and religious spheres of life and of their interrelations, and it is here that the equally different qualities of their inner "openness" achieve real significance. Just as one finds nothing of Kierkegaard's profound distrust of the forms of corporate life and nothing of his doctrine of the leap from the ethical to the Christian sphere of existence, so also one is unable to catch sight of anything resembling his indirectness in Schleiermacher. On the contrary, Schleiermacher's youthful *Soliloquies* could scarcely have been more directly confessional, and even from the letters of his maturity we come to know him as a man who was deeply disappointed if his friends did not recognize his own full and immediate presence in his words and if they themselves did not answer in kind with a wholehearted candidness. There was no self-concealment in his nature. Moreover, as we have seen in *The Christmas Eve*, the author presented the religious and ethical spheres as pervasively penetrating and conditioning each other, so that Christian experience and faith cannot arise in the individual save in and through a social context, a family or group of friends; yet the fabric of social relationships itself is finally expressive of the personal identity and freedom that are bestowed upon the individual through faith and regeneration. In Schleiermacher's view, only the ever renewed dialogue of self with self can etch upon our lives their common ethical structure and provide the means by which each interlocutor may appropriate his own inalienable identity. However, this identity itself is always more than the ethical sphere can contain, for it expresses the relationship of the individual not only to man but also to God. Consequently, Schleiermacher's style is not one of indirectness in antithesis but directness in polarity.

We have a description of Schleiermacher left by Henrich Steffens, his colleague and friend at Halle, which indicates something of the personal manner that accompanied and supported this style:

> Schleiermacher was, as is well known, of small stature and somewhat deformed, but in such a way that he was scarcely disfigured. He was lively in all of his movements and his facial features were most telling. Something sharp in his glance could, perhaps, rebuff one. He appeared in fact to look right through a person . . . . His face was long; all of its features were decisively drawn, the lips firmly closed, the chin jutting forward, the eyes lively and fiery, the gaze continuously serious, composed and thoughtful. I saw him in the most varied, changing circumstances of life, reflecting deeply and playing, jesting, gentle and angry, moved by joy as by pain; but an enduring, unchangeable calm

> greater and stronger than these passing emotions appeared to rule his soul. Nevertheless, there was nothing rigid in this repose. A soft irony played in his features, a hearty sympathy moved him inwardly and an almost childlike goodness pervaded this visible calm. His dominating reflectiveness had strengthened his faculties admirably. While he was engrossed in the most lively conversation, nothing escaped him. He saw everything that was going on about him on all sides; he heard everything, even the softest conversation of others. Art has preserved his features for eternity in an admirable way. Rauch's bust is one of its greatest masterpieces, and whoever has lived with him so intimately as I is almost startled when he looks at it. Even in this moment, it often seems to me as if he were there, nearby me, as if he were about to open his firmly closed lips in earnest converse.[1]

Steffens' recollection of his friend is of all the more interest because it is obviously a likeness in which we can recognize the author of *The Christmas Eve.* Just as in that dialogue Schleiermacher emphasized both the importance of the fundamental religious mood (*Stimmung*), in which the sense of personal identity and humanity are integrated, and the equally basic importance of the dialogical relations among the members of the small group, so also Steffens' image of the author depends chiefly upon the impression that Schleiermacher left of a strongly unified personality whose whole energy was poured into the arts of sociability and of activity in the various circles of his life. This striking agreement clearly suggests that the Christmas dialogue, despite its occasional character, embodied elements that were determinative of its author's style of life and reflection, namely, the ideas of mood/feeling and of the moral nature of man coming to decisive expression in his capacity for dialogue within the corporate forms of human ex-

[1] LS^2, p. 548. Quoted by Dilthey from Steffens' *Was Ich Erlebte,* Vol. V (1842), pp. 141f.; *cf.* English edition, *German University Life,* trans. W. L. Gage, Philadelphia (1874), pp. 136f. Translation my own.

istence. Furthermore, these ideas were not only obviously determinative for the man of 1805/06, but they also mark a continuity of direction in the succeeding years, a continuity that is conspicuous when we compare the brief Christmas piece and the famous dogmatic theology of 1821/22 which contains the controversial and technically brilliant proposal that the proper material of dogmatic theology is the content of the religious feeling of the members of the Christian church. There can be no doubt that the description and analysis of joy, around which *The Christmas Eve* revolves, foreshadow the basic principle of the magnum opus.

But even if the pivotal significance of these two ideas or complexes of ideas is beyond doubt, we have to acknowledge that the bearing of each upon the other is still relatively obscure. Indeed, the failure to recognize that there is *any* relationship at all between the religious and the ethical spheres of life has constituted one of the most grievous obstacles to the interpretation of Schleiermacher to date. The appreciation of him on the part of contemporary theology has in particular suffered from a one-sided approach in which the single element of feeling has been isolated for a critical but unproductive examination.[2] Now, however, the evidence of *The Christmas Eve* alone is sufficient to establish the futility of this line of interpretation. But granted that this is the case, and that each

[2] This one-sidedness is present in the account of Schleiermacher given by H. R. Mackintosh, which is probably the most widely read interpretation of Schleiermacher's theology in the English-speaking world. Mackintosh makes the initial error of suggesting that Schleiermacher thought of feeling as a faculty, standing alongside the faculties of thinking and willing. In the second place, he neglects Schleiermacher's intense preoccupation with history and the historical. The consequence is that Schleiermacher emerges as one guilty of subjectivism: "he was not prepared to take history quite in earnest." *Types of Modern Theology*, New York (1937), pp. 45, 57. One hears nothing in Mackintosh of the Schleiermacher who wrote in his journal: "History is always religious and religion, by its nature, must be historical." "A dialogue concerning the discipline of history, after the manner of the Phaedrus on rhetoric, would have to be very good indeed." "A real historian could well say he would prefer to count peas than have anything to do with the transcendental philosophy." LS[1], pp. 100, 127, 130 in "Denkmale."

element of Schleiermacher's style must be scrutinized in its reciprocity with the other—the religious in the context of the ethical, and the ethical in the context of the religious—, it follows that we shall have to examine not only his theology but also his ethics. For this purpose, we turn now to a consideration of Schleiermacher's idea of the ethical character of life.

§2 THE ART OF INTERPRETATION

A distinguishing feature of Schleiermacher's ethics is its capacity to serve both as a philosophy of history, hence as a comprehensive interpretation of human thoughts and acts, and as a positive basis for particular historical sciences. Nowhere are the realism and the creativity of the ethics better shown than in the lectures on hermeneutics, or the art of interpretation. In fact, Schleiermacher lectured on ethics and hermeneutics concurrently, thereby demonstrating his own maxim that the general and the particular disciplines can grow in depth as well as scope only when they grow apace. We shall, accordingly, examine his ethical principles in both of these forms and take up first of all the art of interpretation, in order that we may have before us a concrete example as we later encounter the fundamental formal principles upon which he articulates his idea of man as the image of being in the historical cosmos.

Schleiermacher's lectures on the method and aims of interpretation were based on a considerable experience with the whole gamut of problems implicit in translation and critical, historical inquiry. Such historical criticism, which he broadly defined as the technique of investigating and judging the authenticity of written documents, proceeds hand in hand with its companion science, hermeneutics, or the discipline of understanding correctly the content of the discourse of another person. The effort to distinguish between the genuine works of Plato and the pseudo-Platonic dialogues, like the effort to disentangle the theology of St. Paul from the merely Pauline, can be successfully prosecuted only if the critic grasps what Plato or Paul intended to communicate. The discerning and defining of the intention of the author and of his particular relation to the linguistic symbols in which he clarified and executed that intention are the unique tasks of hermeneutics. As such, the discipline of interpretation is obviously of the utmost importance to all of the departments of culture that depend upon a living connection with the past.

Characteristically, however, the road by which Schleiermacher arrived at his idea of the discipline lay through his own personal history as well as through his scholarly training. We have only to recall Steffens' picture of his friend, as one who not only conversed but also lived in his conversation, to understand that Schleiermacher must have drawn heavily upon his own experience for the formulation of his principles of interpretation. We know from his autobiography that the intensity of inward, personal piety in the Moravian community embued him as a youth with a sensitivity to nuance and tone in the utterances and gestures of others. He was acutely conscious that he lacked some of the religious experiences presupposed by the Moravians, and he was given to comparing his own psychic state with that of his school mates.[3] It is also evident that first as a tutor in a noble family and later as a frequenter of the literary and intellectual salons of Henriette Herz and her circle in Berlin he received informal but effective schooling in the art of earnest and animated exchange of ideas. Steffens' description of Schleiermacher at Halle confirms Schleiermacher's developed virtuosity in such conversation, and Schleiermacher himself briefly adverted to this personal background in an address on hermeneutics before the Royal Academy of the Sciences: "Who," he asked, "could associate with exceptionally lively and witty men without being just as careful to listen between the words as we are to read

[3] Br. I, pp. 7f., 23f. (E.T. I., pp. 7, 26).

between the lines in intelligent and close-packed books . . . who would not want to grasp the inner logic . . . of a significant discourse?"[4] But the meaning of the personal and experiential for his conception of hermeneutics went still farther. As, by his own suggestion, his early, social experience had prepared him for the work of technical interpretation, so he sought to show that the discipline as such is rooted in everyday life, and he advised "most urgently, the interpreters of written works to exercise industriously the interpretation of the more meaningful conversation."[5] Schleiermacher even intimated that a familiarity with the principles of hermeneutics could enhance ordinary social intercourse, "for very often in private conversation, I resort to hermeneutical operations, if I am not content with the usual level of understanding but wish to explore how, in my friend, the transition is made from one thought to another, or if I would seek out the views, judgments, and endeavors that are connected with the fact that he expresses himself in one way rather than in another respecting the subject of our conversation."[6]

Such remarks indicate in part the reasons for Schleiermacher's hesitation in subsuming hermeneutics wholly under the general head of philological science. The act of interpreting appeared to him to be something personal and creative as well as scientific, an imaginative reconstitution of the selfhood of the speaker or writer. Such an effort of empathy must always go far beyond the principles of philological science into the realm of art.[7] But his deeper reasons for criticizing the strictly philological, grammatical approach to the

[4] SW III/3, "Ueber den Begriff der Hermeneutik mit Bezug auf F. A. Wolfs Adeutungen und Asts Lehrbuch," p. 352; (Herm., p. 130). Joachim Wach believes this recognition of the actual extension of the principles of hermeneutics into the domain of conversation constitutes Schleiermacher's first great contribution to the discipline. *Cf. Das Verstehen,* Tübingen (1926), Vol. I, pp. 89f.

[5] *Ibid.;* (Herm., p. 131).

[6] *Ibid.,* p. 351; (Herm., p. 130).

[7] Herm., §9, p. 82.

verbal expressions of others grew directly out of his reflections on history and human nature. Interpretation, Schleiermacher was convinced, does not belong to philology alone, because it has its origin in that nuclear life structure that transcends the vision of every particular science. It is rooted in the constitution of man as an ethical agent. The level of human nature from which it rises is accessible only to thinking that is informed by both empirical and constructive, theoretical interests in man. Schleiermacher believed that each actualization of language through specific speaking and hearing peculiarly exemplifies the ethical balance between individuals and simultaneously enhances it. Speaking and interpreting presuppose participation in a common humanity but at the same time they give a new concreteness to that which is distinctively human in our experience of others and of ourselves.

This is the basic conviction that informs the whole of the development of his thinking on interpretation. It is reflected in the way that Schleiermacher conceives of language as a living organ of our historical existence, so that even in the first division of his treatment of the discipline, which has to do with the strictly grammatical foundations of interpretation, he approaches words in their syntactical contexts not as arbitrary symbols or counters for the exchange of thoughts but as integral members of the internal skeletal structure upon which the flesh of consciousness grows and forms itself. Hence, he insistently asserts in his lectures that there can be no thinking without words.[8] The full implication of this thesis for philosophy constitutes the substance of his lectures on *Dialektik*, which we will have occasion to consider briefly later, but here we can anticipate the discussion that is amplified in that place, and also in his ethics, to the extent of noting that Schleiermacher believed thinking truly exhibits the moral, historical character of human existence because it is an activity that always involves an awareness of the relatedness of the individual to the community of

[8] *Ibid.*, §3-§5, p. 80; *cf.* Braun II, "Brouillon 1805/06," p. 97.

consciousness; it is "that kind of activity of which each person is conscious as something not in himself especially but in all equally."[9] In addition, thinking involves, by its very nature, an awareness of conflict (*Streitigkeit*) or of difference between the judgments of the self and of others. Such conflict is the distinguishing mark of thinking, according to the *Dialektik*, and sets it off from perfect knowing, to which none of the sciences can pretend in their present state. The original situation of the rational self is then a dialogical one. Thinking is the struggle to overcome conflict, and even when it occurs in solitude, the self is playing a twofold role, reproducing the social matrix in which the impulse to critical reflection first arises.[10] Mediation of thought is, therefore, part of the very process of thought itself, and to think means to acknowledge one's own obligation to deposit one's thoughts in the public language in response to the utterance of others, the obligation of both learning and teaching, the obligation, that is to say, of becoming a particular self.[11]

Thinking then is an inner speech, and speech symbolizes the innate tendency of thinking to externalize itself and reconcile the conflict between selves occupying different historical positions. There is a further corollary of this dialogical view of thinking, however, which must also be recognized at this point, since it is so fundamental to Schleiermacher's entire treatment of language and interpretation. Schleiermacher points to it when he observes that language never appears except in an individualized form.[12] Therefore, since all men learn to speak within the matrix of some given, historical language, their thinking also bears the impress of that historical mold. Reason is conditioned by the "natural" organ in which it appears. A number of significant consequences flow from this dictum. One of them, particularly interesting when we remem-

[9] Braun II, 1816, §48, p. 586.
[10] Dial. (O), p. 54.
[11] Braun II, 1816, §57, pp. 592ff.
[12] *Ibid.*, "Brouillon 1805/06," p. 100.

ber that Schleiermacher was the contemporary of Schelling and Hegel, is that we can never expect to encounter a universal and absolute philosophy, simply because there neither is nor can be a universal language.[13] Within the context of the lectures on hermeneutics, however, the meaning of the dictum is simply that there is no access to the mind and the intention of an author or speaker apart from his use of his language, his words, sentences, paragraphs, books, and finally his life's work. Therefore, Schleiermacher declares, the interpreter stands under an absolute obligation to achieve not only a mastery of the grammar of the language into which he is conducting the investigation but also a knowledge of its history and physical conditions. Something of the sense of Schleiermacher's insistence on this point can be conveyed if we say that one duty of the interpreter is to regard his author primarily as an event in the life of the language itself, as a vessel in and through which the language and current literary forms preserve themselves by coming again to public expression.[14] As a homely illustration, Schleiermacher offers the example of talk about the weather, chatter which has little meaningful content but does allow the language to maintain itself through repetition. Language possesses an autonomous power. The meaning of words and expressions is determined by a context that far transcends the identity of the speaker or author. Each language has to be regarded as something of an organic unity, having a life of its own. Individual words are embedded within this organism, and they stand in a web of positive connections with the totality, so that their meanings cannot be easily controlled; the practice of defining words by setting them over against antonyms creates a false impression of the logic of speech. Schleiermacher preferred to describe a word as a historical, dynamic entity whose precise meaning in any given occurrence can be determined only when we consider its relations to the

[13] *Ibid.*, p. 101.
[14] Herm., §5, 3., p. 81.

entire development of the body of speech within which it lives.[15] Even when the individuality of the speaker or writer is more significantly present in his discourse, his language constitutes an inheritance that qualifies his spirit, conditioning the direction and the progress of his thoughts.[16] For this reason, the interpreter must have a thorough knowledge of the author's language in order that he may be aware of the limits of the latter's mind and that he may avoid anachronisms in his exegesis of the text. In sum, the interpreter must so comport himself in his own dialogue with the author that he always remains fully conscious of the latter as one who is both objectively and subjectively conditioned by the language of which he is an instrument and by the total historical complex in which he lives.[17]

The sweep of the objective and subjective historical side of the method is symbolized in Schleiermacher's assertion that the "task can also be expressed in this way: to understand the text just as well as and then better than the author himself understood it."[18] This assertion points to the fact that the interpreter must bring to the level of conscious appreciation a great deal in the history of the language an author employs that the author himself takes for granted and to which he responds only on an unconscious level. However, both his personal and scholarly experience would have prevented Schleiermacher from wholly identifying the aims and principles of interpretation with this objective and subjective "historical" method. Schleiermacher knew that an author, engaged in writing, understands the words he is setting down as something both larger and more limited than a representation of the meanings implicit in the language he has inherited. The total production is also his own deed, arising out of his own inner history, and this history is one that cannot be encompassed within the author's lin-

[15] *Ibid.*, §1, 8., p. 92.
[16] *Ibid.*, §5, 1., 2.; §6, 1., pp. 80f.
[17] *Ibid.*, §18, 1., 2., p. 87.
[18] *Ibid.*, §18, 3., p. 87.

guistic inheritance. We must, therefore, regard the author as an agent who conditions his language, even though he is also being conditioned by it. The interpreter must, then, undertake to acquaint himself both with the individual moments that constitute the history of that author and with the form within which those moments have been organized by the author. This endeavor leads the interpreter toward the author's own sense of identity and purpose. The realization of such a goal dictates that the interpreter focus in his own mind the individuality of the author, again including many elements that resided in or affected the latter only unconsciously, and to that end the interpreter must supplement the grammatical-historical method by a parallel approach called by Schleiermacher psychological interpretation.

The psychological method is no less rigorous than the grammatical and, for that matter, no less historical, although the kind of history with which it deals is certainly of a more elusive nature. Its object is the author's decisions, his freedom. This kind of history cannot be studied and reconstructed except in the closest connection with the other. Something of the relation between the two methods is conveyed by Schleiermacher's characterization of the complete goal of the psychological method as "the thorough understanding of the style." Style, he goes on to explain, reflects both the inner and outer history of the author in their unity. "We are accustomed to understand by 'style' only the way in which the language is handled. But thoughts and language always inform each other, and the distinctive way in which the object is grasped informs the arrangement [of the elements of the composition] and thereby also the handling of the language."[19] Part of the task of the psychological method is to analyze the rôle played by the form in which the author chooses to organize and present his thoughts—the so-called "technical" method. But the other, the "pure psychological," which is the endeavor to understand the full significance of the author's

[19] *Ibid.*, §3, p. 108.

initial decision to make this particular communication, is doubtlessly the more basic, since modes of reflection and composition constitute relatively uninformative data unless we are able to see why and how they have been adopted as instruments by a particular rational will.

As one follows the development of the psychological method, therefore, one better understands the reason why Schleiermacher defined hermeneutics as an art rather than as a science. (It is not a branch of philosophy, he adds, because it is no longer the fashion to claim it as a department of logic, for the philosopher "seldom interprets, though he himself believes that it is necessary that he be interpreted.")[20] Hermeneutics is a science, to be sure, in the sense that all of its principles require a thorough justification and must satisfy the criterion of internal consistency, when taken together. Furthermore, the practitioner of interpretation seeks to serve the furtherance of knowledge rather than the canons of taste. Nevertheless, interpretation is also of the nature of art, particularly in view of the fact that it rests decisively upon certain talents that all men may possess latently, but only a few in the requisite measure. The first of these talents is the ability to know language not only extensively or by the comparative method but also intensively, the ability to feel language as a living reality and to penetrate "into the core of the language in its relation to thought." The second is the capacity to know men as individuals, again not only extensively but also intensively by the direct understanding of the "genuine meaning of a man and his distinctive characteristics in relation to the [essential] idea [*Begriff*] of the man."[21] On Schleiermacher's terms, it is even true that these "intensive" talents, and particularly

[20] *Ibid.*, §2, 1., p. 80.

[21] From student notebooks, SW I/7, *Hermeneutik und Kritik*, p. 17. Schleiermacher's reason here for calling interpretation an art, because it requires a knowledge of individuals and hence transcends the idea of science, is an anticipation of the idea of history that we find in Wilhelm Dilthey, Ernst Troeltsch, Benedetto Croce and R. G. Collingwood.

the latter, must assume a definite priority over the extensive linguistic and historical branches of the discipline because no communication, whether it be written or vocal, is ever meant to be taken merely as an aggregate of symbols but rather as an organized representation of its author's historical intention, as an effort to bridge the distance between the self and the other. Just as, therefore, we all are on occasion "virtuosi of conversation," having presentiments of what the other person wants to say and constructing the evolution of his thought before we have heard the whole utterance, so in the interpretation of written texts the exegete must divine the intention and total purpose of the author as he reads the individual parts of the composition.

When we are dealing with written documents, of course, we are not compelled to be intuitive or "divinatory" in precisely the same way as in conversation, for we have the advantage here of being able to deal with the whole composition before undertaking the interpretation of its individual parts. However, the advantage is only relative because every literary whole is itself only a fragment of the larger whole of the author's life, and every author, like every man, is an individual who stands in and is qualified by an infinite number of relations to his world. To reconstruct the individuality of the author by selecting out of this potential infinity those relations that are most important to him and arranging them in their proper order is an exercise that needs for its successful completion an acute and instinctive knowledge of men. From the historically limited and finite point of view of the interpreter, the author necessarily appears as a contingent being. There is no way in which he can be wholly deduced from generic humanity or even from his nation and generation. Our knowledge of him, therefore, must remain less than exhaustive, confronted with a residual mystery of his individuality. As a consequence, the precise juncture in his inner history from which his communication arises, be it autobiography, historical narrative or epic poem, must also remain partially shrouded in the sheer contingency of his inner and outer being. The interpreter has no alternative, therefore, except to complement his ordinary or scientific knowledge of his author by an attempt to grasp the life-unity of the author directly, to call into play his intensive knowledge of men or—as Schleiermacher more frequently speaks of it—his talent for divination.

When Schleiermacher comes to the point at which he must specify the character and procedure of the divinatory method more closely, he is suggestive rather than precise. The perils of relying upon a direct and intuitive knowledge of the author's identity are obvious, however, and consequently Schleiermacher emphasizes that it must be controlled by a parallel "comparative" method, which is correlated with the divinatory method in the following way. The divinatory method seeks to grasp the individuality of the author by transforming the interpreter himself into the other. It is based upon the sensitivity that every man has for all others, a sensitivity which, Schleiermacher declares, "appears to rest only on this fact, that each individual carries in himself a minimum of all others."[22] A knowledge of self is therefore indispensable to a knowledge of what lies in others. We find Schleiermacher saying the same thing, in somewhat different circumstances, as he writes to Eleonore Grunow: "But how much is involved in the ability to see a man rightly, dear friend, and what things! The man must know himself, and not only that, but he must also have discovered everything in himself. True simplicity and innocence will never attain to such a knowledge of men. But he who has found in himself—if only an element, in which nevertheless its true nature lies—of perversion and corruption and then also a trace of greatness and nobility, and then is frivolous enough to construct in his fancy the whole form out of this suggestion—look you, such a person is fitted for the knowledge of men."[23] The divinatory method requires that

[22] Herm., §6, p. 109.
[23] Br. I, p. 342 (E.T. I, p. 330).

one recognize elements of the other in the self; but this recognition is prompted by the interpreter's interest in comparing the object of his interpretation with himself. A fully developed comparative method, on the other hand, attempts to arrive at an understanding of the individuality of the author by setting him alongside of other men with whom he shares important characteristics and then isolating his individualizing features. But such a method of classification implies that we recognize the general character of the author by an immediate intuition; otherwise we become involved in an infinite regression of comparisons. Hence, the comparative involves the divinatory method also.[24] In short, each approach entails the elements of the other and the employment of one necessitates that we take up the development of the other in order that in our knowing of men we neither fall prey to fantasy nor persuade ourselves to rest content with generalities. The dialectical relationship of the two methods means that interpretation is a never ending work.

We shall pursue Schleiermacher's theory of interpretation no further, despite the fact that it contains many features that are noteworthy both by reason of its place in the history of hermeneutics and because of its bearing upon the principles of interpretation espoused by contemporary theological existentialism.[25] Here, we are interested in the *Hermeneutik* as a concrete exemplification of

[24] Herm., §6, p. 109.

[25] Schleiermacher's place in the history of hermeneutics is examined by Wilhelm Dilthey; *cf.* "Die Entstehung der Hermeneutik," *Gesammelte Schriften*, Vol. V, Stuttgart (1961); also Joachim Wach, *op. cit.* Dilthey's own categories of historical reason, *Hineinversetzen, Nachbilden, Nacherleben*, etc., represent further development of Schleiermacher's method. There are a number of affinities between Schleiermacher's idea of interpretation and the hermeneutics of contemporary theological existentialists; *cf.* Rudolf Bultmann's essay, "The Problem of Hermeneutics," *Essays, Philosophical and Theological*, trans. J. C. G. Greig, London (1955), and the hermeneutics of Bultmann's pupils as described in part by James M. Robinson in *The New Quest of the Historical Jesus*, Naperville, Illinois (1959). The distinguishing between an existential and a historical method, of which Bultmann and his heirs make much, echoes faintly the more dialectical relationship between the divinatory and grammatical modes of interpretation in Schleiermacher.

the style that informs Schleiermacher's own perspective, and, in this connection, the last-mentioned point in the exposition above provides us with a summary statement of the import of the whole. The dialectic between the divinatory and comparative methods, through which the interpreter is required to come to an increasing knowledge of himself as he reaches after the inner meaning of the author, indicates that the discipline of interpretation arises out of and belongs to the dialogue of life with life, which, whether it be between speaker and hearer or author and reader, is the marrow of our historical existence. Hence, while the problems posed by historical criticism dramatize the importance of interpretation as a discipline, interpretation itself far transcends the limits of criticism and historical research and will never be brought to perfection until the sum of our words reveals the identity of all men without remainder. Hermeneutics systematizes and refines the human processes of disclosure and appropriation through which societies grow toward a clearer and more lively unity. This is the reason that the welfare of the church, for example, requires the constant development of the art of interpretation. The apprehension of the common life in the church, the life and the Spirit of Christ, can occur only when the religious consciousness is awakened to the meaning of the language in and through which it is related to the historic church; and the proclamation that originates in Christ and founds the church, together with the theology that serves it, also presupposes such an awakening consciousness of language.[26]

The dialectic between the divinatory and comparative methods, repeating as it does the more inclusive dialectic between the technical and pure psychological and then between the psychological as a whole and the grammatical-historical methods, illustrates concretely the close correlation between Schleiermacher's

[26] SW I/7, *Hermeneutik,* pp. 261f. (from student notebooks) & Gl., §15-§18. "From the beginning Christianity has shown itself as a language-building principle." Send., p. 60 (642).

development of the particular historical discipline of hermeneutics itself and his view of human nature in the historical cosmos. The form of the discipline and its subject matter correspond, and the unceasing need for this correspondence exhibits another reason why hermeneutics can never be brought to perfection, since it must share in the incompleteness of history. At the same time, however, and in partial contradiction of this dialectical or polar structure, the reader of these lectures has to acknowledge that another style also exerts a shaping power throughout the *Hermeneutics*, sometimes directly and sometimes more gently. This second style arises out of Schleiermacher's temperamental nisus toward unity or completion; it is the trait of his mind that his interpreters have called his Spinozism. The actual, abiding significance of Spinoza in Schleiermacher's own history constitutes just such a problem in the understanding of an author as he himself discussed in his lectures. That Schleiermacher, in common with the philosophical Romanticism of his day, found a genuine inspiration in Spinoza's vision of the Being who is at once *natura naturans* and *natura naturata* stands as an indisputable fact of his own history, to which his earliest publication *On Religion* bears a witness with its failure to draw a distinction between God and the world and its tendency to speak of the infinite universe as divine.[27] Furthermore, that even in subsequent years this early conatus toward a final unity still exercised a forming influence upon his mode of thinking is also undeniable. The point in question, however, is not the fact of what we may, for purposes of convenience, continue to call Schleiermacher's Spinozism but rather its influence upon his spirit. Did it survive as an unassimilated body, containing an at least implicit disruptive threat to the consistency of the historical texture of the thought exemplified in the lectures on interpretation? Or did Schleier-

[27] For Schleiermacher's indebtedness to Spinoza and his differences from him, see Dilthey, LS², pp. 358ff. Schleiermacher explains this point as due to the rhetorical nature of the language used in *On Religion*. *Cf*. Reden, E.T., p. 103.

macher succeed in bringing this early heritage into an harmonious and constructive relationship to the idea of dialogue that has figured so importantly in *The Christmas Eve* and the *Hermeneutik*? Within the limits of the latter, the answer to the question would have to be twofold. So far as the structure of the interpretative method is concerned, its dialectical balance seems to remain undisturbed, and in fact Schleiermacher insists that the findings of the interpreter can never be regarded as final; hence the dogma (of hermeneutics) that there is only one correct exegesis of a text is false, and the goal of a perfect understanding of the author's meaning can be only approximated.[28] The idea of an ultimate, organic unity of meanings stands on the methodological level as a theoretical presupposition only, necessary to the actual life of the discipline; but it is not to assume an operational function or to become a pretext for intuiting a particular synthesis of meanings where there is no warrant for such.[29] Nevertheless, we also find hints of Schleiermacher's own disposition to use the ideal of unity as a criterion of reality, so that his perspective on history is informed by a definite bias. "Our mode of viewing each person as a whole," he wrote to Eleonore Grunow, ". . . of believing in the existence of dissonances in human nature, but not of incongruities; and not in total transformations, but only development and improvement—this method is identical in us both, and is undoubtedly correct."[30] An example of this tendency occurs in his judgment that of all the four Evangelists John is the most likely to have been an eyewitness of Jesus' ministry because his narrative has a more personal, historical unity;

[28] Herm., §18, 4, p. 88; §4, p. 108.

[29] Schleiermacher carefully qualifies the application of the traditional concept of "the analogy of faith" used in biblical interpretation to obtain doctrinal harmony from the diverse components of the New Testament. *Cf. ibid.*, "Erster Theil," §22 - §30, pp. 101ff. In his lectures on the life of Jesus, he cautions: "We have his self-consciousness of the unity of his life as a fundamental presupposition, but no one is in possession of the continuity of his life in its temporal evolution." SW I/6, p. 36.

[30] Br. I, pp. 329f. (E.T. I, p. 319).

it presents that of Jesus which the oral tradition could have least successfully preserved—the dialogical.[31] The truth, of course, is that Schleiermacher could more easily recognize himself in John than in any of the synoptists. As his friend and editor remarked: "Schleiermacher belongs to the class of those [interpreters] who are far more strongly inclined towards a distinctive individuality of apprehension, than to self-surrender; who rather draw over the author to their own position, than allow themselves to be drawn by him."[32]

Keeping these observations in mind, we may conclude this brief examination of the *Hermeneutik* by stating that Schleiermacher has here shown the essential problem of the critical historian to be none other than a systematic analysis and mastery of the dialogical situation in which we live from day to day as particular historical beings in a determinate world, a world that potentiates our own feeling of selfhood as we become increasingly aware of our relatedness to other selves through the common structures of humanity.

§3 CRITIQUE OF ETHICAL INQUIRY

In the lectures on hermeneutics, Schleiermacher has in effect presented the literary monuments of the past as deeds symbolizing the moral lives of their authors and the language that spoke through them, and concomitantly he has defined the task of interpreting these lives through their deeds as being itself a moral act.[33] Consequently, when we consider these lectures together with the Christmas dialogue, we see a fundamental consistency. The frame and humor of Schleiermacher's own inner world govern both the

[31] SW I/8, *Einleitung ins neue Testament,* p. 219.

[32] F. Lücke, "Reminiscences of Schleiermacher," *Brief Outline of the Study of Theology,* p. 33.

[33] *Cf.* August Twesten's introduction to Schleiermacher's ethics, *Grundriss der philosophischen Ethik,* Berlin (1841), p. xv., note.

manner in which he approaches the past and its historical remains and his attitude in the midst of the edifying friendship and sociability that make up the present. It is a world of past and present set in motion by the striving of reason to understand, that is, to grasp the real in its particular self-disclosures and, in the process, to arrive at a more inclusive moral equation between the interpreting self and all the others that make up its world. But to say this is to affirm that the *Hermeneutics* is fundamentally a scientific expression of its author's characteristic and innermost ethical spirit. There is nothing else in Schleiermacher's authorship—with the exception of his *Brief Outline of the Study of Theology*—that offers as rewarding an insight as this into both the inclusive and the critical qualities of this guiding interest of his in the nature of man as agent in an historical world, the interest that in practice was the axis of his view upon reality and informed his systematic reflections not only on interpretation but also on all the other social and historical sciences that now fill his collected literary remains.

If we ask why Schleiermacher's ethics should have lent itself so well to the interpretation of other selves, part of the answer lies in the fact that he did not content himself in his ethical reflections with purely formal principles but instead sought to understand the rôles of material values, of concrete goods. Like Augustine, he found the truest image of human nature reflected not in a man's notion of what is right but in the object of his love. This fact is all the more noteworthy when we recall that Schleiermacher lived in the age of "practical reason," the generation dominated by the voices of Kant and Fichte calling men to hearken to the pure sense of duty that lies at the core of their humanity. Indeed, Schleiermacher's own youthful philosophical efforts were critical reactions to Kant's ethics, and there is no doubt that he was one of those who listened most attentively to these philosophers of practical reason. The response that these voices elicited, however, assumed a significantly different form, for Schleiermacher rejected the Kantian-

Fichtean accent on duty as the principal phenomenon of the moral life and of our sense of humanity and instead organized his own ethical reflections around the idea of the highest good.

Schleiermacher arrived at his formulation of the idea of the highest good through his critical study of Kant and under the influence of the Platonic dialogues he was busy translating. The thinking of the former was embarrassed by an inner contradiction, Schleiermacher believed, because it stipulated as integral to the moral life the idea of the perfect highest good as the union of virtue and happiness; yet a premise of Kant's ethics was that the moral life is entirely independent of the affective side of human existence.[34] Schleiermacher himself, consequently, rejected Kant's sharp distinction between the empirical and the rational-moral self. A second defect or further extension of the same error in Kant's reasoning appears when we recognize that either the idea of the perfect highest good is an idea of pure reason, as Kant claims, in which case it cannot be identified with a particular content such as happiness; or the content of the highest good must be derived from the actual material of ethical activity and not from pure reason.[35] In the development of his own ethics, Schleiermacher chose to identify the highest good with the content of ethical activity and to deny that reason can entertain a pure, a priori idea of it.[36] But while Kant provided Schleiermacher with a vigorous, critical impetus, it was quite evidently Plato who inspired his true creativity. In *The Republic*, "the most glorious composition of antiquity" to Schleiermacher's mind,[37] Plato places the good at the apex of the hierarchy of forms as the source or principium of the order and

[34] *Cf.* Herman Süskind, *Der Einfluss Schellings auf die Entwicklung von Schleiermachers System*, Tübingen (1909), p. 2.

[35] *Ibid.*

[36] Braun II, 1816, §19, p. 569. "We have no special knowledge of the highest good as the unity of the being of reason in nature, save this knowledge of the mutual co-inherence and penetration of all individual goods."

[37] LS¹, "Denkmale": "Ueber das höchste Gut," p. 15.

intelligibility of the world. All that exists, then, to the extent that it does exist, participates in and reflects the good; and our own humanity, to the degree that it is a true realization of human nature, culminates in a love for this good that orders our souls and the soul's commerce with the world. This conception of man, as being an analogue of the divine world and as having the capacity to govern himself both inwardly and outwardly according to the pattern of the eternal ideas, Schleiermacher judged to be the most significant albeit undeveloped statement of the idea of the highest good in the history of ethics.[38] Naturally, however, in view of the bent of mind that we have already seen exemplified in his criticisms of Kant, Schleiermacher did not follow Plato in the latter's teaching about the transcendence of the supreme idea of the good with its attendant doctrine of the tragic imperfection of every concrete embodiment. Instead, he concentrated upon the community of finite agents in which reason becomes actual, that is, functions as reason by indwelling and organizing nature through man himself. Here we have the context for Schleiermacher's idea of the moral agent, the agent that as a producer of goods is good in himself and vice versa—the counterpart to Kant's "end-in-himself." Kant's "end-in-himself" is the rational will moved solely by the timeless and purely formal law: "Act so that the maxim of thy will can always at the same time hold good as a principle of universal legislation." Schleiermacher, on the other hand, defines ethical being (*Für-sich-zu-Sezende* [sic]) as a member of a community organically constituted of rational wills together with the sum of their productivity, and the goodness of these wills or agents lies not simply in their holy respect for the timeless moral law but in their contribution to the total human content of the community.[39] According to this view, moral agency is not so much conformity to a universal, selfsame maxim of reason as it is the actualization of the (rational)

[38] SW III/1, *Kritik der bisherigen Sittenlehre,* p. 176.
[39] Braun II, 1816, §102 - §104, p. 507.

nature of humanity in a unique, concrete form. Hence, not only rationality but individuality is ethically significant.[40] And, indeed, so much is directly implied by the very idea of a community of such agent-ends, for a community does not arise out of an aggregate of individual examples of humanity who are only quantitatively differentiated. Schleiermacher regards humanity as an organism of such moral agents who are not only vessels of reason but unrepeatable symbols of it and organs of its productivity. This organism, furthermore, includes not only single persons but larger corporate persons in which the single are rooted, such as family, nation, university and church, and these latter too are ethical entities nourished by and nourishing the whole organically fashioned system. Such a construction of the discipline of ethics is obviously not Platonic according to the letter but only in spirit; its object is the highest good, but the highest good is this organic system itself of dynamic beings.[41]

All of these considerations are reflected in the characteristic language of an early statement of the relations to each other of the various types of ethical theory. "The highest good," he wrote in his sketch for the system in 1805/06, "is the cosmography, the entire organization of the doctrine of virtue is the dynamic, the doctrine of duty is the speculative view through which the whole arises."[42] The idea of duty is a critical tool, to be employed after the fact in the analysis of an act; the idea of virtue is merely a formal expression of the living motions of the moral agent, related to the latter as

[40] *Ibid.*, §8, p. 565. One of Kant's gravest faults, in Schleiermacher's eyes, was his failure to see that by excluding personality from the province of ethics he vitiated the reality of the community to which he appealed under the name of the kingdom of ends. *Cf.* SW III/1, *Kritik der bisherigen Sittenlehre*, pp. 21ff., 63. Georg Wehrung believed that Schleiermacher's estimate of Kant rested only upon the first two critiques but not on *The Critique of Judgment*. *Cf.* Wehrung, *Die Dialektik Schleiermachers*, Tübingen (1920), p. 16.

[41] *Ibid.*, §104, p. 507.

[42] *Ibid.*, "Brouillon 1805/06," pp. 84f.; *cf.* also "Ethik 1812/13," §83 §108, pp. 256ff.

in mathematics the formula is related to the actual line. Both ideas point to nothing more than single moments in our understanding of the human response to man's intuition of his place in the cosmos. The fundamental insight toward which we strive, and which ethics seeks to clarify, is determined by the concrete order of being as it includes and affects the self-becoming of the person. In the spirit of Plato, Augustine and Jonathan Edwards, Schleiermacher believed the moral life to be a coming to know and to love that which is. But the scope of such an endeavor, especially as it is suggested by this definition of the highest good, is obviously so wide as to make of ethics a virtual philosophy of history, if not more. And, in fact, philosophy of history is Schleiermacher's meaning, when he speaks of ethics as the "science of history or of intelligence as appearance."[43] Ethics must, to be sure, "comprehend and record all truly human action,"[44] but Schleiermacher understands human action as the motion of love, as the human response to the order of being, and as the further definition and actualization of that order in the proprium of the self.[45] Therefore, it is neither the comprehending and recording of universal order in itself nor the study of mere personality; rather, ethics is the science of that order in personality and of personality as the chief organ of that order.[46] It is the expression of the "becoming of the world from the standpoint of reason,"[47] but, as we shall see, for all that, it is not an absolute science, inasmuch as the standpoint of ethics is itself involved in that becoming. Consequently it is a philosophy of history that is

[43] *Ibid.*, p. 80.

[44] *Ibid.*, 1812/13, §12, p. 246.

[45] *Proprium* is used here and elsewhere to translate Schleiermacher's term, *Eigenthümlichkeit,* which is equivalent to *proprietas* and could reasonably be rendered by either of the English words *propriety* or *proprium.* The latter has not lost its alien sound, but the former has come to connote the conventions of a given society and consequently does not lend itself to the expression of the idea of the inner, irreducible essence of individuality. Circumlocutions are also used, such as underivable selfhood, innermost individuality, etc.

[46] Compare §17 and §81 in Braun II, 1812/13, pp. 247, 255.

[47] *Ibid.*, 1816, §66, p. 500.

bound to its place within the horizons of history itself. However, this conception of the scope and status of the discipline will emerge more clearly, when we take account in somewhat greater detail of Schleiermacher's derivation of ethics from the order of being and knowing as it appears in our consciousness.

Schleiermacher sets out to describe the order of being by taking his departure from a polarity that he conceives to be the most universal of all, the polarity of ideal and real.[48] As the terms *ideal* and *real* are used here, in this initial and most abstract statement of the polarity, they do not so much stand for two theoretically separate orders of being, after the fashion of the Aristotelian distinction between form and potentiality. Rather, Schleiermacher intends to point to the fact that all finite being represents less than a pure or absolute unity. It represents only a relative unity whose actual existence cannot be derived from its form nor its form from its existence. The polarity of ideal and real is the expression of the fact that all that falls within our experience is involved in becoming and can consequently never be seized by the intellect or the will and reduced to a single term. Both form without matter and matter without form transcend our experience, and therefore we cannot assign a metaphysical priority to either one or the other.

The derivation of this polarity is not speculative, Schleiermacher explains. It is simply entailed in the fact that our own existence is a soul-body existence,[49] an existence itself exhibiting only a relative unity in which body is body by virtue of its penetration by an active forming principle, and soul is soul by virtue of the presence in it of consciousness, or—in equivalent language—the presence to it of "real" being.[50] Hence, it is that our own constitution prevents us from attaining a metaphysical reduction of the elements of experience to pure reason or pure matter. For, if we take

[48] *Ibid.*, §40, §41, p. 495.
[49] *Ibid.*, 1812/13, §27, p. 248.
[50] *Ibid.*, 1816, §50, p. 533. For a closer definition of real, *cf.* below, pp. 99ff.

body as the most immediate exemplification of the real, then it follows that real being, as it enters our experience, appears as an analogate of body and consequently implies an equally original active principle informing it. And, if we take soul as the most immediate exemplification of the ideal, then it likewise follows that soul, insofar as we can objectify it in thought, is always dependent upon the presence in itself of real being in the form of consciousness of such, whether it be of our own body or of a more remote object. Stating the matter in a general way, and overlooking for the time being the distinction between the rational activity of knowing and that of willing, we may say that being is given only in and through knowing and knowing only in response to being. Consciousness is not a manifestation of pure reason but of reason individuated in a body and set in motion, as it were, by an object, and real being is not a thing-in-itself secluded behind the appearances but it is being responsive to the search of consciousness for an object.[51]

It will be well to emphasize at this juncture that Schleiermacher makes no attempt to adduce an absolute intuition or knowing in which we become aware of a ground of being and of the ideal and real poles of finite being arising directly out of it. On the contrary, in conformity with his stipulation that all actual or historical knowing is involved in this polarity,[52] Schleiermacher stands fast against the claim of the absolute idealists to transcend the subject-object relationship. We have reason, he says, only in the form of personality.[53] He is, of course, fully alive to the fact that the polarity between knowing and being is derived ultimately only from his analysis of consciousness itself and he cannot offer a demonstration of its logical necessity, for the form of consciousness is

[51] Schleiermacher's full account of the matter here involves the inclusion of the organism of perception in the cognitive process. This bodily organism is not created *ex nihilo* by reason but is an instrument adapted by reason to its purpose. So, in itself, it exemplifies soul in body and body in soul; it is an image of the polarity of ideal and real in knowing.

[52] Braun II, 1812/13, §20, §21, §22, pp. 247f.

[53] *Ibid.*, §81, p. 255.

not susceptible to logical proof; it can only be described. Consequently, Schleiermacher can do no more than point to consciousness and declare that we find ourselves therein in two forms, as thinking activity and as that which is thought, as self-active and as modified and informed by external being. This argument is circular, indeed, and its persuasiveness rests only on the testimony of self-consciousness, namely, that knowing is given in and through being yet as something different from it. In this connection, it is possible to cite additionally the fact that in the act of willing or doing we also are oriented on being, and willing permeates and conditions thinking; but we have not thereby broken out of the circle of self-consciousness.[54] However, Schleiermacher did not lack means to defend the plausibility of his construction, if not its logical necessity, for the issue at stake here affects his entire position at its very center. And even though it is in the *Dialektik* that he sets forth his defense, the reasoning involved belongs as much to the foundations of his ethics as to his philosophy of thought. The defense is in actuality an appeal to the fact that Schleiermacher regards as axiomatic: thinking is dialogical. It begins with the premise of the *Dialektik*: thinking is driven by a will to know, by a will to grasp the object at the roots of its existing-in-such-and-such-a-way. Thinking presents itself as being moved by a virtual pathos for being in itself. It aspires toward the final unity of the ideal and the real. But the phenomenon of thinking, as a given and ever renewed activity, is the proof that this will is not satisfied and that the thinking self remains in a situation of striving to know, which is expressed by the self's conflict with others concerning the object of thought. Indeed, as we have already seen anticipated in the hermeneutics, Schleiermacher regards all thinking, from the highest or purely philosophical to the most informal, as a more or less stringent effort to conduct a dialogue for the reconciliation of differing judgments and concepts. If we accept this descrip-

[54] Dial., §101 - §103, p. 53.

tion of conflict as the matrix of thought, then we are obliged also to acknowledge the fact that each participant in the dialogue must be present in the individuality of his thinking to the other(s), so that the evident differences distinguishing the position of each provokes on the part of each a comparison of himself with the other(s). But the very possibility of such recognition of differences and of a comparison implies that there is a common, perduring object present to the thinking subjects, an object which is distinct from their thinking itself.[55] This defense, however, is essentially only a restatement of the fundamental thesis of the ethics. We have reason only in the form of consciousness, and our knowing is a response to being; it is an appropriation of it ideally, but it does not constitute an identity with being. These statements are, in

[55] *Cf.* Dial. (O), p. 315. The foregoing explication of the relationship to being inherent in knowing is based on Odebrecht's reconstruction of the lectures of 1822, from student notebooks. Aside from the student notebooks, the warrant for this reconstruction lies in the fact that we have in Schleiermacher's own lecture notes of 1822, which are in the form of comments on the outline of 1814, a treatment of willing and being that suggests the logic explicated above. This treatment of willing and being is prefaced by the remark that the argument even back in 1814 should have been worked out in closer parallelism to that for thinking and being, a parallelism that we presumably have in 1822. *Cf.* Dial. (O), p. 279; *cf.* also Dial., p. 426. One may infer, therefore, that the argument for thinking and being in their relationship to each other embodied the logic we have here, although from Schleiermacher's own hand we have only the brief suggestion that the agreement of thinking to being "is given necessarily with the presupposition of a plurality of individuals" (1814). Again, there is the assertion that we can consider the question of the relationship of thinking to "something outside of ourselves" only from the standpoint of the presupposition that "conflicting conceptions presuppose a plurality of individuals who think" (1822). *Cf.* Dial., pp. 53 and 386. In the same cycle of notes from 1822, Schleiermacher continues by saying that the same thing obtains also "if one takes his departure from conflicting conceptions in the same individual: he himself becomes an object thereby for himself, in his doing, as then doing and being, as object of thinking, everywhere behave wholly in the same way." The argument is further applied to the ability of thinking to return to an object of thought and to repeat the first process of appropriation, "that is to say, thinking corresponds to its object. If we designate this also as being, nothing more shall be thereby declared than the persistence of the object for thinking." Dial. (O), p. 137.

effect, an affirmation that thinking and striving to know, and therefore all of the sciences, arise in a relationship of mediacy, in time and space, which is to say that they arise in history and nature.[56]

Speculative and abstract as Schleiermacher's point of departure may first appear, then, one of its most immediate and important functions both for his treatment of ethics and for his idea of the sciences at large is the limitation that it thereby places on all thinking and striving to know. Neither ethics nor any other science is directly concerned with God or the absolute being, for the absolute as the ground of both the ideal and the real cannot fall within the field of consciousness defined by the polarities of ideal and real, subject and object, reason and nature. The object of real knowledge is real or polarized being. This is not to say that finite being does not point to an absolute ground; for from the beginning, with the publication of the *Speeches on Religion*, one of the distinguishing features of Schleiermacher's view was his doctrine of the individual entity as an image of the All, and this doctrine continues as a cardinal principle of the ethics. Likewise, it is essential to Schleiermacher's position to affirm that all rational activity, both knowing and willing, is an expression of the absolute ground of consciousness, and the *Dialektik* devotes considerable attention to the postulation—as over against a demonstration—of such a ground along the lines of the foregoing discussion of the relation between being and knowing. The significance of the delimitation here drawn is that all real knowing transpires within the world and is bounded by human history.[57] The positive statement of this delimitation is to the effect that all of the sciences are dependent upon

[56] Braun II, 1812/13, §82, p. 255. The rejection of time and space as a priori forms of intuition is part of the difference between Schleiermacher and Kant, and it is related intimately to Schleiermacher's view of the pivotal significance of individuality.

[57] *Ibid.*, §1, §2, p. 245; *cf.* also *ibid.*, 1816, §§79ff., pp. 503ff. The last mentioned point recurs throughout the *Dialektik* and is especially evident in the "Einleitung," the only portion of the *Dialektik* that Schleiermacher prepared for the press himself. For example, *cf.* Dial. (O), pp. 40f.

real being both for their possibility and their development. Science is descriptive in nature, though it is not merely descriptive. The negative statement of the delimitation is to the effect that none of the disciplines receives its aims and principles from any highest or universal knowledge. Insofar as it is possible to speak at all of a highest science, one must say that its actualization awaits the completion of all the real sciences in their reciprocal relatedness to each other.[58] We may remark incidentally here that it is this conviction that prompts Schleiermacher to assert the independence of theology from any particular philosophy, not in the sense of an absolute independence, for every discipline must be affected by its sister sciences, but in the sense that both the orthodox theologians and idealist philosophers deny by their reduction of doctrinal truth to the language of a particular metaphysics. How can such a simple dependence be asserted, Schleiermacher asks, when it is the several disciplines themselves, both individually and in their interdisciplinary dialogue, that are the instrument through which language and hence thinking are purified and cultivated?[59]

To say that the sciences are descriptive in character means that we cannot construe the principles and procedures of the sciences a priori but only in an empirical dependence upon the being that the sciences endeavor to understand. Our thinking does not attain to certainty through the employment of innate ideas; it must always be open to the possible criticism implied in newly discovered data.[60] The science of ethics is deeply affected by this restriction, particularly insofar as it must perform the functions of a philosophy of history, for it is thereby debarred from becoming autonomous and assuming a lofty prophetic and prescriptive role. But this restriction arises directly out of Schleiermacher's point of departure in the ideal-real polarity as given in the soul-body form

[58] *Ibid.*, 1816, §5, p. 488, but see the whole discussion here, §1 - §21.

[59] "The society of sciences (*wissenschaftliche Verein*) is the knowing activity (*Erkennen*) that builds language." *Ibid.*, 1812/13, §67, p. 273.

[60] For Schleiermacher's discussion of innate ideas, *cf.* Dial. (O), p. 151.

of our existence. For by virtue of the soul-body form of our existence, we are enabled to think only as conscious or embodied souls and to know ourselves as bodies only through the adaptibility and conformability of body to the soul's work of thinking and willing, symbolizing and organizing. This co-inhering polarity, as we have seen, defines both our inner and outer horizons and nowhere vanishes.[61] If this is the case, however, then reason is given to us in and through our natural constitution, and embodiment and consciousness cannot be set aside as accidents in the life of the soul affecting it only tangentially; they are rather integral to its life. Otherwise, as Schleiermacher says, the soul would be "merely a nameless something next to matter, the place of ideas."[62] In actuality, however, it is not nameless but is always the soul of a particular man, of a member of a particular family or nation and race; it is rooted in a temperament and participant in a destiny. The point of departure in the ideal-real polarity consequently makes impossible a sharp and absolute line of demarcation between reason and instinct or passion, between history and nature. History and nature converge in man, and man's history as the sum of the movements of his soul reflects that nature at every moment, while nature depends on him for its recognition and completion. Hence, the study of man as an historical agent must take account of the fact that he is not an absolute agent, for he receives his temperament, his talents, his tools such as language, etc. by virtue of the "accident" of his time and place. We have already met with one example of the import of this restriction in Schleiermacher's hermeneutical thesis, that the interpreter must raise to the level of consciousness much that remained at the unconscious or natural level in the author or speaker, for the intentions of the latter can be fully grasped only when the interpreter can fully describe him in his

[61] Braun II, 1816, §50, p. 533. Where the polarity seems to disappear, Schleiermacher reasons, we no longer have an entity that is real for us.

[62] *Ibid.*

passive as well as active identity. For the discipline of ethics at large this same restriction means that ethics, as the science of human action or—more comprehensively—as the endeavor to understand all finite being both in relationship to and from the standpoint of human agency, is dependent on the science of nature or "physics."[63] Man is not an ethical agent to be recognized on the basis of the principles of ethics alone, but he is a bodily organism whose description ethics must receive from "physics" or, as we might say today, empirical anthropology.[64] The material of his agency is not simply the maxim of his will but that which is naturally given, the soil, the family, the tribe, etc. Ethics is always dependent, therefore, on the sciences that deal with nature as such and on the sciences that address themselves to all the forms of organization and corporate life that stand between the "natural" and the intentions of the individual. Theology would express this polarity of his existence by affirming that man is a creature. For the discipline of ethics, its significance lies in the fact that ethics itself is thereby limited; it can at no time pretend to a greater wisdom or insight than its sister science of nature permits it by virtue of its own progress, and, similarly, ethics can never transgress the limits of the present development of the intermediate descriptive, historical sciences in order to postulate what reason demands for the sake of an a priori conception, such as the notion of a transhistorical vision of God. Ethics has to do only with "earthly, resisting life."[65]

At the same time, however, physics is likewise dependent on ethics, for the "natural" is a relative concept whose full meaning appears only when we have clearly in view the character of the

[63] *Ibid.*, 1812/13, §28, p. 248. "Ethics is, accordingly, the representation of being under the power of reason, that is from that side in which—in the coinherence of the polarity—reason is the active term, and the real that which is acted upon; and physics [is] the representation of finite being under the power of nature, that is, as the real is the active term, and the ideal that which is acted upon."

[64] *Ibid.*, "Brouillon 1805/06," pp. 81f.

[65] *Ibid.*, 1816, §62 - §74, pp. 537ff.

beings for whom nature is nature. And, by the same logic, the descriptive, historical sciences can proceed no farther than permitted by the idea of history given to them by ethics. So, the sciences in their interdependence demonstrate the dialogical nature of all thinking and striving to know.

This last-mentioned, dialogical interdependence of the sciences underscores another aspect of Schleiermacher's conception of human reason that is important both for the form of the ethics itself and the idea of man that is ingredient to his theology. The underscoring here is of the fact that reason is not only limited by the polar nature of finite being, so that, unable to reduce being to a final unity, it must supplement each approach to being by a complementary science; reason is also internally limited by its position in time and society. Our thinking does not begin with absolutely clear and distinct ideas, as Descartes would have it, any more than it begins or ends as though its embodiment were extraneous to its proper operation. The ideas with which we commence are only relatively clear and distinct. They are so for those who are able to enact the same processes of appropriation;[66] but as the distance grows between the distinctive modes of apprehension characterizing two or more individuals, societies or cultures—of which language is, perhaps, the most significant index—the self-evidence of these ideas wanes, or the ideas that are self-evident assume a different form. Here we see Schleiermacher taking a fundamental cognizance of the inherence of knowing in the knower. Knowing is not only a response to being but it is also the deed of an agent, and it bears in itself all the traits that define his individuality, the marks of all the polarities between his own irreducible selfhood and his family, nation, university and society. Hence, each person in his striving to know is expressive of the way in which a multitude of relations converge in him uniquely. These relations converge in him uniquely because no other person occupies exactly the same

[66] *Cf.* "Einleitung in die Dialektik," Dial. (O), §4, pp. 24ff. *et passim.*

position in time and space and because no other proprium can appropriate these relations in the same fashion. There is, therefore, when we think, a relativity that belongs as indefeasibly to our thinking as does our sense of participating in an activity that belongs equally to all men.[67] This relativity of knowing and knowledge, and of volition also, for that matter, reflects the situation of man as a being who is always both an individual personality and the race. He is a being whose identity includes in its range both the underivable essence of his uniqueness and the form of his species together with all the intermediary spheres of human life through which this essence and form are mediated. If then we posit as the goal of thinking such a completed knowledge as all men may share in alike, departing from the same principles and attaining to the same conclusions, that goal will have to be something else than a knowledge in which the individuality of the thinker is expunged by the dominating presence of pure reason; it will be a knowledge inclusive of the individuality of every thinker.[68] Therefore, the acknowledged relativity of all striving to know does not so much betray, for Schleiermacher, the ineluctable shadow of skepticism as it declares the necessity for each knower to cultivate a full consciousness of the way in which his own position modifies his thinking and of the way in which he is also modified by all of those other knowers who oppose him.[69] The necessity of being aware of the modifying presence of opposing knowers is exemplified in the hermeneutical theory we have briefly detailed above, for the interpreter using the divinatory method has incumbent upon him the duty to take cognizance of the principles and results of the opposing grammatical interpretation of the words he seeks to make come alive. The necessity of being aware of the efficacy of one's own presence in one's own knowing is illustrated in the maxim that

[67] Dial., §127, p. 69.
[68] *Ibid.*, §91, p. 47.
[69] *Cf.* footnote 63 above; also Braun II, 1812/13, §3, p. 245.

Schleiermacher provides: every discipline must attend to its own history, whether the discipline in question be interpretation, ethics, dogmatic theology, or some other.[70] Progress in inquiry and understanding requires that the scientist consciously carry in himself the history of his endeavor. And in this fashion, through dialogue with the present and the past as it exists both in the self and in the other opposing selves, the intrinsic openness of striving to know becomes a critical tool for the preservation of the integrity of knowledge and of the knowers out of whose life it arises.

§4 SUFFERING AND DOING

In the preceding sketch of the form of Schleiermacher's ethics we have seen reflected the movements that distinguish all human striving to know. In the subject matter we encounter man and mankind in the dialectic of life, seeking the appropriate expression of the power (*Kraft*) and eros of human existence. The real purpose of the ethics is to furnish the reader with the characteristic patterns traced by this dialectic, and if we were to make use of the mathematical imagery to which Schleiermacher himself was addicted, we should have to say that these patterns resemble neither geometrical forms nor the arbitrary motions of random particles of energy but rather are better likened to the open curves of the parabola or hyperbola, figures that are determinate yet never to be reduced to a finite set of coördinates. Or, if we borrow from Augustine who in the *City of God* alludes to the life of the human race as a river and again as a torrent, we should have to compare Schleiermacher's ethics to the analysis of the currents and whirlpools, which in their several motions and countermotions never-

[70] Braun II, 1812/13, §5, p. 245. *Brief Outline of the Study of Theology* is the finest illustration of this point with its application of the principle to the dialectic between church history and systematic theology in the section on "philosophical theology."

theless compose themselves into one system of energy running on toward a common end. But the metaphor of the river of life does not license us to superimpose here the view that is to be found in the older scholastic and Greek theology, in which the economy of the life of mankind is presented as merely the diremption and return of divine energy to its source. Human history is not the devolution of a pure and undifferentiated power. It is better compared to an organism wrought by the power of formation, and this power of formation gives shape and impetus to the processes of history solely in and through personality.[71] Consequently the object of Schleiermacher's ethical inquiry is not the naked energy that posits the cosmos but the creative logos as it indwells mankind and its members.

The object of ethical inquiry is, accordingly, the person, the historical, moral agent. The agent is a being with universal dignity and value, for he is endowed with a universally recognizable rationality. But this endowment of rationality is not extrinsic to his existence as an individuated being; it is rather constituted in his inward and peculiar identity.[72] So much follows from the fact that the person is an image of the universal logos but as such reflects the logos in a unique way, thereby contributing to the total content and wealth of all human history and culture. Construed in this fashion, the individual man appears as an end-in-himself and something more. He is a citizen and freeholder among all other men because he has a share in the universal property of reason. But this property, in turn, receives its own final historical identity in the character of the holder. Hence, each citizen or agent plays a rôle in the appropriation of his own identity and in the mediation to others of that indispensable endowment that constitutes them as men also. To be sure, this agent and end-in-himself is also out-

[71] *Ibid.*, §81, p. 255.

[72] The irreducible, inner identity of the self, expressed most immediately and fully in feeling, is not the accident of time and space but is directly created by reason, which posits itself differently in each man. *Cf.* below, pp. 116ff.

wardly determined and individuated by time and space as well as by all of the natural conditions embraced therein. He is not a world citizen, therefore, save insofar as he participates in and arises out of the life of an epoch, a civilization, a people, a family, etc. But, once again, these conditions of his nature and outward individuality are not merely the results of the astonishing, but in itself ethically insignificant, variety of nature; they are the raw material in need of being shaped by the inner self (the proprium), in need of being appropriated and organized into the instrumentality of the individual's true existence as a living co-creator of human history and culture.

We may fairly describe the individual person as an historical image of the universal, but we must immediately underscore the fact that he is a dynamic image. He suffers and he freely acts. He suffers not merely or primarily in the narrow sense but to the degree that he is placed and does not place himself, that he is embodied and does not embody himself, and that he is consciousness and, in the subject-object duality of his consciousness, is bound to both of these given poles of his life. In this sense, he is a passive, suffering image: a point of focus, a reflector and a symbol of the life and energy that converge upon him. But the function of the image is also to be a clarifying concretion, a renewed embodiment and fresh communication of life. For ethical inquiry and reflection, consequently, which must interpret the suffering as well as the deeds of the person as a form of his agency, the existence of man is a constant becoming and deepening in and through his activities of bearing, exemplifying and symbolizing, on the one hand, and a constant communicating afresh and extending and so reshaping the power and order of life, on the other. Ethics, therefore, finds the life of man to be founded upon and expressive of a fundamental duality of receiving and setting forth or communicating; the ethical agent lives in the reciprocity of inheriting and endowing in a community of persons. Lacking either one of these basic forms of agency, his life declines below the status of a true image of being in becoming or—in the words of *The Christmas Eve*—of man-in-himself.

The dialectic of suffering and doing is present throughout the material exposition of the ethics. It appears at the very outset, for example, in the sections concerning the human functions of organizing and knowing, of representing and recognizing. Traditional philosophy would speak of the two faculties of will and intellect, but Schleiermacher's approach cannot be easily translated into the terms of "faculty" psychology, since he has in mind not two abstract and more or less discrete capacities but two functions of the total self, which deeply interpenetrate each other throughout. This much is indicated by the choice of the word *organizing* which, instead of directing our attention to something in the self that is opposed to reason or is a-rational, denotes the appropriating and shaping power of the self. Accordingly, organizing and knowing stand respectively for the whole self in its willing and its striving to know. But the self that comes to be in both of these activities can never abide in one of them alone; it must always pass over into the other, so that the willing-shaping self becomes the striving-to-know self, and the knowing self the willing. This interpenetration appears clearly in both of the functions named. If we examine it from the standpoint of knowing, it becomes manifest when we perceive that knowing is founded upon a will to appropriate the "other." Knowing expresses the thrust of volition and of love. It is a *recognizing*. (The word that Schleiermacher uses here is *Erkennen.*) And, at the same time, willing discloses its true nature to be not a blind movement of the self but the setting forth of the self, the deed of stamping the self's identity upon such being as has the capacity to be organized by the rational agent. Thus the will to communicate arises in response to the recognition of the structure of the "other," and knowing is the response to a movement of the will.[73]

The agent-self that emerges here conforms to the description

[73] Braun II, 1812/13, §6, p. 259, *et passim.*

of human existence that lies at the basis of Schleiermacher's conception of ethical inquiry and of all the sciences. It is a rational consciousness that is informed by its embodiment, a subject given only in the polarity of subject and object. The self in willing or organizing and in knowing or recognizing is oriented on being. Willing or organizing is, to be sure, that activity in which the agent-self freely inscribes its own identity upon being and appropriates it to its own uses; while knowing is the endeavor of the agent to subordinate himself in a disciplined fashion to objective being, to let himself be determined, as it were, by the object.[74] But the interpreter of Schleiermacher's ethics cannot oversimplify his conception of the moral agent here by stating as a generalization that in the former activity the self exercises its freedom and in the latter is determined by the object. Rather, it is the case that since each activity is the presupposition and the issue of the other, we have to conclude that the living self is as such both relatively free and relatively determined. Thinking then is finally as much the deed of the self and as much declares its initiative as organizing, and organizing as much reflects the determinedness of the self by the objective world as thinking. In short, the entire temporal content of conscious life enacts itself in the reciprocity of bearing and exemplifying, on the one hand, and of extending and reshaping the material of life, on the other.

The direct implication of this rendering of human life on the pattern of a reciprocity of determination and freedom is that Schleiermacher can make no room in his ethics for a doctrine of absolute freedom. The self is always a self over against other being; it is a self with a world, and the articulation of the one grows only apace with that of the other. The exclusion of an absolute freedom and the firm insistence that man is a creature whose existence in such and such a particular way is always prior to his freedom is of the greatest moment for Schleiermacher's idea of religion, to which

[74] *Cf.* Dial. (O), p. 228, and Gl., §3, 3.

the propositions, borrowed from ethics, that provide the introduction to the dogmatic theology testify. Without a doubt, Schleiermacher is not a philosopher or theologian of radical freedom, and the reader has no choice but to acknowledge that the self Schleiermacher outlines with his principles of ethics is through and through a determined and dependent being. Furthermore, he is determined by and dependent upon not only the external objects of his willing and striving to know but also the conformation inwardly of his own nature. The critique of the limits of ethical inquiry has already shown this, and it is indicated by the order of discussion that he adopts in his analysis of the fundamental modes of agency falling under the aegis of ethical inquiry, for he is obliged to present the thinking and willing agent as one who is himself, anterior to all his own activity, the deed of a prior agency. The all-important soul-body form of human existence is the expression of this dependence and determinedness. This form of our existence teaches us, we have learned, that we have our intellect only as an embodied reason that employs its embodiment as the medium of its commerce with the world. Hence, to be a man does not mean to be a substance harboring a spark of reason but to be a rationally organized nature. If we render this fact as a metaphysical judgment, we say that human existence points to its own genesis in the aboriginal activity of reason as an organizing, shaping power.[75] In ourselves the shaping power of reason discloses itself immediately, and all the self's commerce with the world, through which it becomes genuinely human, is but the development of the pattern of organization with which it is endowed and by which it is defined. This commerce, beginning with man's most primitive and always fundamental relations to the world, can never extend beyond the intellect's capacity to develop its own instrument of knowledge, the body together with its senses and members, in and through which consciousness is related to all other being. Schleiermacher sum-

[75] Braun II, 1812/13, §3, p. 259.

marily states the matter by saying that "mechanics" (the basic organizing relation of man to the inorganic world) and "agriculture" (the basic organizing relation to the organic world) are dependent upon "gymnastics" (the rational appropriation and critical employment of the senses and talents of the embodied self).[76] Hence, the whole range of human activity and life, from its physiological basis to its most creative apex in the pursuit of knowledge, is articulated upon and limited by the pattern of its own given organization. The structure of our being is the limit of our thinking and willing. Therefore, the universe is not destined to become the mere organ of human nature; for inasmuch as the organization of our human nature has to be regarded as a product of the cosmos, the cosmos must be acknowledged as something that is given in the same sense that our nature is given, and like our nature it stands as a limit that cannot be reduced either by our willing or our knowing.[77]

But since with Schleiermacher metaphysical statements never have an independent validity or cogency, we gain a better insight into his meaning concerning the givenness of the self when we turn to the ethical significance of the fact. And, ethically, the import of the fact is that our existence as such is always the expression of the organizing, producing, self-extending wills of other agents, first of all those who make up the family; but ultimately it is also the expression of all the other members of the communities from which the self comes and in which it exists. These agents who bring forth each new individual are not, to be sure, absolute creators or organizers, but their procreative activity exemplifies the true nature of ethical agency, which is the reduplication of the self by means of the common, organic media of human existence, in the community of common life. The child is the symbol, then, of his parents, the pupil of his teachers, the citizen of his nation, and so forth. The individual is the offspring of the joint wills of others,

[76] *Ibid.*, §7 - §12, p. 276.
[77] *Ibid.*, §4, §5, §6, §7, §14, pp. 263ff.

and as such he is already an organized being, and not merely in the minimal sense of inheriting the soul-body form of existence but more fatefully in the sense of receiving this inheritance as it has been qualified by the characteristics and experiences of the communities from which he derives. He reflects the personal identities of his progenitors. And, in this way, each personal life always arises as the compound creation of prior shaping intelligences and recognizing wills, and issues into the stream of life by which this process is perpetuated. To become a self means to appropriate the identity that is given through all these mediators of life, until it qualifies the entire polarity of soul and body and becomes the "style" of the individual's existence.

We may summarize the immediate significance of Schleiermacher's conception of agency, then, by saying that to be an ethical, historical agent means to suffer (in the widest sense) and, in response, to do; to be determined and to determine; to inherit and, in response, to create. Ethical responsibility consists in entering into both of these movements of existence with a full awareness; it is to receive one's identity as it is given and to inscribe that identity upon the common life. Nothing in Schleiermacher illustrates this reciprocity so well, perhaps, as the description of the functions of language we have already encountered in the hermeneutics and *Dialektik*. The tongue that the speaker inherits is his common bond with other selves; it is the premise of his humanity, the basis of his thought. But its very preservation for the commonweal requires that each speaker take up the language into his own life and make of it an organ of his own will to communicate. Through this language the speaker grows into selfhood, receives himself from the community of speech, and, setting forth his own selfhood in the common speech, creates a new moral content for the community's medium of shared life. In this sense, language as an organ and symbol, as an expression of will and vessel of intelligence, is an exponent of the underivable and irreducible ethical and even covenantal quality of life.[78] And what is true of speaking is true of every form that the movement of life produces, whether it be aesthetic, scientific, domestic, political, social or religious. In each of these spheres, the individual exister is the dynamic mirror of the totality, inheriting and re-creating, being formed and re-forming, suffering and doing.

§5 THE SELF IN FEELING

The moral self of Schleiermacher's *Sittenlehre* never appears as, and is not conceivable as, a pure individual. Not only is it the case that the individual is physically posited by the community, but he is psychically dependent as well. The relation in question here is, again, one of limited dependence only; more precisely it is another relationship of polarity or of co-inherence. As Schleiermacher explains in his lectures on psychology, our own affirming of ourselves as I's or as selves is not the function simply of the continuity of our own memories, for our memories are not coextensive in time with our actual existence as individuals. The sense of an inner unity of selfhood is aroused in each person through the recollections and descriptions of him given to him by other persons or Thou's standing over against him.[79] By virtue of this co-inhering polarity of community and individual, the character of the former comes to qualify every significant activity of the self: its perceiving, speaking, thinking and doing. Only by acknowledging the extensiveness and intensiveness of the community's participation in the individual is it possible, to Schleiermacher's mind, to grasp the meaning and the reality of communities at all. But, for all that, the individual is still an integral and independent being, standing over against the community in a genuine polarity.

[78] *Ibid.*, 1816, §57, pp. 592ff.

[79] SW III/6, *Psychologie*, pp. 14f. All experience that presupposes a positing of the self involves a Thou. Schleiermacher discards the *nicht-Ich* of his contemporaries in favor of the *Du* as the designation of that which genuinely opposes the I. The *nicht-Ich* is simply a negation of the I. *Cf.* p. 18.

Like the ideal-real, mind-body polarity, the polarity of self and community occupies the place of an axiom in Schleiermacher's ethics. In fact, we can interpret it as but the other side of the former, insofar as Schleiermacher could defend the validity of the ideal-real polarity only by appealing to the social matrix of all thinking. The import of this second polarity is that the community does not come after the individual, and neither, as we shall see immediately, does the individual come after the community. Schleiermacher steadfastly avoids the error of constructing a philosophy of history that relegates either term of the polarity to a secondary status. In effect, then, he refuses to follow either Hobbes or Hegel in his thinking about man and organized society. Schleiermacher's basic criticism of the social philosophy that attempts to place the community second is that it thereby gives to the community an ethical and historical foundation that is arbitrary at best. The social contract theory of the nation or state, for example, employs the myth of an original, absolutely free covenant on the part of individuals, whereby they limit their own inherently illimitable pursuit of life for the sake of an orderly and secure corporate existence. The social contract supposes that the freedom and morality of the natural man are antithetical to social forms. In fact, however, one has to see the community as an expression of human freedom, rather than as a denial or arbitrary limitation of it.[80] And, obviously, Schleiermacher with his conception of ethics as the doctrine of the organic system of goods could never allow a fundamental form of social coöperation, such as the state, to be relegated to the level of an accidental historical phenomenon. History does not begin with individuals as such but with individuals in communities.

The thinking at work in this criticism of the social contract myth bespeaks the attitude that Schleiermacher holds toward all basic social forms. Neither the national unity and state, nor the

[80] Braun II, 1812/13, §§89ff., pp. 335ff. There is, however, a relative truth in the social contract theory, to the extent that it criticizes the identification of the ethical essence of the state with the *Obrigkeit* or ruling class. *Cf.* also *ibid.*, "Brouillon 1805/06," p. 82.

church, nor the universities and academies, nor the more vague but no less important associations of men comprehended under the rubric of free sociality (*Geselligkeit*) are intelligible as the products of artificial compacts. They all, like the most basic of the forms, the family, belong to and are rooted in the ethical, historical life that emerges in the individual. In actual fact, Schleiermacher understands the individual person as a virtual microcosm of the social macrocosm that entails these various spheres. The family, the national unity, the church, etc. are themselves persons in dialogue with whom the agent lives. The reason, whose activity in and through ethical personality constitutes the meaning of history, is not fully manifested until these larger persons are also represented in the dialectic of life.[81] Such a construction of the individual-community polarity means that under Schleiermacher's hands the ethical agent never stands over against the state or any other of these forms as though it were an alien and autonomous entity. On the contrary, he bears a responsibility for it that is consonant with his own moral sense; since the individual and corporate persons participate in each other, there can be no sharp distinction between private and public responsibility, and neither one can claim a higher or different morality from the other.

In view of the fact that each and all of these spheres of social life arise out of and express the moral nature of the individual, Schleiermacher cannot allow an absolute distinction to be drawn between them. He was, to be sure, an ardent defender of the independence of the church over against the state, and likewise he championed the freedom and integrity of the university against the interference of the government. Each of these social forms possesses its own birthright and enjoys the freedom that belongs to the free pursuit of its own goals and execution of its own duties. But at the same time, each of them has something of all the others in itself. The church, for example, must incorporate something resembling

[81] *Ibid.*, §72, p. 273.

the civil organization in its polity; again, the state must embody something of the religious disposition of its people. It is evident that all institutions must comport themselves in their relations with one another according to the morality of free association.[82] And all these spheres or forms are to be found germinally in the family itself and represent the further articulation of the individual-community polarity that comes to its original manifestation therein.[83]

The Christmas Eve provides us with an illustration of the way in which these social forms blend into one another through their common inherence in the family. In that early work, Schleiermacher did not include a statement on the integrity of each of the communities; so much is really taken for granted by the author. He is more concerned to picture the family, free society and the Christian community in the ecology of historical, human existence. And we should note also that the fate of the national unity of the German people is introduced into the background of the dialogue from time to time. It is a mistake, then, to interpret Schleiermacher's intentions in *The Christmas Eve* to be limited to the informal portrayal of the true church or of the ideal family.[84] Rather, his purpose is to call attention to the fact that none of these social forms is dispensable from the viewpoint of an adequate philosophy of man, that each informs and sustains the other, and that the life of the individual must embody a full participation in all.

But an individual who is able to move freely in a plurality of ethical spheres is larger in his identity than any one of these spheres, and, for that matter, transcends all of them collectively. The polarity of individual and community is not merely a device that Schleiermacher employs in order to limit the scope and authority of the community; it is a genuine polarity, with the consequence that the inherence of the community in the individual is

[82] *Ibid.*, §74, p. 273.

[83] *Ibid.*, §71, p. 273.

[84] Karl Barth holds that the group of family and friends in the work is meant to be the real church. *Cf. Die Theologie und die Kirche*, pp. 119f.

but one side of the ethical equation that Schleiermacher describes in his doctrine of the highest good. The counterpart is the movement from the individual toward the community. The Christian church, for example, depends upon the reformations wrought in it and upon it by individuals, as Schleiermacher explained in his Christian ethics.[85] The individual functions not only as a symbol of the corporate whole but as the agent who reshapes the life of the whole church. Schleiermacher firmly rejected the division of the membership into those who are passively joined to the body and those who actively oversee its life. He might have said the same of any of the corporate bodies that make up the form and substance of human life. And, again, what he wrote of the state in his ethics he might have applied to the family and the church, namely that it is "the possessing community and the common possession."[86] This construction of human existence as an oscillation between receiving and communicating means that nothing is genuinely inherited or possessed until it is taken up by the individual agent and wrought upon again. Ethical personality exists only in the reciprocal motions of being-for-the-self and being-for-the-community; or, more precisely, ethical personality exists only in the mutual informing of these two movements of the self.[87] Therefore, in living and doing for the sake of the community, in suspending the self's own self-enclosed identity, as it were, the moral agent is not acting as a neutral, historically indifferent vessel of the life of the community; he is not the victim of Hegel's "cunning of history." Rather, he is acting out of his own inalienable and underivable inner individuality and in so doing achieves a heightened sense of the same. Membership in a community is the function solely of a *person*, a being who, though, externally individuated by time and place and psychically modified by his cultural heritage, also differentiates

[85] SW I/12, *Die christliche Sitte*, pp. 70f.
[86] Braun II, 1812/13, §66, p. 273.
[87] *Ibid.*, §55, p. 271.

himself from all others and at the same time acknowledges such an inward differentiation on the part of every other.[88] A person, in a word, is that kind of being that transcends every community and recognizes that all other members do the same, so that from each member-person the community receives new content and modification of its organization and is thus maintained as an open society, as long as historical life flows in it.

Schleiermacher designates this inner and underivable selfhood that stands within the person, in a co-inhering polarity with the community, as *Eigenthümlichkeit* (proprium); and the mode through which this inner givenness of the self achieves expression and enters into consciousness is *Gefühl* (feeling). *Eigenthümlichkeit* is thus the quality of individual existence that opposes—but does not contradict—the participation of the community in the person (*Gemeinschaftlichkeit*). And feeling is the vehicle of this special quality of existence, of this given, irreducible individuality, this inner unity of the self that underlies all the temporal moments of the self's existence but that never issues into a direct and complete outward manifestation in any one of them. This feeling, as Schleiermacher described it in another place, "is the original expression of an *immediate* existence-relationship."[89]

As the expression of an immediate existence-relationship, feeling arises out of the self in its totality. Consequently, the relationship informing feeling is something quite different from any of the particular relations inhering in the self-world or individual-community polarities. Schleiermacher describes this aspect of feeling in §3 of *The Christian Faith*, the locus of his famous definition of piety, in which he discriminates between knowing and doing as particular functions of the self, oriented upon particular objects, and feeling as a state of consciousness that is independent of and anterior to the subject-object relation. It is, he writes there, an "im-

[88] *Ibid.*, 1816, §71, pp. 604f.
[89] Send., p. 15 (586). Italics mine.

mediate self-consciousness," in distinction from the self-consciousness that is mediated by the world and society. However, we would be mistaken in interpreting Schleiermacher, were we to conclude that he has anything more than a descriptive distinction in mind here and that he intends to indicate a nucleus of the self shut up in an inviolable privacy. This piety, which he defines as a qualification of feeling or of immediate self-consciousness, appears to be last in the order of analysis, and it is independent of the subject-object relation in the sense that it expresses that which in the self the subject-object relation presupposes rather than produces. Nevertheless, such feeling always manifests itself in association with relations to society and the world. In agreement with his polar style of reflection and analysis, Schleiermacher presents both feeling and the inner, underivable selfhood it expresses as graduating into the more public self and the functions of thinking and doing that are informed by community and world. His intention in isolating this modification of feeling is to point to the fundamental state of consciousness that expresses the basic unity of the self's existence within which the dialectic of a particular life with other lives occurs. Each act of willing or organizing and of thinking or striving to know displays, as we have noted, a relative freedom and a relative determinedness of the agent. According to the vocabulary of *The Christian Faith*, self-consciousness contains two elements, a positing-of-the-self-by-the-self (corresponding to relative freedom) and a having-been-posited-in-a-particular-way (corresponding to the relative determinedness of the self).[90] But the "feeling of absolute dependence," which is the content of pious feeling, refers to that absolutely original having-been-posited-in-a-particular-way to which there is no responding freedom. Feeling of this order indicates more than the sheer "happened-ness" of the self; it symbolizes the life-unity within which the reciprocal moments of suffering

[90] Gl., §4,1. Schleiermacher's terms are: *ein Sichselbstsetzen* and *ein Sichselbstnichtsogesetzthaben*.

and doing transpire. It is not a mystical or a-cosmic state of mind but the consciousness of the unity of the self that is given within experience rather than derived from it. In order to emphasize that he has more than simple contingency in mind, as he describes the feeling content of piety, Schleiermacher cites the words of his former colleague and friend at Halle, Henrich Steffens: "the immediate presence of the whole, undivided personal existence."[91]

Feeling expresses, then, the unity of the self for which not even the sum of the world's influences upon the individual can account. When Schleiermacher explains that such feeling only apparently disappears, even if the agent seems to be completely absorbed in his thought or deed, and that in reality it always accompanies thinking and doing, he is affirming that the total self is necessarily present in each of the moments of life.[92] He further says that feeling is the point of transition from thinking to doing and from doing to thinking, but as the point of transition it is not the symbol of a qualitativeless self raised above the limits of time and space as a transcendental ego; rather, feeling stands for the being who thinks and wills,[93] for the moral agent in the world.

One of the difficulties encumbering Schleiermacher's discussion of feeling arises from his failure to distinguish between the formal and material aspects of the phenomenon. Consequently,

[91] *Ibid.*, §3,2, note. The full sentence from which Schleiermacher excerpts these words is as follows: "What we call feeling here is the immediate presence of the whole, undivided personal existence [*Dasein*, not *Sein* as the Edinburgh edition of the E.T. might suggest], sensible as well as spiritual, the unity of the person and his sensible and spiritual world." H. Steffens, *Von der falschen Theologie*, Breslau (1823), pp. 99f. The sentence as a whole, together with its context, does not so well agree with Schleiermacher's exposition in *The Christian Faith* as his citation of a part of it would lead the reader to expect. His use of feeling elsewhere, as an aesthetic category, more closely approximates Steffens'. "Feeling is then also a consciousness, also connected with the ideal form of being [a function of reason] and just as much also a consciousness of the coexistence of man with the world." *Friedrich Schleiermachers Ästhetik*, ed. R. Odebrecht, Berlin (1931), p. 34 (taken from a student notebook).

[92] Dial. (O), p. 289; *cf.* also Gl., §5, 3.

[93] *Ibid.*, p. 288.

when he speaks of the feeling that expresses the ultimate life-unity of the self, at times he is referring to the underivable individuality of the person, while at others he is referring to the absolute dependence of the self. Evidently, however, the feeling of absolute dependence, which is the same in every man, has for its content in each man his life unity or particular way of existing, and this furnishes an important part of its quality.

Some additional light is shed on this aspect of feeling as the organ of the self's individuality, if we revert briefly to Schleiermacher's early interpretation of the closely related phenomenon of religious mood in *The Christmas Eve*. When, as we have seen, the conversation of the small company evokes memories of Christmas gatherings and events in the past, the mood that the celebration of the nativity creates is acclaimed by all to be one that arises neither out of the gifts nor out of any other particular element in the festivities. The only origin that can be surmised is the life of a sinless man in times past, the redeemer. The mood itself now embraces the individual member of the Christmas party as well as his world, transforming his identity by infusing it with an original joy and serenity. This new quality of personal existence is given to the individual, and it permeates each separate moment of his life. The members of the dialogue, especially Eduard and Karoline, make a point of the analogy between the mood and music, for as the musical composition does not abrogate the identity of the individual notes but modulates them by introducing them into a new harmonic whole, so the regenerated Christian consciousness takes up pleasure and pain, allowing them to remain what they are but at the same time introducing them into a qualitatively new context.[94] This religious mood of joy represented in *The Christmas Eve* is not wholly or precisely what is meant by personal feeling in the philosophical ethics and *Dialektik* or by immediate self-consciousness in *The Christian Faith*, but it is an important element of the phe-

[94] *Cf.* above, Ch. I, §4, pp. 54f.; also Gl., §5,4.

nomenon, and it serves to interpret the qualitative content of such feeling. The rôle of the mood of rejoicing, as *The Christmas Eve* illustrates it, is to clarify the sense of identity and inner unity and to interpret the relationships of life with life under the aspect of grace. "Mood is," Schleiermacher said elsewhere, "the permanence of religious feeling."[95] It lies on a continuum with feeling and restores, preserves and intensifies such feeling as the sense of the unity and identity of the self. Consequently, while the feeling that expresses the unity of the self is formally the same in all men—it is the "universal form of the self's having itself," we learn in one place—,[96] it also expresses the particular way of existing in which the individual finds himself, his *Sosein.*[97] Schleiermacher wrote to his friend, Lücke, in his later reflections on his use of the word *feeling* in the dogmatic theology, that the term *disposition* appeared to him to be quite close to his true meaning but he had rejected it because of its too practical coloration.[98] What he had in mind was an affective level of existence anterior to all social attitudes and informing them. He had in mind the character of individual existence that we call its style, which determines the quality of its openness toward others and of its return to itself.[99]

Feeling as the form of consciousness that expresses the inner unity of the person possesses a range that is coextensive with personal existence and activity. Consequently, even though the agent is a being in whom the community inheres, no limit can be placed

[95] *Ästhetik,* p. 71.

[96] Dial. (O), p. 288. Student notebook.

[97] *Cf.* below, Ch. IV, §1, pp. 182f.

[98] Send., pp. 14f. (586).

[99] In his aesthetics, Schleiermacher uses feeling somewhat differently, applying it to the ephemeral moments in *Stimmung.* True art is the expression of the latter; it is the expression of the inner selfhood of the artist rather than of a passion. *Stimmung* is closely associated with the artist's style, and, insofar as it lies at the base of every act in which the individuality of the agent is set forth, there is an aesthetic dimension in all of life; or, we may say, the religious, the aesthetic and the ethical identity of the individual are intimately related. *Cf. Ästhetik,* p. 52.

upon the field of his life in which feeling manifests itself and in which, correspondingly, his innermost individuality plays a determinating rôle. We may remind ourselves here of Schleiermacher's statements that reasoning is an activity of which we are aware as something belonging equally to all men and that the goal toward which science aspires, albeit an historically inaccessible one, is a logic in which any and all can fully participate regardless of their particular identities. But the very idea of this goal is conceivable only if the individuality of each participant is included rather than excluded from such perfect knowledge. Hence, even in the most rigorous thinking, the feeling of individuality in the thinker cannot be abstracted from the processes of thought.[100] The particular manner in which he articulates his ideas always reflects the work of his "imagination," that is to say, of his reason as it is qualified by his own inner, underivable unity.[101] Moreover, the aforementioned awareness of thinking as belonging commonly to all mankind is itself a species of feeling-consciousness rather than of thought-consciousness.[102] It is another example of the moral function of feeling that we met in the Christmas dialogue, feeling recognizing and acknowledging the presence of humanity in other beings. Thus feeling and thinking accompany each other and, in reality, coinhere in the same kind of polarity as the individual and the community, and neither is to be found entirely apart from the other, by virtue of their common root in consciousness. Hence, feeling does not stand for the irrational in the self. It is, rather, as much a part of the rational consciousness as the capacity for the most critical and scientific reflection.[103] While feeling has for its final content the innermost and underivable individuality of the self, it nevertheless does not symbolize the arcane, self-concealing element of personality. It too is carried by the nisus of personal consciousness

[100] Dial. (O), pp. 131ff.
[101] Braun II, 1812/13, §163, §220, §221, pp. 302, 313f.
[102] *Ibid.*, 1816, §54, pp. 590f.
[103] *Ibid.*, §52, §61, pp. 589, 596ff.

toward communication and shares in the morality of the agent.[104] The moral function of feeling, as cited just above, emerges as it accompanies the activities of speaking/thinking in the movement of the person toward society, becoming a feeling of common humanity, or a "fellow feeling," or a "consciousness of kind." But that which feeling has to communicate from out of its source is the least communicable thing in the self, namely its otherness, for which there is no wholly precise analogate in any other person. Unlike the thinking activity with which it co-inheres, it cannot set itself forth in the common, inherited language, and instead it issues in gestures, such as the posture of the body and the expression of the face. Inasmuch as feeling also gives rise to communication then, we have in the thinking/speaking and feeling/gesturing self a being who enters into dialogue on two levels. The first is that of thinking setting itself forth in language; the second is that of feeling issuing in these other, more private symbols. The first is a direct communication, for the uttered thought of the speaker enables the hearer to reconstruct that thought by virtue of the identity of language. But the second is an indirect communication, for feeling, insofar as it seeks to express the "otherness" of the self, cannot impart its content through an identical medium such as language but must "reveal" its content in gestures and the like. "Revelation" in this sense is more self-disclosure than impartation, and it induces in the other member of the dialogue not so much a direct understanding as a heightened self-consciousness, a sensitivity to the feeling-content of analogous symbolic gestures in his own life, and an intuition of the other.[105] As speaking seeks to be understood, so feeling seeks to be "divined." And since it is the whole self that is present in such dialogical relations, all communication is both direct and indirect, a matter of revealing and divining as well as speaking and understanding. Here we can cite the method of Schleiermacher's her-

[104] *Ibid.*, §61, pp. 596ff.
[105] *Ibid.*

meneutics with the parallel employment of the grammatical and psychological-divinatory approaches as a concrete illustration. And the ethics shows that this procedure in interpretation is founded upon the conformation of the self in community. Not in historical documents alone, but in the dialogue of life with life, *Eigenthümlichkeit* and its organ *feeling* are present wherever there are thought and deed.

For the sake of the initial comparison with Kierkegaard, we could well describe Schleiermacher's teachings about feeling, in his ethics, dialectic and aesthetics, as his doctrines of "indirect communication" and of "truth as subjectivity." Schleiermacher did not maintain, to be sure, that the holding fast inwardly is more significant ethically than that to which the self holds fast, as we find Kierkegaard doing in his ethical works. But he did affirm that where subjectivity is not present, there we have no real knowing and willing but only historically meaningless recitation of propositions and empty imitation. Truth must be embodied in personal existence and actualized in the dialogue of life with life, and this dialogue is indefeasibly united with the immediate consciousness of selfhood and the presence of feeling. The point at which Schleiermacher most sharply disagrees with Kierkegaard is in his refusal to except any level or hidden recess of the self from this dialogue with others. A reform of the ethical in the name of the religious identity of the self is quite conceivable and finally inevitable, on Schleiermacher's terms, but a suspension of the ethical by the religious sense of duty is quite inconceivable. The self in its inner otherness has finally to acknowledge only God as the ground of its dependence, but this fact does not preclude, to Schleiermacher's mind, the self in its individuality seeking out a society. Indeed, insofar as a heightened immediate self-consciousness is called forth by the self-revealing of other persons, feeling and free society are inseparable moments of personal life.[106] They are the pillars upon which Schleiermacher rests his whole view of the ethical, historical world.

[106] *Ibid.*, §59, p. 594.

Feeling and free society are not, however, the sole foundations of the ethical, historical world. As we have seen earlier in this chapter, Schleiermacher construed the individual as an end-in-himself and an agent who participates in a number of social orders: the family, the nation and state, the institutions of learning, the church, and free associations. He ascribed to each of these forms of social organization a specific ethical character. Some of them are communities in which the aims and character of the community supersede the individuality of its members, without expunging it. Others are essentially communities that serve the individual. Each type requires the presence of the other. Among the former are the national unity and the institutions of learning; among the latter we find the church and free associations. Obviously, then, Schleiermacher did not regard the free play of individuality as the only manifestation of ethical agency and responsibility. His concept of polarity between self and community in the person would not allow him to do so. The national unity is one of those corporate persons within which the single person stands. Its unity is the unity of shared language, tradition, culture and character. It appears to be a more "natural" community than does the church, for example; but it is only relatively more natural or apparently so. The doctrine of Schleiermacher's ethics is that the state is the organizational expression of this unity and depends upon the national character,[107] having no moral right to expand beyond the geographical limits of the latter.[108] (The warnings in the second edition of *The Speeches on Religion* against Napoleon's imperialism mirror this view, and it provides the ethical principle in Schleiermacher's Prussian patriotism.) The institutions of learning constitute the community of

[107] *Ibid.*, 1812/13, §66, p. 273; for the propositions relating to the national unity and the state, *cf. ibid.*, §77 - §145, pp. 333ff.

[108] Hence, no single nation or state can be the sole or chief bearer of the highest good: this latter can be produced only by the human race. For a discussion of Schleiermacher's ideas of nation and state, see Ernst Müsebeck, *Schleiermacher in der Geschichte der Staatsidee und des Nationalbewusstseins,* Berlin (1927).

knowledge that is "the other side of the national unity."[109] Such a definition of the academies and universities is the logical result of the convictions that the pursuit of knowledge is a moral deed reflecting the identity and character of the inquirer and that all knowledge evolves dialogically within the matrix of a given language. Schleiermacher refuses, consequently, to accept the idea of the university as a congeries of disciplines conjoined only by an abstract devotion to truth; in fact, the sciences have a common root in the history of the language, in the character of the national unity, and they can proceed in a genuinely disciplined fashion only when they commonly acknowledge their ethical-historical conditionedness.[110] The task of the community of the sciences is to preserve, criticize and extend the knowledge that lies in the language[111] and so to exercise the rôle of the alter-ego in the national citizenry's dialogue with itself. So conceived and justified, the universities and other unions of learning and teaching belong neither to individuals nor to the state but are independent and only as such can serve the single and corporate persons.[112]

It is in the church and free society that the inner individuality of the single person assumes a more significant part. And, for that reason, Schleiermacher admits, these two "forms" of historical, ethi-

[109] Braun II, 1812/13, §146, p. 347.

[110] Schleiermacher's "Gelegentliche Gedanken über Universitäten in deutschem Sinn" gives his philosophy of the university and of the sciences. The most recent edition of this and others of his pedagogical works is edited by T. Schulze and E. Weniger, *Friedrich Schleiermacher, Pädagogische Schriften*, Düsseldorf (1957), 2 vols.

[111] Braun II, 1812/13, §67, p. 273, and *ibid.*, §146 - §186, pp. 347ff.

[112] The picture of the scientific man as living shut up in isolated work is a gross illusion, Schleiermacher wrote. His thinking is dependent on public means of communication and the achievement of his goal upon his association and coöperation with those occupied in similar work. *Cf.* "Gelegentliche Gedanken," *op. cit.*, Vol. II, p. 83. The dialogue between the public and the scholar is carried out by the individual not as a private person but as one living for the sake of the discipline. And, where the state interferes in the university, the willing and thinking functions of the national unity are "diseased." *Cf.* Braun II, 1812/13, §157 - §161, §172, pp. 350f., 353.

cal life are more difficult to define, lacking as they must the relatively clear basis in the natural endowment of human nature that the national unity enjoys. But from the point of view of ethics, these two are nonetheless of the utmost importance, even though they cannot be thoroughly comprehended by ethical reason alone. They introduce into corporate life the leaven of freedom and of fluidity, not through any arbitrary interference or assumption of hegemony but by virtue of the fact that all of the forms of life are implicitly contained in each, and, hence, free society and the church express and crystallize the immediate sense of individuality and of openness that prevent the life of mankind from degenerating into stagnation. Free social intercourse finds its outlet in "hospitality" and "friendship," forms of human association and of sharing that know no intrinsic limits but only the accidental barriers of enmity or radically different levels of culture.[113] The presence of such a leaven in the academic community is wholly necessary; it is a condition of the growth of science. And, again, it provides the moral impetus and quality for the relations of national entities with one another.

Schleiermacher conceives the church to be the final community of personal individuality, for the religious is the highest grade of feeling.[114] The church is the community in which *Eigenthümlichkeit* is called forth in the reciprocity of "revelation" and "divination." This description is not a definition of the Christian community, however, but only of the ethical function that belongs to religious society as such and without which no culture can be complete and fully alive. Apart from a church, immediate self-consciousness remains partially inchoate, and ethical, historical agency partially stultified. On Schleiermacher's terms, life uninformed by religion is life without style or art; it is merely mechanical involvement in the reciprocal motions of thinking and acting,

[113] Braun II, 1812/13, §68, p. 273 and *ibid.*, §233 - §258, pp. 366ff.
[114] *Ibid.*, §69, p. 273.

inheriting and reproducing, unqualified and unmediated by the inner unity of the self; it is dialogue without self-revelation and divination, and deeds in which the doer leaves no trace of himself. The true office of the church is the development of the means for the stimulation and expression of this highest feeling (or "subjective knowing"). In this sense, it parallels the community of the sciences but, while the latter preserves, criticizes and extends the language that is the organ of thinking, the church's province is the liturgy and all the symbols pertaining to the elicitation and expression of feeling. It is the community, therefore, whose highest tendency is the constant formation of a "treasury of art" or a cultus, a process, however, that is the business of the entire religious community and not of special individuals alone.[115]

There is no thought in Schleiermacher's mind of a theocratic society. He will not even allow the church to claim to be the absolute ethical community;[116] it participates in the same limitations as the national unity, although they do not figure so decisively here; yet it cannot supplant but rather requires the university and free society. Nevertheless, there is scarcely any doubt possible that Schleiermacher attributed to life in the church a significance that transcends any of the other forms of corporate life, just as there is in fact no doubt that he reserved for the religious consciousness the final definition of the self's identity and destiny. His concluding observations in his lectures on hermeneutics from the academic year 1826/27 are to the effect that the last and most enduring impetus to the interpretation of others is the religious.[117] Such an observation bespeaks the center of Schleiermacher's own life and thought. His mobility and activity in government, the university and the national life were predicated on his first and last vocation as a preacher in the Reformed Church, and it is difficult to resist

115 *Ibid.*, §213, p. 362, *et passim.*
116 *Ibid.*, §211, pp. 361f.
117 SW I/7, p. 262.

the conclusion that the system of ethics is just such a representation of his own inner identity in polarity with his society, as he described in the propositions of the *Sittenlehre*.

Perhaps the most frequently cited words from Schleiermacher's correspondence are those in which he wrote that he had always remained a Moravian of "a higher order"; even as a minister of the Reformed communion, as political preacher in Berlin striving to awaken the Prussian consciousness against Napoleon and a Napoleonic peace, as professor in the University of Berlin, which he also helped to found, as an agitator for the liberal reform of the political and social organization of Prussia, as a member of the government bureau of education, as an open champion of the freedom of the church and critic of the King's ecclesiastical policy, as a prime mover in the union of the Lutheran and Reformed Churches in Prussia, and, finally, as the center of a vast circle of friends and head of a family, Schleiermacher left the imprint of his religious temper upon all that he took up and made into his own cause.[118] To his sister, Charlotte, he once explained that his life in the world

[118] Schleiermacher was married to the widow of a young friend (von Willich) in 1808. An account of his life in university, church, state and learned society is given by Dilthey, whose *Leben Schleiermachers* stops short with the Halle period, in his biographical article in *Gesammelte Schriften*, Vol. IV, pp. 354ff. For the political activity, *cf.* Müsebeck, *op. cit.* and Dilthey's "Schleiermachers politische Gesinnung und Wirksamkeit." Adolf von Harnack wrote concerning Schleiermacher's varied interests and activities: "his significance is just as great as spiritual leader in the war for independence and as systematizer of theology and of the *Geisteswissenschaften*, of the university and of the Academy. In the course of my study of the history of the Berlin Academy, I have taken notice of the very numerous memorials that were written in a period of fifteen years in connection with the founding of the new university in Berlin and the reorganization of the Academy, and have worked through the acts of the Academy, for which Schleiermacher was the secretary many years. The result was that Schleiermacher was to be placed immediately next to Wilhelm von Humboldt in stature and importance, that he even surpassed [von Humboldt] in insight into organizing and in direct influence. One may say without exaggeration that both the internal new direction of the *Geisteswissenschaften* and the new direction of the German universities and of the Academy were essentially wholly due to this professor of theology." *Erforschtes und Erlebtes*, Giessen (1923), p. 204.

was as that of a member of the Moravian community.[119] But this need of his to live on the line of intersection between two or more spheres is finally only an expression of his belief that a man is an image of Being and that the unity of his life does not need to be earned but is given. So he could write: "Science and the church, the state and domesticity—more than this is not given to man in the world, and I belong to the happy few that have enjoyed them all. To be sure, it is only in the most recent times, when men divide and separate everything, that such a conjoining is rare; otherwise, every able man would be bold in all things, and so it must be, and our entire effort is that it shall be so."[120] But in time of stress he could also say: "Preaching, with a little leisure and daily bread, is all that I really require."[121]

[119] Br. I, p. 209 (E.T. I, p. 200).
[120] Quoted by Dilthey, *Gesammelte Schriften,* Vol. XII, p. 36.
[121] *Ibid.,* p. 21.

PART TWO

The Christian Faith

Chapter Three

THEOLOGY AS HUMAN REFLECTION

§1 THE DAUGHTER OF RELIGION

When Schleiermacher appeared in the lecture hall at the University of Berlin, instead of reading a polished narrative of his completed thinking, he spoke to his students from simple notes and laid everything before them "as problems" to be thought through again in their presence. He was by nature, David Friedrich Strauss later recalled, decidedly one of those men in whom liveliness and a quicksilver-like mobility predominate. If he spoke from the pulpit, a tone of solemnity counterbalanced this vivacity; but in lecturing his manner was restless as he moved from one idea to another, examining each now from this side and now from that, until he would have made his auditors dizzy had it not been that his power of speech seemed to hold the listener by the hand and help him over the fissures. "Imagine now," Strauss added, "the task of capturing such a lecture in writing. It likens itself to that of photographing a dancer in full motion."[1]

The spectacle and problem that Schleiermacher presented to his hearer argue the reasonableness of his own conviction that an interpreter must take the words of another (even when the other is

[1] D. F. Strauss, *Gesammelte Schriften,* ed. Eduard Zeller, Bonn (1877), Vol. 5, p. 9.

a scholar) not only as scientific "notices" but also as living moments of the speaker's personality, and understand such moments in the context of the life from which they issue. Doubtlessly, few readers of the great book of Schleiermacher's maturity, *The Christian Faith, presented systematically according to the basic propositions of the Evangelical Church,* have encountered at first glance the quicksilver personality of the writer.[2] But that also is only as it should be, at least to its author's mind, for systematic or dogmatic theology first and foremost seeks to express the heart of the church community and not of the individual theologian alone. Yet there is a principle of interpretation that Schleiermacher offers, analogous to the one mentioned above, which obtains for the Christian community and its theology, and apart from an understanding of it *The Christian Faith* will seem to be little more than an elaborate but impersonal exercise in formal theological dialectic. The principle is that theological discourse is likewise a life-moment of the corporate Christian body, and however scientific an aspect it may present to the world, its meaning and meaningfulness can be

[2] *Der Christliche Glaube* first appeared in 1821/22 and in revised form in 1830/31. The changes in the 2nd edition are of interest for the professional student of Schleiermacher, though, as might be expected, they constitute elaborations, replies to criticisms, and accentuation of certain themes such as that of the second Adam. *Cf.* H. Scheele, *Die Theorie von Christus als dem zweiten Adam bei Schleiermacher,* Naumburg a.d. S. (1913) and compare, for example, §110, 1st edition, with the parallel §89 of the 2nd edition, where what is implicit in the 1st edition is not revised but made more explicit. But no real alterations in direction or substance are evident. "Concerning my dogmatics, I can say that at least in the first part not one stone remains standing on another, and that nevertheless it is entirely the same." Schleiermacher to Graf Alexander zu Dohna, 10 April 1830, *Schleiermacher als Mensch: Sein Wirken, Familien- und Freundesbriefe, 1804 bis 1834,* ed. H. Meisner, Stuttgart/Gotha (1923), p. 357. *Cf.* also *Schleiermachers Briefwechsel mit J. Chr. Gass,* pp. 219f. Except where otherwise noted, all of the following references are to the revised edition, and the reader may consult it in either the original German or the English translation. Where the English translation is not as faithful as desirable, or where relevant material is to be found only in the critical German edition by Martin Redeker, *Der Christliche Glaube,* Berlin (1960) 2 Vols., I have so indicated in the footnotes.

grasped only by those who also are moved by the experience that the Spirit creates in the church.

Theology issues out of the life-matrix of religion, and Schleiermacher was puzzled, therefore, by those who evidently believed that theological learnedness and insight preceded piety. Was not "our Luther's" theology also manifestly "the daughter of his religion?" he asked of his friend Lücke. "Even though one can no longer say in general that [faith] remains hidden from the wise, do we not have every reason to thank God that he has revealed it pre-eminently to the children, that is to say, to those whose piety could not be worth much, if it had to rest on a complex of ideas?"[3] Schleiermacher himself steadfastly endeavored to make his own theological reflection subserve the appropriation and furthering of the Christian life and, conversely, to debar it from the fatal pretension of having created that of which it was merely the offspring. To this end, he prefixed to *The Christian Faith* the following lines from Anselm of Canterbury, as the motto for the whole:[4] "Nor do I seek to understand in order that I may believe, but I believe in order that I may understand."—"For he who does not believe does not experience, and he who does not experience, does not understand." Theological thinking is, according to Schleiermacher, reflection upon and clarification of believing experience.

As reflection upon believing experience, theology is at bottom nothing else than the disciplined and critical thinking of those men to whom has fallen the responsibility of guiding and vocalizing the common life shared by believers.[5] And this in turn means, for

[3] Send., p. 16 (587). Schleiermacher wrote two lengthy epistles to his former pupil, Lücke, in 1829, explaining his mind on the criticisms he had received of the first edition of *The Christian Faith*. These *Sendschreiben über seine Glaubenslehre an Lücke* provide an unusual commentary on the work by the author himself and an apology for the second edition.

[4] These lines have not been included on the title page of the Edinburgh edition of the E.T.

[5] Therefore, practical theology stands at the apex of the theological curriculum. *Cf.* KD, Pt. III.

Schleiermacher, that if the thinking of such men is uprooted from the soil of the common life and needs of the church, the content of their thinking can no longer be called theology, and its elements fall to the lot of other sciences.[6] Such a conception is obviously not hospitable to the notions that theology is a self-explanatory and self-evident discipline or that it can exhibit any cogency apart from the historical life out of which it arises. It is furthermore unsympathetic to the view that theology is required as a species of synthetic higher wisdom or philosophy of the human spirit that fills the vacuum of life's meaning by spinning inferences *ex nihilo* in the lacunae of other, established sciences. Theology does not exist by virtue of the default of other disciplines but solely on account of the reality and urgency of its own subject matter. Schleiermacher also rejected the claim that in fact theological thinking is the architectonic impulse of the mind, giving to all knowing its principles and limits and acting as the science of all human sciences. If the latter state of affairs were the case, it would be incumbent upon the theologian to show how the particular categories and intuitions with which he works are implied in and presupposed by the mind's work in all of its endeavors and how all judgments are latently theological in character. But such a transcendental philosophy of religion was no part of Schleiermacher's intention. In actuality, Schleiermacher could even eschew the term *systematic theology* precisely for the reason that, when applied to the teaching of the Christian church, it encourages the presumption of a universally valid system of knowledge of which the intellectual content of the Christian faith is, then, one part.[7] The necessity of theology as a part required by the larger whole of human knowledge or as a premise of an incontestable, universally accepted conclusion is no more demonstrable than is Christianity itself.

[6] KD[1], "Einleitung," §6.

[7] SW I/12, *Die Christliche Sitte,* pp. 7f. While Schleiermacher uses the word *dogmatic* in the text of *The Christian Faith,* he pointedly omits it from the title. When we measure the work against our contemporary usage of the terms it appears to be more nearly a systematic than a dogmatic theology.

It was, to be sure, as we have seen and shall notice again, far from Schleiermacher's mind to sequester theological thinking from all contact with other sciences or to shut up the import of religious faith within the church alone; but he was tirelessly insistent on the fact that the rise of theological reflection is comprehensible only in the context of the historically mediated religion of the Christian community. Therefore, the theology that Schleiermacher himself prosecuted and that *The Christian Faith* exemplifies in a classic fashion can be appreciated only if the reader is mindful that it is a massive attempt to expound the substance of Christianity in a wholly positive and nonspeculative fashion. In a word, the author's aim was to be empirical, and empirical to such a degree, moreover, that his data be accessible not only to professional colleagues and to scholars but also to every man upon whom the communication of the gospel has worked. (In this respect, although theology is a historical science, it cannot be compared to the science of history.[8]) The material of theology is simply that which is at hand for everyone who has believing experience. It is the Christian religious self-consciousness. "Christian faith-propositions are," he explains accordingly, "conceptions of Christian religious soul-states set forth in speech."[9]

Nevertheless, if Schleiermacher could admonish his critics and interpreters that his theological method was nothing if not wholly straightforward and empirical,[10] it is soon evident to the reader that he cannot expect to find in *The Christian Faith* the familiar sort of empiricism that, for example, he encounters in William James' casebook, *The Varieties of Religious Experience,* the study that has exerted so wide an influence upon more recent efforts to reconstruct theology as a science of religion. Even though James may superficially resemble Schleiermacher, at least to the extent that he also adduces "feeling" as the root of religion, the

[8] Gl., §28, 2.
[9] Gl., §15.
[10] Send., p. 21 (593).

American psychologist and philosopher has nothing of Schleiermacher's sense for social and historical relations, so that, in contradistinction, James investigates a species of religious experience belonging to the individual solely, a religious experience that is, therefore, essentially esoteric, amorphous and incommunicable. James tried to be not only clinical in his attitude toward his material but sympathetic as well. However, in the latter regard he was not especially successful (witness his classification of theists as "tender-minded"), for James was at heart a moralist. This fact, no doubt, made the phenomena that he described seem even more alien and impenetrable than they were. Therefore, much of the discourse that purported to grow out of religious experiences appeared to him as hopelessly inadequate, for he interpreted it as surging up from the underground of the ineffable, and the ineffable cannot, of course, be communicated. Hence, he proposed to replace traditional theology, the discourse of religious faith about religious faith, with a new "science of religion," meaning thereby science about religious phenomena. Among other possible counterparts to Schleiermacher's magnum opus, with which American readers may be familiar, the thought of Jonathan Edwards, especially as it is presented in his *Treatise on Grace* and *Treatise Concerning Religious Affections*, offers a far more instructive comparison. Though Schleiermacher would have adjudged Edwards' treatises as far too "anthropopathic" and Edwards certainly would have found Schleiermacher much too constrained in his rendering of the content of the soul, both of these men sought not only to speak reasonably about religion but also, and at the same time, to speak from within its heart. The hiatus between feeling or religious affection and discourse that so struck James did not exist for Edwards and Schleiermacher. These two not only shared a common idea of human nature, which Edwards stated as the conviction that "affections [are] the springs that set men agoing, in all the affairs of life, and engage them in all their pursuits . . . he that has doctrinal knowledge only, without affections, never is engaged in the business of religion";[11] but they also agreed that theological discourse can remain faithful to the stuff of human religion and still be coherent, that theology can unite the affectional and rational dimensions of human nature and therefore need not subsist either upon mere semantic and logical conventions nor upon esoteric and incoherent attestations of mystery. The point of view espoused by these two men enjoins the theologian that if he is to present Christianity at all, he must, in the very act of talking about it, permit it to be recognized as a faith and style of living that pertains to and clarifies the affective, feeling self; and if he is to describe Christianity as a religion of redemption and new birth, then the new nature must be delineated in categories that are intelligible as well as affecting. Both Edwards and Schleiermacher, therefore, embraced a specific kind of empiricism. The datum they scrutinized was neither the religious phenomenon abstracted from its total subjective meaning nor the subject isolated from his natural and social world, but it was rather the psychical content of awareness that fills the self in and through the nexus of its existence-relationships and that thereupon reduplicates itself and symbolizes itself in these very relationships. The object of their empiricism was, in brief, the believer receiving and imparting the impulses of faith in the visible, historical communion of saints. This kind of empiricism appeared to Schleiermacher to be the only alternative to the establishment in the church of a gnosis-Christianity, a faith based on privileged intellectual powers or arcane information and hence requiring a "priesthood of speculation."[12] He avowed his empiricism, therefore, as a part of the armory by which he was defending and strengthening Protestantism. What theology is able to give and ought to give is an idea of the clarified humanity that all who have

[11] *Treatise Concerning Religious Affections,* ed. John Smith, New Haven (1960), p. 101.

[12] Send., p. 16 (588).

believing experience can immediately perceive and understand as a humanity coming to be in themselves through the communication of faith in the church.

While, therefore, theological reflection and language are subordinate to the concrete, universally accessible matter of religion, it is obviously not the case that Schleiermacher supposed such reflection and discourse represent the intrusion of tolerable but nevertheless alien academic, speculative interests upon the domain of the soul. The whole view of human nature, history and culture that he set forth in his ethics and the conception of thinking and knowing to be found in his philosophy contravene such an interpretation, and the bearing of these disciplines upon the relation of language to religion may be stated in the often repeated principle of the ethics and philosophy: speech is the outer side of thinking and thinking the inner side of language. That is to say, the rational processes in and through which the individual attains to consciousness of his humanity are dependent upon the symbols of the public language, and the public language receives its moral content and its personal significance through the employment made of it by selves in community. But since Schleiermacher permitted no absolute barrier to divide feeling, as the voice of the innermost self, from the thinking and doing through which the individual participates in the communities of his society, feeling must also play its part in social intercourse. Religious feeling inevitably seeks the means of communication, and consequently, insofar as theology is simply the self-conscious employment of language by and on behalf of the subject of religious feeling, it is as natural a mode of human reflection and discourse as any other. The abuse inflicted upon it by the scholastic mentality, which mixed speculative ideas into the language of faith, should not be allowed to obscure that fact, and Schleiermacher in actuality aspired to write a theology that would be free precisely of the alien elements with which scholasticism encumbered itself.[13] He regarded Christianity, especially in its Western branch, as the religion above all others that has cultivated an interest in its own language. On the one hand, it seemed to him, Christianity presupposes for its propagation a relatively advanced stage of linguistic culture;[14] but, on the other, it has also from the very beginning shown itself to be a language-forming agency.[15] And this last-named point is of the uttermost importance for understanding his intentions as they are embodied in *The Christian Faith*, for the interpretation of Schleiermacher's theology customarily is so preoccupied with his initially startling use of human feeling that it overlooks the conspicuous pains the author takes at the outset of his enterprise to explain the relationship between theology and language. Yet in fact, Schleiermacher conceived of the task of theology as the self-conscious execution of the language-forming capacity with which Christianity is imbued; and, of the thirty-one propositions making up the introductory material to the corpus of the work, four concern themselves principally with the relation of the Christian religion to speech, while the topic arises in many of the others as well, particularly in those dealing with the use of philosophy.[16]

The key to the author's theological concern for language and its employment lies in his conviction that the entire content of the Christian religious self-consciousness is intrinsically related to and determined by the person of Jesus of Nazareth, whose whole work "was conditioned by the communicability of his self-consciousness by means of speech, and similarly Christianity has always and everywhere spread itself solely by preaching."[17] A more detailed examination of Schleiermacher's doctrine of Christ belongs to an-

[13] For Schleiermacher's opinions on scholastic theology, see Gl., §16, postscript; §28, 3 and "Erwählung," pp. 461f.

[14] Gl., §15, 2.

[15] Send., p. 60 (642).

[16] Gl., §15 - §18.

[17] Gl., §15, 2.

other place, but here it is appropriate and important to take notice of the fact that he did not have in mind the notion that the words of Jesus may be divorced from his person, or that—as later Protestant liberalism had it—the religion taught by Jesus could be distinguished from the religion about Jesus.[18] On the contrary, Schleiermacher maintained the preaching of Jesus to be the single most important or typical form of his work and his work was to communicate himself.[19] Underlying this view of the redeemer is a fundamentally Johannine christology, in which Word (*logos*), Life (*zoë*) and words (*rhēmata*) are comprehended as three aspects of the person of Christ, who, as the Word, is Life, possesses the power to impart life, and in proclaiming and founding the kingdom of God proclaims and gives himself.[20] Consequently, in construing Christ primarily as a preacher, Schleiermacher was not suggesting—in a fashion contradicting the premises of his idea of religious faith and theology—that the Christian church is first and foremost a school occupied with the preservation of divinely sanctioned truths and doctrines, an inference that might be prompted by some of the christological references in the early *Speeches on Religion* but that does not fit at all the analysis of the religious consciousness in *The Christian Faith*.[21] Rather, when he stipulates that Christianity arises out of the preaching of Christ, he means by *preaching* an act more inclusive than discourse about ideas; preaching is the expression of Jesus of Nazareth's identity before God and the vehicle of his communication of his own life. Therefore, so little is the preaching that constitutes the living essence of Christianity merely externally related to the person of Christ that it is in

[18] *Cf.* SW I/6, *Leben Jesu,* p. 251.

[19] *Ibid.,* p. 130.

[20] *Ibid.,* p. 293; *cf.* also, e.g., the sermon on John 1:1-5, in *Homilien über des Evangelium des Johannes,* SW II/8, pp. 5ff.

[21] *Cf.,* e.g., Reden, p. 283: "the truly divine element is the glorious clearness to which the great idea He came to exhibit attained in His soul." (E.T., p. 246).

reality the presence of Christ himself in the church, and the presupposition of *The Christian Faith* as a whole is that the church lives in and through the *kerygma* of Christ. Thus Schleiermacher's christological principles reflect, perhaps more clearly and pointedly than any other element of his theology, the firm convictions that word and life are inseparable and that if the former is to be apprehended and understood and appropriated only through participation in the latter, nevertheless the latter (i.e., life) without the means of implanting itself *humanly* in the hearer (i.e., as a communication) is impotent. All of which is to say that Schleiermacher interpreted the import of the logos-christology of the New Testament as a christology of communication from God rather than as a christology of an idea of God. And for these reasons, he was evidently bewildered by those who asked why God did not impart himself entirely and immediately rather than through the form of a communication, as though the divine self-disclosure and self-giving were absolute rather than an act of God in relation to humanity.[22] In this respect, the present-day reader cannot help but note that Schleiermacher differed from his own contemporary idealist colleague, Hegel, who made the knowledge of God to be a knowledge of God by God (hence, literally absolute), and he also thereby differs from Hegel's great successor, Karl Barth. But Schleiermacher was equally unsympathetic with the orthodox tendency to make over the revelation of God into a message from God, a body of doctrine, as though the impact of Jesus Christ upon men had been and is primarily cognitive and as though what Christ came to share was a theology rather than his own "God-consciousness" or relationship to God. Even if we supposed that the teaching of an idea about God or a system of doctrine was the point of his activity, Schleiermacher argued, still a system of doctrine purporting to be revealed or "supernatural" could only be understood as part of a larger whole, namely, the life of the revealer who works directly

[22] Gl., §10, postscript.

upon us through a "total impression" of himself on our own self-consciousness.[23]

Hence, while Schleiermacher's whole orientation on religion as an affective condition of man in his feeling or innermost self-consciousness prevented him from venerating the detached word either of Jesus or of the apostles, as being in and of itself a receptacle of divine inspiration and efficacy, he obviously had a due regard for the word as the means of communication. And since, furthermore, speaking is the outer side of the feeling, thinking self, he was bound to find in theology a natural and inevitable creation of the religious community that arises out of and receives its sustenance from preaching. Under these circumstances, it is not surprising that he could characterize theology as existing first and last in the interests of preaching and further affirm that all true doctrine must be traceable not only to the preaching of the church but also, and decisively, to the self-proclamation of Christ.[24]

In actuality, then, theology, in what Schleiermacher called its "dogmatic" form, is but one more manifestation of the communicative impulse that gives rise to Christian preaching, though certainly it is not identical with that preaching since its task is not only to set forth the affective religious states of the soul but to do so in the form of scientifically qualified propositions. In this sense, theology is preaching-faith's descriptive science of itself.

§2 THEOLOGY AS THE COUNTERVOICE OF THE CHURCH

This idea of theology is naturally fraught with decisive consequences for the whole tenor and execution of *The Christian Faith*. The first of these appears in the use that this theology makes

[23] *Ibid.* For the hermeneutical principle involved, *cf.* above, Ch. II, §2.

[24] Gl., §19, 1 and postscript; §15, 2. This is one of the points at which Brunner most seriously and consistently errs in his account of Schleiermacher, alleging that the author of *The Christian Faith* had no regard for the Word of God but only for inner, subjective states of immediacy to the Absolute. *Cf. Die Mystik und das Wort,* Ch. 3; and above, Ch. I, p. 45, n. 55.

of Scriptures, which for all practical purposes meant for Schleiermacher the New Testament. The exegetical approach to theological exposition is conspicuously absent, as is also the proof text method.[25] Schleiermacher's reason for the avoidance of these procedures is close enough to the surface of his thinking: it lies in his conception of "dogmatic" or descriptive theology as the declaration, in highly articulated form, of the faith of the church in the present age. To be sure, he not only made nominal provision for but also actively practiced the type of theology that does properly have the Bible as its object, but exegetical theology is not the function of "dogmatics." In wholly Schleiermacherian fashion, *The Christian Faith* stands in a relationship of independence and reciprocity with such exegetical theology.[26] Therefore, so far as the theology by which the Christian community reflects upon the content and means of its declaration of faith in its here and now is concerned—and so far, therefore, as the principal or "dogmatic" function of theology is concerned—the reader discovers in Schleiermacher's execution of it no echo of the *sola scriptura* that twentieth-century theologians so often identify as the distinguishing mark of Reformation Protestantism. (Schleiermacher's Protestantism is the Protestantism of *sola gratia* rather than of the exclusive authority of the Bible.) This refusal to adopt Scriptures as the primary object of theology is to be explained in part out of the fundamental idea of the relation between word and life that we have already come upon. The word is the interagent of life and as such indispensable to its communication; the Bible, correspondingly, "is the original translation of the Christian feeling, and," Schleiermacher felt able to add in good conscience, "for this very reason [it is] so firmly established that it allows us only to understand it and unfold it ever more. As a Protestant theologian I will permit no one to encroach upon my right to unfold it."[27] But as the interagent of the life that

[25] Gl., §27, 3.
[26] Gl., §19, postscript.
[27] Br. II, p. 351.

was in Christ and that Christ imparted in founding the church, the Bible is not the object, rather it is the instrumentality, of that life-communication. The new life in which the members of the Christian community share remains prior to the book that stands as the first collective expression of that corporate existence. Consequently, while Schleiermacher recognized that apart from Scriptures the historical continuity of the church threatened to be dissolved,[28] at the same time he predicated his systematic thinking upon the conviction that it is still only by immediate confrontation with and participation in the *communicated* that the *communication* also is truly received. Just as those disciples of the first generation, about whom he spoke in one of his sermons, understood the words of their Master only because they had already been chosen by him and drawn into his sphere, so the disciples who are at a remove of eighteen centuries likewise are enabled to understand not alone out of the words themselves but out of the life that is mediated through them.[29] Systematic theology cannot of itself bring Scriptures to life, and for this reason the pure, individual text as the object of theological reflection remains dumb. Such theology can only explicate the total context in which the Bible and all Christian communication are prized, namely, the religious consciousness of the Christian communion.

In part, however, the relation here of *The Christian Faith* to Scriptures also reflects the fact that the conceptual framework of the religious consciousness, as §24, §25 and §27 make abundantly clear, is something quite other than a simple Bible-determined structure. It has become historically differentiated. The epoch of the ecumenical councils and great controversies over the nature of Christ and the Godhead together with the Reformation and the rise of confessional documents have created in Christendom a variety of communions bearing distinguishing and identifying marks,

[28] *Ibid.*
[29] *Cf.* above, Ch. I, p. 47.

and each of these communions has, in effect, become a historical personality. Thus, while the Bible, insofar as it is the original translation of the Christian consciousness into public language, remains the normative guide for all the constituent branches of the church catholic, it cannot lift from the individual communions their responsibility for appropriating and clarifying their own historically given identities, even as they acknowledge their dependence upon the written deposit of the earliest church's faith. For a church approaching Scriptures stands in the utmost need of a clear and firm grasp on its own doctrinal convictions, their order and interrelation, if it is to recognize the doctrinal import of the book.[30] But it is "dogmatic" theology that is charged with just this task, in Schleiermacher's view of the theological curriculum, namely, the task of elucidating and systematizing through concepts the entire content of the religious self-consciousness of the church in its particular time and place. For these reasons, *The Christian Faith* is predicated upon the assumption that the work of critically expounding the content of the faith that is being preached is larger than, though not independent of, the exegesis of the Bible.

Schleiermacher's use of the Bible is, however, only symptomatic of his wider- and deeper-reaching idea of the true nature of theological thinking. Proposition 19 in the introductory portion of *The Christian Faith* reduces the idea to technical proportions: "Dogmatic theology is the science that systematizes the doctrine prevalent in a Christian church at a given time." But behind this

[30] *Cf.* the first edition of the *Glaubenslehre*, §1, 5. The relationship here of exegesis to dogmatics is typical of Schleiermacher's manner of establishing connections between disciplines. Exegesis uninformed of the present circumstances of dogmatics cannot adequately interpret the theological content of its texts, but dogmatics, being more dependent upon and reflective of "secular wisdom," ought not to control exegesis. Likewise, dogmatics will not be complete until exegesis of Scriptures has attained perfection and the religious consciousness of the early church is thoroughly understood (Gl. §27, 3). But, again, this earliest Christian piety will not be fully comprehended until the validly Christian, in all other historical forms of the church, is similarly comprehended. See also the discussion of "philosophical theology" in *Brief Outline of the Study of Theology*.

summary declaration lies the vision of theology as the voice of the living, historical church. To be sure, Schleiermacher obviously did not confuse technical theology with preaching, nor did he allot to it the nurturing of the experience upon which alone faith rests securely; that also "comes only from preaching."[31] Nevertheless, the theological business of exhibiting the interconnections between the doctrines obtaining in a particular church community at a particular time involves far more than the simple clerical task of inscribing propositions upon the pages of an ecclesiastical textbook. In its own way, theological reflection is no less dramatic than the office of preaching, for Schleiermacher's conception of his work really gives to dogmatic theology the work of crystallizing the living consciousness of the church, even as it sets forth the contents of that consciousness in speech. The character of this task is hinted at in §19, which qualifies its assertion that dogmatics systematizes the doctrine obtaining in a church by adding "at a given time," so making clear that the pace of history demands that this work be commenced ever anew. Its dynamic character is also betrayed in the position within the theological curriculum to which the author assigns dogmatics, to the third division of historical studies, where it falls under the rubric of "the historical knowledge of the *present* conditions of Christendom."[32] And it is further reflected in his assertion that, of all the theological disciplines, dogmatics stands in the most intimate relationship to "secular wisdom,"[33] a relationship whose necessity is dictated by the fact that dogmatics, in bringing to explicit awareness the contents of the church's religious self-consciousness, must always face the changing configurations of the human spirit that make up the church's context. All of these indi-

[31] SW II/8, p. 106.

[32] KD, Pt. II, Division 3. (Italics mine.) The other discipline belonging to this division is the knowledge of the social circumstances of the Christian church in the present, called by Schleiermacher "Church Statistics."

[33] Gl. (1st edition), §1,5.

cations point to the fact that Schleiermacher's idea of theology is imbued with a deep historical sense which, more than any other single feature of his thought, obtains for him the position of father of modern Protestantism. Accordingly, the commission that he lays upon dogmatics is to organize and focus the content of the *present* consciousness of the *historical* church. (*The Christian Faith* itself was written to do precisely this for the newly formed Union Church of Prussia.) The goal of the theologian is, therefore, no longer to speculate about the supernatural and to seek to erect time-impervious ontological systems and hierarchies of being, out of which the church may then extract eternal metaphysical justifications for its sense of what is its due from society. His goal is now, rather, to bring together in orderly fashion the elements of the community's religious consciousness and so to fix in concepts and propositions the Christian identity of that community and its members, in order thereby the better to enable the church to give an account of itself both to its own constituency and to the world. We may interpret the import of this idea by saying that, if it is the business of preaching to confess faith and to exhort others to faith, the business of the theology exemplified in *The Christian Faith* is to examine the confessional and hortatory language of preaching (and also of hymns, the liturgy, etc.), less as a censor than as a Socratic partner who is concerned that contradictions, inconsistencies and superfluous connotations be purged and that in the process the integrity of the consciousness out of which this discourse arises be more steadily acknowledged.[34] Theology is the countervoice of the church. Consequently, the dialogue of theology with the church is unending and, in its work of drawing forth the content of the Christian consciousness and representing it in the clearest fashion humanly possible, theology must play the rôle of critic.

[34] The relationship of dogmatic language to the language of preaching is discussed in Gl., §16, 1.

§3 ECCLESIASTICAL CRITICISM

The task of criticism devolves upon theology in this rôle in a twofold fashion. First of all, theology is prompted to raise the question of style to its uttermost pitch, the question about which words, concepts, and symbols and which arrangements thereof provide appropriate vessels of expression and representation of the Christian self-consciousness in a particular church. Schleiermacher refers to this fitness of a faith-utterance to function as an accurate representation of the content of the Christianly determined self-consciousness "in a given time" as the "ecclesiastical value" of the theological proposition.[35] This question of style is fundamentally one of identity. What is Christianity? What is the specific Christianity of this communion, and, therefore, what are the limits that circumscribe the concepts and symbols appropriate to this faith's confession of itself? The author's earlier *Brief Outline of the Study of Theology* assigned fundamental queries of this type to a separate theological discipline which he called philosophical theology, the branch of theology whose perennial business it is to seek out all pseudo- or un-Christian elements in the particular church in question, and to exhibit, on the other hand, the presence of essential Christianity in that same communion.[36] He conceived it as a never ending enterprise that must grow apace with the data of church history, a discipline it presupposes and for which it provides the critical tools.[37] It is an enterprise, furthermore, which must be carried out by all communions, each one for itself, since essential or absolute Christianity can never be identified with any one Christian denomination or generation but only with the entirety of all genuine effects of the work of Christ in inaugurating the Kingdom of God. This fundamental and character-defining kind of theological criticism thus involves a perpetual dialectic between the historical manifes-

[35] Gl., §17.
[36] KD², §32–§68.
[37] KD², §89.

tations of Christianity and the evolving canon of true Christianity by which a church and its theologians are guided. *The Christian Faith* as an instance of "dogmatic" theology really presupposes the work of this philosophical theology, and accordingly, Schleiermacher here simply stipulates that the ultimate boundaries beyond which no theological reflection and instruction can go are drawn by the four classical heresies of docetism, adoptionism, Manicheanism and Pelagianism,[38] while the proximate boundaries and more specific marks of ecclesiastical identity are to be found in the symbolical books and catechisms of the communion in question.[39] (To be sure, as we have seen, the Bible underlies all of these marks of identity, but they in turn furnish the guides for the approach to Scriptures in that particular church.)

Even though *The Christian Faith* is not primarily philosophical theology, many exceedingly critical stylistic matters remain to it for disposition, as it executes its dogmatic task. For example, quite apart from the fact that a conception offering itself for theological employment may show no sign of violating the classical Christian character of the church's religious consciousness, there is still to be settled the question whether it stands in an intrinsic relationship to that consciousness and the life that produces it or whether it is in reality superfluous. The book contains several conspicuous illustrations of this type of critical evaluation.

The most famous of these instances of criticism—though not the most drastic—is without doubt Schleiermacher's treatment of the doctrine of the Trinity. He relegated the doctrine to a secondary status. In doing so, he did not say or suggest that the doctrine is without "ecclesiastical value," although the pages devoted to the trinitarian formulae are filled with critical observations concerning the inadequacies of the classical terminology. Schleiermacher was convinced, for example, that it is impossible perfectly to balance the preservation of the unity of the Godhead with the declaration

[38] Gl., §22.
[39] Gl., §27.

of the absolute equality of the three persons. He did not believe that any of the classical definitions of the trinitarian being of God had achieved the goal toward which Athanasius originally aspired. But what most disturbed Schleiermacher was the tendency to adopt a particular formulation of this doctrine of the Godhead, which is so beset with difficulties in any case, and to make it the point of departure for the determination of other more crucial statements, especially the doctrines of the presence of God in Christ as the redeemer and in the Common Spirit of the church.[40] In this fashion both the doctrine of the redeemer and of the Spirit in the church are too easily made to bear the burden of the speculative peculiarities of the trinitarian language; it is a procedure that represents an inversion of the actual order of knowing, since the foundations of Christian faith rest not upon the terms "eternally begotten," "unbegotten," etc., but rather upon the experience of God in Christ and in the Spirit as well as upon the feeling of absolute dependence. The consciousness of God is given only in and through these relations that inhere in our Christian self-consciousness, and we have no criterion by which to distinguish the being of God in himself, therefore, from the being of God in relation, in the aforementioned senses.

For these reasons, Schleiermacher looked upon the doctrine of the Trinity as an unfinished doctrine, as one whose determinate expression was always open to revision in the light of exegetical theology and of closer examination of experience and as a doctrine that at best combined concrete elements of the Christian religious consciousness but that as a whole in itself did not directly embody a specific single element in that consciousness. Consequently, the doctrine properly belongs at the conclusion of *The Christian Faith*, as a summary, for its authentic content is nothing else than the body of theological exposition of the whole of the faith.

In a similar vein, Schleiermacher also subjected the traditional language of church symbolical statements about the person of

[40] Gl., §172, 1.

Christ to a searching criticism. The terminology sanctioned at Chalcedon, with its inclusion of *physis* (nature) and *hypostasis* (subsistence) for the definition of the constituent elements of the person and status of Christ, carries with itself many scientific and metaphysical connotations that not only create grave difficulties for Christian thinking about the redeemer but that also raise the question whether the terms themselves are accurate representations of the Christian religious self-consciousness in its relationship to Jesus Christ. Proposition 95 therefore warns that the "ecclesiastical formulae concerning the person of Christ need to be subjected to continual criticism." And in the immediately following paragraphs Schleiermacher lays the foundation of his reinterpretation of the intention of classical christology and of what he believes to be the substance of New Testament christology by discarding the two-natures formula and stressing the unity of the person of Christ. He construes the perfectly regnant God-consciousness as the dwelling of God in Christ, and this then is Schleiermacher's equivalent for the notion of the divine nature of the redeemer. The result of this critique is a doctrine of Christ as the last Adam and the heavenly or life-giving, spiritual man; but of this we shall take notice in the following chapters.

Another, technically more startling, criticism appears at the very outset of the substantive discussion of Christian dogma, where Schleiermacher asks if the traditionally distinguished articles concerning creation *ex nihilo* and the preservation of the world express appreciably different facets of faith. He concludes that the two terms are merely two conceptual modes of one fact of the Christian self-consciousness.[41] Many other instances of this kind of criticism occur throughout, such as the discussion and reinterpretation of the belief in original righteousness and in the perfection of Adam,[42] and the reader may suppose that Schleiermacher would have

[41] Gl., §36–§38. The way to this conclusion is clearly pointed by Calvin's treatment of creation and divine government or providence.

[42] For discussion of this criticism, see below, Ch. IV, §2.

wielded his Occam's razor even more insistently, had he not wished to soften the radical appearance of his work. Indeed, according to the logic prevailing here, it would theoretically be feasible to include in dogmatic theology only such propositions as describe the state of the Christian religious consciousness as such and to omit all those having to do with divine attributes or the world's original constitution, because these latter kinds of statements inevitably encourage the tendency to abstract God or the world from the relations in which alone they are known in faith and so lead to gratuitous speculation about matters unessential to piety.[43] If such statements about the attributes of God or the original condition of the created order must be included, then the arrangement of the exposition should make clear that as expressions of Christianity they stand on a level different from that of the basic propositions of faith.

But these various questions about the "ecclesiastical value" of particular concepts and the attendant debates about their intrinsic necessity finally point beyond themselves to a far more fundamental and significant interest on Schleiermacher's part: his occupation with the principles of the economy and organization of the Christian religious consciousness as a whole. The proper and most economical arrangement of the parts that would at the same time best exhibit the integrity and vitality of the whole of the content of faith evidently struck him as the most effective means for clarifying and preserving the identity of the Christian community and Christian man in the intellectually and socially tumultuous days of the early nineteenth century, especially in the face of the rise of the natural and historical sciences with their latent threat of cultural and intellectual imperialism. One of the most decisive of all "stylistic" questions confronting theology was, therefore, the question concerning the principle of the order of exposition of systematic theology as a whole. "For according to my view," he wrote in the

[43] Gl., §30.

first edition of his *Glaubenslehre,* ". . . that which can above all endow a textbook in the Christian faith with unique worth . . . is the order and structure of the whole in which the individual propositions are placed."[44] Ought redemption, then, or creation be treated first? Ought God's love or his omnipotence take precedence? No other issue is more fundamental to the method of modern theology than this, as Karl Barth's *Church Dogmatics* demonstrates today. It entails the question about nature's relationship to grace, and Schleiermacher, fully aware of the far-reaching consequences that his own answer to the question would inevitably bring with itself, hesitated long before committing himself. As it turned out, however, he remained to the end ambivalent about the actual solution he adopted.[45] We shall have occasion later in Chapter V to look more closely into the roots and scope of this problem, but here it is apposite to note the precise shape this question assumed in his mind. Is, for the Christian consciousness, the creation the context for the appropriation of Christ's redeeming work? Or are the person and work of Christ the presupposition of the Christian's confession of faith in God as creator? While this question is as old in biblical and Christian thought as the idea of a divine plan for history, it presses more acutely in *The Christian Faith* than hitherto in systematic theology, because it is no longer the blatantly speculative query whether God, in his secret and eternal counsels, ordained creation for the sake of Christ or the atonement for the reparation of creation; it is now a matter of the actual configuration of the historical religious self-consciousness of the Christian community. Wherein, Schleiermacher asked of himself, does the fundamental unity of that consciousness lie? Does it lie in the Christian's sense of creaturely humanity, in his "feeling of absolute dependence"; or does it consist of his trust in the person of Jesus Christ? Should the Christian render an account of his own hu-

[44] *Loc. cit.,* "Einleitung."
[45] Send., pp. 30ff. (605ff.).

manity and—by inference—of the humanity of others by saying that his relationship to Jesus of Nazareth is the presupposition of that humanity? Or should he take his departure in the created nature shared by all his fellow creatures and articulate the meaning of Christ into that common possession? None of the responsibilities of the reflective theologian is more important than the putting and answering of this question, for obviously nothing else so profoundly touches the sense of identity that the church must bring to explicit consciousness as it faces its own work and deploys its own energies amid the rapidly devolving courses of social, political and intellectual history in modern times. Schleiermacher was, therefore, scarcely misconceiving the nature of the contribution he believed himself to be making in his published theology when he suggested that its greatest value would lie in the "order and structure of the whole." The problem of order arises directly out of the constitution and exigencies of historical life, and the inquiry into that order is inquiry into the true nature of that life. It is incumbent on the reader to attend with commensurate pains, therefore, when *The Christian Faith* states the principle on which its author's order of thinking is predicated: "Christianity is a monotheistic faith, belonging to the teleological type of religion, and is essentially distinguished from other such faiths by the fact that in it *everything* is related to the redemption accomplished by Jesus of Nazareth."[46]

There are, to be sure, many exceedingly important methodo-

[46] Gl., §11. (Italics mine.) *Cf.* especially part 3: human bondage and redemption through Christ constitute not merely one element among many others in the Christian self-consciousness but rather that to which all others are related. There is, of course, a contradiction between this apparent declaration of Christocentrism and the conventional movement of *The Christian Faith* from creation to redemption to church. But Schleiermacher was aware that this simplified direction of exposition was barely translucent to the deepest currents of his thinking, and he attempted to warn the reader to that effect in §29, which states, in turgid language, that creation is not merely the presupposition of redemption but is apprehended through Christ. The corresponding paragraph (§33) of the first edition is clearer on this score. Nevertheless, this ostensible solution of the problem of order is still attended with grave difficulties in the *Glaubenslehre*. *Cf.* below, Ch. V.

logical issues contained in this definition of Christianity, and we shall return to it for further discussion in the following chapters. What is of particular interest at this juncture, however, is the fact that Schleiermacher points to the work of the redemption by Jesus Christ, that is, to the most real of all the relations to the Christian consciousness in which Jesus stands, as the agency or power that affects the entirety of the religious self-consciousness. In one sense, this proposition seems to be saying that the unity of the Christian consciousness is dependent upon Jesus of Nazareth, or, more precisely, upon his work-relation to the self-consciousness of the Christian. But this implication should not be taken to carry in itself the further suggestion that the very humanity of the Christian is derived from Christ alone and that apart from Christ humanity remains entirely inchoate. At least, additional documentation is necessary to establish this further inference, although, as we will see subsequently, there is a nisus in Schleiermacher's theology towards this position. The immediate import of this definition of Christianity and the Christian religious self-consciousness is, however, that the clarity of the Christian self-consciousness is the effect of the relation to Jesus the redeemer, to whom nothing in human nature is alien or beyond his power of touching and affecting and ordering. We have here a species of Christo-centrism, though it is not the Christo-centrism of Karl Barth's *Church Dogmatics*. The unity of the Christian religious self-consciousness is *dependent* upon the redemption wrought by Jesus of Nazareth, *historically dependent*, but it is not derived from Christ. It is derived from God the creator. Schleiermacher parallels Calvin on two scores here. On the one hand, Jesus Christ effects the restoration, the collecting and refocusing of the mind's diffused and darkened relation to God, just as Scriptures perform this task according to Calvin in *The Institutes of the Christian Religion*.[47] On the other hand,

[47] *Cf. Joannis Calvini, Opera Selecta,* ed. P. Barth and G. Niesel, Vol. III, Monachii (1957, 2nd edition), Bk. I, Ch. vi, i. "ita Scriptura confusam alioqui Dei notitiam in mentibus nostris colligens."

from the standpoint of the Christian religious self-consciousness, looking backwards, as it were, we see that it is just as true for Schleiermacher in *The Christian Faith* as for Calvin that Christ the redeemer appears to the reconciled self as having been eternally decreed by God and as having always been the true agency of God's final completion of his work of creating the self.

§4 SCIENTIFIC CRITICISM

Such reflective questions as the foregoing are bound up, however, with still another kind of criticism that the theology of *The Christian Faith* is called upon to exercise in its rôle as the translator of the religious affections into carefully considered propositions. Schleiermacher refers to this second species of criticism, whenever he speaks of the responsibility of theology for ascertaining the "scientific" as well as the "ecclesiastical value" of theological propositions.[48] The scientific value of a theological term is its clarity and consistency with the whole vocabulary that the theologian employs in his rendering of the Christian consciousness, and, obviously, in practice the ecclesiastical or descriptive faithfulness of a proposition and its "scientific" adequacy cannot be settled independently of each other.

A paramount instance of scientific criticism obtrudes from the very heart of the methodological problem of order, whose importance for Schleiermacher we have already recognized. The criticism has to do with the meaning of "nature" and the "natural," and it thrust itself upon Schleiermacher's attention for the same reasons that prompted him to deliberate over the proper sequence of the exposition of the doctrines of creation and redemption. For in the same way that theological tradition prescribes that the first article of the creed, "I believe in God the Father Almighty," shall also be the first topic of dogmatic or systematic theology (so that creation

[48] Gl., §17.

precedes the redeemer and redemption), it dictates that the theologian shall subsume the matter of these articles into the scholastic schematism of the natural and the supernatural. But, if Schleiermacher was already convinced that the actual Christian religious self-consciousness receives its historical unity and sense of life and meaning from its relationship to Christ, then he had to entertain the possibility that the norm of all the self's relationships and hence the whole force of the "natural" and the proportions of the "natural" were profoundly qualified for the Christian consciousness by the Christ-relation. Schleiermacher could not raise the question about the order of theological exposition, therefore, without suspending the self-evidence of the natural/supernatural schematism and setting out to obtain greater clarity and consistency for the term "nature" and its cognates in theology. The urgency of the problem is obvious, for the manner in which the "natural" is conceived and delimited affects a host of sensitive areas into which every theologian of the church must venture, including the disposition of belief in miracles, belief in the verbal inerrancy of canonical Scriptures, and ultimately the Christian man's fundamental conception of the manner in which the Son of God shares in adamic humanity. The resolution of the nature/supernature dichotomy or tension through the clarification of the meaning of the term *nature* is bound to affect these and other problems because it calls for a fresh examination of the points of reference by which nature as the system of interconnectedness of finite entities and events is identified. If, for example, the biblical picture of Christ is adopted as the norm of what is appropriate and hence natural for this nexus of entities and events we call nature, then nature itself will include a multitude of occurrences that from a non-Christian point of reference would be described as unnatural or supernatural. Schleiermacher did not accept every biblical text about Christ as normative, but he did believe the Christ of the New Testament, particularly the Christ of the Fourth Gospel, to be one who, instead of being determined by a prior system of nature, is the illumination of and the revealer of a "larger" system of nature. Consequently, while he was sufficiently a child of the Enlightenment not to accept the miracle stories of the various Gospels as the attestations of the divinity of Christ, he was also sufficiently critical of the rationalism of the Enlightenment and so deeply informed by the central tenet of Johannine and Pauline christology, namely that Christ is the incarnate principle of life, that he did not simply reject the miracles wholesale. Instead, he treated the miracles as instances of events that appear "natural" in the light of Christ as the head of the created order. In effect, he returned to the New Testament ideas of wonder and of faith as the key to grasping the true meaning of such events. And he further suggested that events apprehended in and through the relationship of the religious self-consciousness to God and to the redeemer may well appear as wondrous against the background of what had hitherto been known and understood of nature, and still they might be regarded as open to investigation and future understanding without thereby losing their wonderful character, that is, their relationship of meaningfulness to faith.[49] The very presence of this problem of nature and the supernatural makes even more intelligible why Schleiermacher should have insisted simultaneously that theology is only the offspring and servant of popular religion and yet that it must always push beyond the level of inherited and popular religious language, be it that of hymns or homilies, in order to achieve precision.[50] Such purification of terms is no more than the fitting and necessary extension of the tendency toward self-consciousness and self-criticism that is implicit in the use of all language by a community of persons.[51]

Schleiermacher prescribed for his theology a dialectical ap-

[49] *Cf.* Gl., §14, postscript, and §47, especially part 3. For the manner in which Schleiermacher relativized the doctrine of the inspiration of Scriptures under faith in Christ, in a similar fashion, see §14, postscript, and §128–§132.

[50] Send., pp. 59f. (642f.).

[51] Gl., §18.

pearance under such circumstances, because the procedure of criticism requires that all the while the theologian is moving between his scrutiny of the content of the religious consciousness and the outward face it turns in its language toward the community and the world, he must also reconcile the elements of its vocabulary and conceptual framework to each other. As he often explained in his hermeneutical theory, his ethics and *Dialektik*, he had discarded the notion of the absolutely self-evident, the "clear and distinct ideas" formula of Cartesian thought, and had insisted that self-evidence is always historically conditioned and that clarity is a matter of relation. Accordingly, nature did not present itself to him, even within religious discourse, as a quiddity to be accepted and employed without being examined; on the contrary, as he wrote to the philosopher Jacobi, "I have placed myself on the footing to demand of someone else the proof of where nature has its limit."[52] Despite the literal sense of his words here, of course Schleiermacher did not mean that the limits of nature were no concern of his but only that the meaning of the term was indeterminate and its scope had yet to be exhausted. But if this is the case, then it is impossible to be certain a priori about that which contradicts nature or purports to be above nature. The traditional theological distinction between nature and supernature therefore seemed to him clumsy and incapable of genuinely productive use in theological discourse. It is one of those inherited notions that promise and hint at more than they are able to reduce to logic. For example, Schleiermacher reasoned, nothing pertaining to the Christian religion could be said to be *absolutely* supernatural, for the absolutely supernatural must of necessity be contradictory and destructive of human nature and, so, contradictory also of the very premise of the Christian faith, namely, that Jesus Christ was a man sharing *our* humanity. There must lie in human nature at least the possibility of receiving the divine, he argued, although by this he did not

[52] Br. II, p. 350 (E.T. II, p. 281).

mean that men or mankind produced the redeemer, anymore than that mankind creates its own nature, but rather that this possibility must be in human nature according to the wisdom and eternal decree of its Maker.[53] But then the supernatural is only relatively supernatural; or, alternatively, one may ask, where indeed are the limits of the natural? To be sure, there is also reason for denying that Christ and all that is related to him in the Christian religious consciousness is simply a natural fact, if by natural is meant a fact that is wholly explicable within the terms of that which precedes its appearance. The very meaning of Christ for the Christian is that he is "original" in history, and that he cannot be explained by the context against which he appears, for it is the context that receives its illumination from him.[54] Thus, while Schleiermacher's attack on the notion of the supernatural resembles the argument of those English Deists who wished to discredit the suprarational status of revelation by showing that the absolutely suprarational must be the absolutely mysterious and unassimilable and, therefore, irrelevant, he did not share the Deists' confidence that nature at large is comparable to a mechanism into which the mind can see with the lucidity that it enjoys in dissecting its own mechanical inventions. Everything that affects the human consciousness and is assimilable by it, regardless of the origin of the powers by which that assimilation occurs, is in one sense natural; while in another, even the whole of nature itself—what rational theology is pleased to call Nature—is supernatural, because human reason does not and cannot make it but can only receive it as given and then endeavor to understand it.[55] Therefore, *The Christian Faith* can stipulate, no matter how great the difference between Christ and our own

[53] Gl., §13, 1.

[54] Gl., §10, postscript.

[55] Gl., §13, postscript. To a lifelong correspondent, Schleiermacher wrote: "Everything is natural, in one sense, and supernatural, in another. Even that the Son of God became man must be natural, in a higher sense." Br. II, pp. 322f. (E.T. II, pp. 250f.).

adamic humanity we are not prevented thereby from regarding the incarnation of the Son of God as a "natural fact."[56] The manner of expression all depends on what one takes to be the center and basis of the natural. So far as the task of the Christian theologian is concerned, his procedure is relatively clear. It is to describe as faithfully and systematically as possible the contents of the Christian religious self-consciousness, and since the unity of that consciousness is not the pure, numerical unity of the monadic individual but a *self*-consciousness whose entire contents are related to the redeeming work of Jesus of Nazareth, the theologian must reproduce as best he can that living, historical kind of unity in which the relation to Christ has become integral and has assumed an organizing power. It is, then, in this relation that he must seek the meaning of the natural, at least insofar as the natural stands for essential and normative humanity. But this religious consciousness is certainly not produced wholesale by the Christian man himself or by his community, any more than is the consciousness of the world so produced; rather, it is first of all given, just as Christ himself and the relation to Christ are also given and hence are not of men's own making. Consequently, in following out the topography of the Christian religious self-consciousness, the theologian finds himself in a real world that is no longer amenable to, or relevant to, the schematisms of the scholastically minded and the controversies between the orthodox supernaturalists and the rationalists. In this vein, Schleiermacher could further explain himself to Jacobi, then: "If my Christian feeling is conscious of a divine spirit in me that is something other than my reason, I will never cease to search it out in the deepest depths of my soul's nature, and if my Christian feeling is conscious of a Son of God who is different from the best of us in another way than by being still better, so will I never cease to search out the genesis of this Son of God in the deepest depths of nature and to say to myself that in all likelihood I shall com-

[56] Gl., §13, 1.

prehend that other Adam just as soon as I do the first Adam or Adams, whom also I must accept without comprehending."[57]

This dialectical treatment of nature is but one of many instances of the "scientific" criticism that Schleiermacher executes in the course of *The Christian Faith*, yet at the same time it must undoubtedly be taken as the most important and ramifying of them all. The position that he thereby establishes between naturalism and supernaturalism enables him, as we have already seen, to reject the New Testament wonders as miraculous and still to retain them or at least the possibility of them insofar as they are not independent witnesses to but effects following from the nature newly present in Christ himself. And many other tactical advantages similarly accrued to him, in his effort to steer a course between the outright naturalism of the left and the desperate supernaturalism of the right in the Protestant Christendom of his day. But what is of immediate additional moment here is to observe how the function of criticism that Schleiermacher so highly regarded and liberally practiced both symbolizes and further accentuates the human tenor of his theology. Theology consists of human acts of thinking and reflection on divinely given matters. Such self-criticism, as this, symbolizes and accentuates the freedom and gusto with which theological thinking ought to be carried out, to his mind. This is an aspect of *The Christian Faith* that is of an importance equal to the casting of dogmatic theology in the rôle of preaching-faith's descriptive science of itself and the employment of it as the countervoice through which the self-consciousness of the church rises to the clarity and integrity demanded by the times.

The freedom of theology is rooted in the original fact that theology is the daughter of religion. Christian theology is the daughter of a particular religion, to be sure, but nevertheless it is coeval with the humanity of the theologian, for a man's humanity is always given to him in this or that specific historical configura-

[57] Br. II, p. 350 (E.T. II, p. 281).

tion. Therefore, the scientific status of theology is secure, as secure, at least, as that of any other discipline, for none of them enjoys the authority of a superscience. All alike arise out of man's confrontation with the historical givenness of his condition and the needs of the human situation. The hegemony of the mind is conferred upon none but only the right to grow apace in the mastery of its own matter, through openness and the clear realization that there is work for it to do. For Schleiermacher, theology is human reflection, necessitated by the Christ-relation that reposes in and permeates a man's feeling of utter dependence on God. Reflection such as this cannot remain deaf or indifferent to the other occupations of men in society and the other uses to which they turn their reason. As the countervoice to preaching, through which the self-consciousness of the church rises to a clarity and integrity commensurate and congruent to the demands of the times, it is obvious that theology is and must be affected by this social context and these employments of reason. The self-criticism that the Christian religion cultivates in theology, as it ascertains the "ecclesiastical" and "scientific" value of its linguistic and conceptual tools, is manifestly a response to the historical character of the life of the church. Were this not the case, the fixing of the identity of the church would not be its perennial problem.

The dialogical interrelatedness that Schleiermacher posited in his ethics and *Dialektik* as the general situation for all the sciences holds no less firmly in the case of theology, therefore, but, if anything, more so, even with respect to that most agitating of all acknowledged or unacknowledged kinsmen, philosophy. The sense of mutual independence and openness that dogmatics can afford within the theological curriculum is equally possible and indispensable here. The identity of faith is not threatened by fraternization. Schleiermacher did show deep suspicion toward both scholastic theology and the idealists of his own day who took up the matters of religion in their own philosophy and sublimated doctrine into eternal truths of the speculative intellect. But his hostility on these occasions was directed at the confusion of religion and philosophy, not at the principle of communication between theology and philosophy. On the contrary, Schleiermacher was capable of displaying a certain carelessness on this score, so that if his dialectical handling of nature or any other term shows that he has learned some of his logic from the philosophers and if *The Christian Faith* takes on a certain philosophical appearance, that should not be cause for alarm, to his way of thinking; whoever penetrates below the surface will recognize the theological substance,[58] and when dogmatics has better mastered its own business, "so extraordinary a question as whether the same proposition can be true in philosophy and false in Christian theology, and *vice versa*, will no longer be asked, for the simple reason that a proposition cannot appear in the one context as it appears in the other: however similar it sounds, a difference must be assumed."[59] The theological proposition can always be reenacted and tested from the standpoint of religious feeling. Meanwhile, the only genuine causes for alarm are the mistaken views that arrange theology and philosophy hierarchically or, again, those two mental attitudes that are only apparently opposite: the perpetual hope of the theologian that the latest philosophical system will solve all of his dialectical problems and the perpetual trepidation of the theologian before all philosophical influence.[60] In the same letter to Jacobi quoted above, Schleiermacher described himself as a man possessing both feeling and the power of understanding and likened his own existence to an ellipse with these two foci and then to an equilibrium that really consisted of the oscillating motion of two waves; finally he chose the phenomenon of electricity, enormously fascinating at that time, as a metaphor for stating his credo concerning the relationship of

[58] Gl., §28, especially part 3.
[59] Gl., §16, postscript.
[60] Gl., §28, 1.

the "head" and the "heart": "Understanding and feeling . . . stand, within me, outside each other, but they touch and form a galvanic pile. For me, the innermost life of the spirit consists only in this galvanic operation by the feeling in the understanding and by the understanding in the feeling, wherein, however, both poles always remain deflected from each other."[61] This particular metaphor does much to illuminate the spirit in which he could also say that his philosophy and dogmatic theology were, therefore, "firmly resolved not to contradict each other, but just on this account both will never be completed."[62] Philosophy and religion are each entirely original manifestations of human nature, the one of reason seeking knowledge, the other of feeling disclosing man's dependence. They can hardly be set over against each other as contradictory forms, for reason and piety do not belong to the same level of human existence, which is the vain assumption of those who forswear the one for the other. Nor, on the other hand, are they so disparate that a man can pretend he is not the same person who is now reflecting philosophically and now reflecting theologically upon the content of his religious consciousness. Consequently, Schleiermacher might have countenanced the aphorism of Pascal concerning the reasons of the heart that reason does not know but never the line often attributed to Tertullian: "I believe because it is absurd." The supposition that faith and reason must be mutually destructive belongs to as faulty an analysis as does the nature/supernature dichotomy. Yet, the ultimate agreement between understanding and feeling, to which every fully self-conscious thinking man must aspire, cannot be produced from either side alone, but must occur spontaneously in and through the growth of human stature and the providence of history.

These remarks by Schleiermacher the theologian concerning philosophy set him off from much present-day theological suspicion

[61] Br. II, p. 353 (E.T. II, p. 284).
[62] Br. II, p. 351 (E.T. II, p. 283).

of the sister discipline, and likewise from those who hold to philosophy in one form or another as the indispensable propaedeutic to the doctrines of faith. His view, however, was not founded on any naïveté concerning the politics of the university and the possibilities therein for interdepartmental harmony. Schleiermacher was, after all, a colleague of Hegel's, and, beyond that fact, he was not particularly optimistic about the immediate profit that the theologian could obtain from a Kant or a Fichte.[63] But if he could not borrow wholesale from these contemporaries, he learned from his own criticisms of them, and his indebtedness to the classical philosophers was a matter of record. Furthermore, he recognized that there has been between the two disciplines the bond of a common language, for theology has always taken from philosophy, though also from law and other spheres as well, the better to execute its responsibility of refining the popular language of piety. It has done so with perfect propriety, in Schleiermacher's opinion, provided the subsequent qualifications and employment spring from genuinely theological motives, and one need only recall Tertullian's *persona* or the *homoousion* of Nicea or the concept of dread in existentialism to recognize the validity of his contention. In this way, he bespeaks his own confidence in the independence of the interests of faith and in the ability of these interests to maintain a relationship to other disciplines that is edifying but neither slavish nor fearful nor arrogant. The necessity of this relationship and of the critical function of theology out of which it arises is, in the last analysis, due to the fact that the work of theology can never be finished in history. Theology is rooted in the piety of particular human communities and their idioms in particular conjunctions of time and place. In this sense, and in the light of the foregoing, one may fairly ascribe to Schleiermacher the intention of exhibiting the

[63] *Cf.* Send., p. 60 (643). All theological borrowing from philosophy should, naturally, be selective, spread widely rather than concentrated in one system or school, and be done self-consciously. *Cf.* also Gl., §28, 1.

thoroughly—not merely—relative and human character of all theological reflection and discourse, that is to say, their relatedness to and complete dependence upon the life of the Christian community on its unceasing way to becoming the kingdom of God, which is a life that theology may express conceptually and so partially clarify but never wholly control or exhaust. All of this is symbolized by the full title of his greatest work: *The Christian Faith, presented systematically according to the basic propositions of the Evangelical Church.*

Chapter Four

RELIGION

§1 MAN AS RELIGIOUS BEING

The Schleiermacher who could describe theology as the daughter of religion and characterize it as an inevitable expression of human self-consciousness must obviously take account of religion not only in his philosophy of culture but also in his theology itself. In fact, like Calvin before him, Schleiermacher freely exploited the conception of man as a being in whom his creator has sown the seed of piety.

This high estimate of religion almost necessarily opens a wide gulf between Schleiermacher and the present-day reader, particularly the reader who comes to *The Christian Faith* with the shibboleths and party manifestoes of recent Protestant theology still echoing in his mind. To such a reader difficulties are likely to appear immediately upon commencing *The Christian Faith*, in the series of paragraphs that Schleiermacher himself described as the "definition of the place" of Christianity,[1] where he first sketches human feeling as a religious phenomenon. Here, in §3 and §4, Schleiermacher speaks of piety as a constitutive element of all human self-consciousness. Accordingly, in the eyes of his modern

[1] Send., p. 55 (636).

critics, he seems to be preparing to ask his readers to accept a general position that in effect betrays the distinctive character of Christian faith. Thus, in §3, he stipulates that piety or religion "considered purely in itself" is neither a knowing nor a doing but a "determination of feeling or of the immediate self-consciousness," and then he proceeds in §4 to define piety more closely as a "feeling of absolute dependence." But very soon thereafter, in §11, he presents Christianity as a particular historical manifestation of this feeling or mode of self-consciousness, the entire content of which is related and referred to the redemption wrought by Jesus of Nazareth. It is at this point that the difficulties assume a specific shape and import for the modern reader. The basic problem may be stated in its simplest form as follows: what in Schleiermacher's mind is the relationship between the abstract conception, "piety considered purely in itself," and the specific, individual self-consciousness that is determined by the historical figure of Jesus of Nazareth? Which is the more important for Schleiermacher: the general definition of religion or the particular character of Christianity?

Schleiermacher's less sympathetic critics have answered this question by suggesting that in these introductory paragraphs he embroiled himself in a dilemma that has since become perplexing in the extreme to philosophers of religion and many theologians. By ranging Christianity as a particular historical faith alongside a general definition of religion as such, the critics argue, Schleiermacher forces the reader to choose between two mutually incompatible attitudes toward Christianity. Either he may assent to Schleiermacher's method of treating Christianity as one religion among many or he may assent to Schleiermacher's conviction that Jesus Christ is redeemer and that Christianity is therefore absolute. He cannot do both things consistently. The fact that Schleiermacher himself did not hesitate to embrace Christianity within his definition of religion in general and at the same time to give Christianity a unique and absolute superiority merely indicates that either he was incapable of perceiving the difficulty inherent in his plan or else he was unwilling to admit its presence. If the reader chooses the first alternative, then, even though he adjudges Christianity to be the best of all religions, he must still draw the conclusion that as an instance of the universal form of human piety it is empty of all transcendent authority.[2] Or, if he clings to the finality of Christianity as faith in God's redemption of mankind through Christ, the reader must deny the validity of Schleiermacher's original approach to the matter, his attempt to treat Christian faith within an analysis of the affective content of the general religious consciousness. In a word, the crucial difficulty that the present-day reader is likely to discover in *The Christian Faith* is its author's combination of an empirical, descriptive attitude toward religion in human nature with a belief in the transcendent origin and final superiority of Christianity.

In point of fact, however, this basic problem which Schleiermacher thrusts upon the present-day reader and interpreter actually entails two elements, and they must be adequately distinguished if the characteristics and original direction of Schleiermacher's theological thinking are to be kept in sight. The first of these is the element of authority. The second is taxonomy or the philosophy of the relation between an individual and its class. Consequently, in order to assess the validity of Schleiermacher's procedure, the interpreter of *The Christian Faith* must recognize that the objection to Schleiermacher's combination of an empirical, descriptive method with a belief in the final superiority of Christianity rests upon *two* prior assumptions which are not connected in a logical fashion but do coexist in the theological mind of our own generation and testify to the intellectual history of Protestantism since World War I. The first of these is the conviction that has crystallized into an

[2] This criticism, which has become typical, has been voiced most insistently by Emil Brunner in *Die Mystik und das Wort* and in *The Philosophy of Religion*, trans. A. J. D. Farrer and B. L. Woolf, London (1937), pp. 38f., 42f. *et passim.*

axiom: religion as a human phenomenon cannot be the vehicle of God's self-disclosure, cannot be the means of communicating "saving truth," and therefore, by its very nature, lacks the power and authority of revelation.[3] The second of these grounds is the equally nearly universal belief that the individual phenomenon is differentiated from its order by accidents alone, and therefore the classification of Christian faith in God through the redeemer, Jesus of Nazareth, under the form of piety is tantamount to reducing Christianity to an instance that is essentially identical with all other religions and only accidentally different from them.[4] Clearly, each

[3] Under the influence of Barth, of Brunner and, more recently, of Dietrich Bonhoeffer, many Protestant theologians simply assume without further questioning that religion is opposed to revelation and therefore to Christian faith. Barth's original attack on religion appears in his *Commentary on Romans* (2nd edition). Brunner first gave his programmatic distinction between religion as a psychological, evolutionary-historical phenomenon and revelation as a non-historical, non-psychological, transcendent Word in *Erlebnis, Erkenntnis und Glaube,* Tübingen (1923, 3rd edition). Bonhoeffer wrote, "We are approaching a wholly religion-less era. . . . How can Christ be the Lord also of the religion-less? Can there be religion-less Christians? If religion is only a garb of Christianity . . . what then is a religion-less Christianity?" "The Pauline question, whether circumcision is the condition for justification means today, in my opinion, whether religion is the condition for salvation. Freedom from circumcision is also freedom from religion." *Widerstand und Ergebung,* ed. E. Bethge, Munich (1958, 8th edition), pp. 178f., 180f. To be sure the "religion" that is attacked by these various writers has various meanings; nevertheless, the effect of this concerted criticism has been to create a deep suspicion and radical distrust of all the word stands for. Among contemporary theologians writing in this ethos created by Barth, Brunner and Bonhoeffer, see, for example, Carl Michalson, who distinguishes two kinds of "religion": "mysticism" (Schleiermacher's *Frommigkeit* interpreted through Brunner) and "penultimate mysticism" (existentialism); the first he rejects as wholly spurious, while the second he adopts as the despairing state of mind through which men must necessarily pass in order to perceive the possibility of radical, eschatological Christianity. *Cf. The Hinge of History,* New York (1959), pp. 106f., 122f., *et passim.* George Forell, under the spell of the general Barthian reinterpretation of Reformation Protestantism, moves from the statement that "it is the unanimous witness of classical Protestantism that all men are law breakers," to the flat statement that for "the great Reformers religion is man's attempt to ignore the situation created by general revelation. . . . For Protestants *human religion* is an effort to domesticate Almighty God." *The Protestant Faith,* Englewood Cliffs, N. J. (1960), pp. 42f., also pp. 53f.

[4] This is part of Brunner's thesis against Schleiermacher; *cf. The Philosophy of Religion,* p. 39.

of these assumptions is of a widely ramifying kind, and each is fundamental to systematic theological thinking. They are not, however, coördinate, and we therefore must treat them separately, turning first of all to the nature of religion, as Schleiermacher conceived it and presented it in *The Christian Faith,* while reserving discussion of the general and the particular for the next chapter.

The reader can better appreciate the place that religion occupies in *The Christian Faith* if he remembers that the antithesis between religion and revelation, which has become an unquestioned principle of theology in recent years, is absent from this work and from the thinking of its author. Unlike his counterparts of the twentieth century, Schleiermacher was not in search of a theology of revelation, and this fact alone creates a certain likelihood of misunderstanding when the present-day reader puts his own theological questions to Schleiermacher. Whatever answers he receives he will have to translate with the intervening history of ideas in mind.

It would never have occurred to Schleiermacher that the category *religion* was in itself compromising of Christianity or that religion as a human phenomenon stands in radical contradiction to faith mediated through Jesus Christ and the Spirit of God. Such treatment of religion and Christian faith is a peculiarity of our own age, made possible in large part only by the profound change in attitude toward the human soul that took place during the later nineteenth century. In this respect, the student of theology today can never overestimate the violence that Ludwig Feuerbach, Feodor Dostoevsky and Sigmund Freud, together with other less obviously revolutionary figures, have done to the continuity of Protestant theological history. The rediscovery of the tortuously involuted character of the human psyche and the treatment of this psyche as a kind of "underground" from which the dogmas and myths of religion arise has robbed religion of its authority and made even a "Christian" religion permanently suspect in the eyes of many contemporary thinkers. For example, with his simple suggestion that the doctrines of the church are the objective expressions not of the mind of God but of human needs that can be analyzed and explained psychologically, Ludwig Feuerbach shot an arrow at his adversary, Hegel whom he regarded as a theologian in disguise, and it still transfixes the bowels of theology today. It is quite true that Feuerbach's criticism pierces most deeply into that variety of theology which shares with Hegel an intellectualistic notion of religion and tacitly assumes that the goal toward which religion strives is preeminently, if not solely, conceptual knowledge of God; the association of religion with psychological needs and the human "underground" in general is most damaging to that idea of Christianity which is concerned above all to guard the intellectual purity of its concepts and doctrines. But then it is also true that the continuing capacity of Feuerbach to wound indicates that the theology of our own times is still mainly preoccupied with a pure conceptual knowledge of God, a knowledge, that is to say, the authority and origin of which are uncompromised and that can be easily reduced to dogmatic proportions. Therefore, it is highly significant that Karl Barth, who embodies the spirit of systematic theology in this generation, reacts to Feuerbach and his logic not by discounting but rather by emphasizing the doctrinal, conceptual character of Christian faith. Barth's reply to Feuerbach consists simply in rejecting the premise that human religiousness has any part to play in Christian faith. Christian faith, he explains, is indeed knowledge of God, but it is a knowing in which God alone is active, and Barth casts religion as a human capacity or disposition in the rôle of the false prophet of Baal who must be slain for the honor of God.[5] Religion, as Barth declared in his famous pronunciamento, is "crim-

[5] There is, furthermore, a heavily doctrinal cast to the knowledge of God comprised in Christian faith, as Barth presents this knowledge. See, for example, his treatment of the doctrine of the Trinity in *Church Dogmatics*, I/1 (*The Doctrine of the Word of God*, trans. G. T. Thomson, New York [1949], §8, 2), where Barth extracts the doctrine directly from Scripture in a fashion reminiscent of scholasticism; or see his statements describing "pure doctrine" as "event" and as the "fulfillment of the promise given to Church proclamation." *Church Dogmatics*, I/2 New York (1956), p. 768 and §22, 2, *passim*.

inal arrogance" against God, and insofar as Barth typifies and moulds theological opinion in our times, religion no longer symbolizes the remnants of the implanted knowledge and acknowledgment of God or the dimmed "memory of God" that revelation in Christ restores and enlarges. Instead, it has become the name of the intractable concupiscence that perennially turns Adam aside to listen to the voice of the serpent in his own bosom rather than to the Word of God.

By reason of his times, Schleiermacher was, of course, unacquainted with the work of Feuerbach and his successors, and, probably by reason of his personality, he was largely innocent of any direct knowledge of the great human "underground" to which these later figures guided their own generations. In an important sense, therefore, he was not hampered by certain serious obstacles that would stand in the way of any one who might undertake his theological program today. Nevertheless, the conception of religion that appears in the pages of *The Christian Faith* is not necessarily rendered obsolete for us today by these later developments; its relative validity does not depend solely upon the fact that it was formulated in a time and by a temperament removed from Feuerbach and Dostoevsky. On the contrary, it is a carefully fashioned idea that Schleiermacher employed in order to render with fidelity the subject matter of theology as he conceived it, namely, the Christian life under God on its way to being conformed to the image of Christ. It is, moreover, an idea of religion that is not vulnerable to Feuerbach's criticism that the subject matter of theology is in reality psychology, simply because Schleiermacher makes plain at the outset that religion is not the name for an absolutely objective and therefore authoritative knowledge of the Absolute; therefore it is impossible to find in his "ostensibly" objective doctrines of God and Christ a "covert" doctrine of human nature. In fact, religion, according to *The Christian Faith*, is not primarily conceptual knowledge at all, nor the relics of the same, but it is the name for that universal problematic of human existence that can never be satisfied by concepts alone, even the purest and most encompassing, but only by an inwardly appropriated reconciliation of the two realities that press in upon the self-consciousness: the world-relation in which man finds himself and the relation to the power that posits him. It is neither the subject as such nor the object as such but it is the self and its relationships that are apprehended, partly through knowing and doing and feeling together and partly through feeling alone, of which Schleiermacher speaks when he speaks of religion.[6]

The proportions of Schleiermacher's idea of religion begin to appear as he makes himself increasingly insistent upon the point that religion is fundamentally man's affective response to the relationships into which the whole of human nature is bound, as the choice of the phrase, "feeling of absolute dependence," in itself suggests. It is to the manner in which this relatedness of human existence and religion are entailed in each other that the reader of *The Christian Faith* must closely attend.

Our previous examination of the idea of feeling as Schleiermacher developed it in the philosophical ethics and in the *Dialektik* has indicated that the interpretation of feeling as a faculty is precluded by virtue of the fact that the content of feeling is coterminous with the life-unity and identity of the individual. In the lectures on ethics, Schleiermacher was intent primarily upon exploring the co-inherence of individuality and community, and it was in that connection, therefore, that he had occasion to adduce the phenomenon of feeling as the inner expression of the underivability of the self. In the *Dialektik*, his purpose was to analyze

[6] For these reasons, Schleiermacher would oppose crisis theology today, just as surely as he opposed absolute idealism in his own times, for crisis theology, in both the persons of Brunner and Barth, maintains the same epistemological position as absolute idealism. Brunner early recognized this affinity and stated it forthrightly: "God can only be known through God; that is the fundamental thought common to the idealistic and the Christian doctrines of revelation." *The Philosophy of Religion*, p. 39. Brunner goes on to say, of course, that idealism differs from Christianity, by locating God within human subjectivity.

the structure of consciousness and to elucidate the function of feeling as the expression of the abiding identity of the subject in the reciprocity of its cognitive and volitional relations to the world. Here in the dogmatic theology, however, Schleiermacher returns to the phenomenon to scrutinize it in still another, though closely related, connection: in its bearing upon the question of the "whence" of human existence. The focus of this theological investigation is, of course, upon the feeling of being absolutely dependent, a form of consciousness that *The Christian Faith* makes no attempt to educe from any prior fact or principle but simply isolates, describes and clarifies as something given.

By characterizing religion as an immediate self-consciousness and a feeling of absolute dependence, Schleiermacher actually offers a formulation that is more lapidary than explicit, and it stands in need of somewhat careful analysis. There are at least four aspects of the phenomenon which require separate mention, and it is important that no one of these be allowed so to preoccupy the reader that he loses sight of the others. First of all, then, the use of the term *self-consciousness* points to the fact that in Schleiermacher's mind religion has to do with the way in which the self is present to itself. The language that §32 employs underscores this aspect of the phenomenon: the Christian religious self-consciousness always includes "an immediate self-consciousness of finding the self as absolutely dependent."[7] The note that Schleiermacher appended to his original definition of religion in §3 also emphasizes this same fact. Feeling, we there learn, stands for the immediate presence of the entire, undivided personal existence, sensible as well as spiritual, the unity of the person.[8] Secondly, the self that is present to the self in this mode of consciousness is the underived self. This is the import of Schleiermacher's explanation that reli-

[7] The Edinburgh E.T. is somewhat misleading in its translation of the German in this proposition.

[8] Gl., §3, 2, note. *Cf.* above, Ch. II, p. 123, n. 91.

gion is an "*immediate* self-consciousness," by which he means that the self in question here is the self that is not qualified by or determined by specific objects and energies located in its world. It is the self in its original identity, in its being-in-such-and-such-a-way (*Sosein*). This is the identity that the self has to discover and actualize in the world but that it does not derive from the world. In the third place, and again as the choice of the phrase *absolute dependence* indicates, the self that is so apprehended is, in effect, apprehended as having been posited. Hence, the self is present to itself not as the object of its own will but as thrust into existence by a causality that it cannot reduce to the terms of any specific concept. Not only does religion name the fundamental way in which the self finds itself or relates to itself then, but religion also names the fact that the self finds itself in a feeling of absolute dependence, which is a feeling that bespeaks involvement in a relation not susceptible of comparison with any of the intra-finite relations of historical existence. "What I understand by religious feeling," Schleiermacher explained in his letters to Dr. Lücke, "by no means derives from conception [*Vorstellung*], rather it is the original expression of an immediate existence-relationship."[9] Thus, in the phrase *absolute dependence* the substantive word conveys the sense of relation that Schleiermacher believed to stand at the center of self-consciousness, and the adjective *absolute* expresses the fact that this relation determines personal historical existence not in this or that particular capacity alone but in its entirety. *The Christian Faith* makes this relational dimension of religion even clearer, when it proceeds to interpret this feeling as a feeling of the "whence" of personal existence and stipulates that here one has precisely the datum to which we refer when we speak of being in relation to God.[10]

Finally, the reader must take note of the fourth and all-impor-

[9] Send., p. 15 (586).
[10] Gl., §4, 4.

tant facet of Schleiermacher's apprehension of this phenomenon: religion is located first of all in feeling and not in an idea. The discussion of Schleiermacher's conception of theological thinking has, of course, already made this side of his understanding of religion clear, and all of the quotations above allude to this fact in one way or another, as does much of the language of the paragraphs following §3 and §4. Therefore, religion does not take its rise from an idea of God, but rather "the whence of our . . . personal existence [*Dasein*], which is co-posited in the self-consciousness, shall be what is indicated by the word, God, and this is for us the truly original meaning of the same. . . . God signifies for us simply that which is the co-determinant in this feeling and to which we trace our being-in-such-and-such-a-way [*Sosein*]."[11]

At this juncture, the import of our analysis of the feeling of absolute dependence may be summarized as follows. Piety or religion is the name of the level of self-consciousness that is the most decisive of all—not, to be sure, in the order of temporal development of self-consciousness but in the order of importance, when personal existence and destiny are our chief concern. This level of consciousness has for its content the irreducible givenness of the self. It is a consciousness of the self prior to all of its specific social and practical relations, though, of course, Schleiermacher would never have argued that these social and practical relations are merely external to the self. This consciousness, moreover, involves a feeling-sense of dependence or a sense of having been posited in-such-and-such-a-way. Clearly, such a characterization precludes the possibility, adopted by the radical or absolute idealists such as Schelling, of interpreting finite self-consciousness as presupposing an immediate intellectual intuition of the Absolute.[12] Schleiermacher does not permit any cognitive dissolution of the finite-

[11] *Ibid.* Slightly altered from the E.T.

[12] *Cf.*, for example, "Vom Ich als Prinzip der Philosophie, oder über das Unbedingte im menschlichen Wissen," *F. W. J. von Schellings sämmtliche Werke,* Stuttgart (1856), Div. I, Vol. I, §8.

infinite distinction, for it is the relation and not the identity of the terms that he stresses in his description and analysis. Consequently, the religiousness that is native to man, constitutive of his nature, and the fundamental problematic of his existence is not to be confused with any supposed intuition of, or immediacy with, the Absolute. That which is immediate to the self is simply and solely the self as dependent. Therefore Schleiermacher believed himself to be under no obligation to prove that that upon which the self feels dependent is God. This necessity does not arise, because the name *God* obtains its first denotation precisely from this feeling: "to feel oneself absolutely dependent and to be conscious of oneself as being in relation to God is one and the same thing."[13] If the reader insists that the word *God* cannot be dissociated from some idea, then Schleiermacher's reply is to say that the idea which underlies the word is simply the expression of the feeling of absolute dependence and the first and most direct reflection upon it.[14]

Schleiermacher's famous definition of religion is, therefore, not so simple as at first glance it might appear. Its brevity should not be allowed to hide the scope of the conception of human nature in its multifold relatedness that is actually present in *The Christian Faith*. For insofar as religion is a mode of self-consciousness, it involves the fundamental way in which the self is present to itself; and, again, insofar as this presence of the self to the self bespeaks a "whence" or utter dependence of the self, it symbolizes the relationship of the self to God.

But even this twofold relatedness does not exhaust the senses in which religion entails being in relation or dependence. Schleiermacher's special use of the qualifying word *absolute* (*schlechthinnig*) expresses still another dimension of religion as relation, which requires as close examination as did feeling and dependence. To be sure, *absolute* may be read throughout the work as simply a re-

[13] Gl., §4, 4.
[14] *Ibid.*

minder of the irreducible givenness and hence of the radical finitude of the self. However, it also stands for a particular aspect of the relatedness of the self which neither the word *feeling* nor the term *dependence* sufficiently convey. *Absolute* stands for the fact that the relationship to God is perceptible as an ingredient of self-consciousness only because it exists along with other relationships from which it distinguishes itself in kind. That is to say, the absolute relationship presupposes, in the order of awareness, relative relationships; hence absolute dependence presents itself in consciousness only along with the feeling of implication in a nexus of relative dependencies. So important is this fact for the entire structure of *The Christian Faith*, that Schleiermacher makes it axiomatic that the "God-consciousness" or feeling of absolute dependence can never appear except in conjunction with a moment of time or—what amounts to the same thing—with a specific relationship to the world.[15] Clearly, therefore, on these terms it is the case not only that the religious consciousness cannot be segregated from the other relations inhering in personal, historical existence, but also that religion is inclusive of these relations, so that, in fact, the relative superiority of a given religion depends to a large extent upon the clarity with which it develops the world-consciousness and upon the degree to which it discriminates between the God-consciousness and the world-consciousness, while at the same time securing them to each other in a stable relationship.[16] One may translate *The Christian Faith* into the language of creedal theology by saying that the basal knowledge of God afforded by the religious consciousness is a knowledge of God as creator of all things visible and invisible, and the finite consciousness can never dissolve or abstract from this relationship.

The importance Schleiermacher attached to this construction of piety is considerable, to say the least. On the one hand, it under-

[15] Gl., §5.
[16] Gl., §5, §8.

lies the entire structure of the book and, on the other, it constitutes his defense against the charge of pantheism, which was immediately and frequently brought against him.[17] Nevertheless, his argument for this interpretation of religion purports to be nothing more than a statement of the facts of self-consciousness, as might be expected, rather than a speculatively constructed ontology of human existence developed specifically for the purpose of avoiding the pitfalls of Spinozism or of any other metaphysics. (And this, of course, is in keeping with his conviction that theology arises directly out of reflection upon the contents of the religious consciousness and never enters into dialogue with philosophy in order to become a rival metaphysics.)

The self that Schleiermacher regarded is always involved in thinking and willing, in suffering and doing.[18] Personal existence is a complex of mutually implicated moments of free action toward another and of being determined by another. However, while these two series of moments fill the temporal consciousness, neither one exhibits an obvious priority over the other. It would be possible, Schleiermacher suggested, to think away the "other" that always coexists with the subject in actual self-consciousness; but the result would be only a notion of "indefinite agility" without "form or color."[19] Consequently, even if we abstract the self from its other or not-self, we do not arrive at an intuition or feeling of immediate and unconditioned freedom in the self. To be convincing, moreover, the ascription of such freedom to the self would require that the self enjoy an awareness of producing itself and of exercising power over the very possibility of the existence of other particular beings. But the self is not its own creator nor does it have the power to contradict the given existence of other beings.[20] Therefore, the feeling of freedom can never be anything more than what

[17] *Cf.*, for example, Send., pp. 23-30 (596-604).

[18] *Cf.* above, Ch. II, §4; also Gl., §3.

[19] Gl., §4, 1.

[20] Gl., §4, 3. *Cf.* also Redeker, Vol. I, p. 27, note C.

it appears to be in our consciousness, a feeling of relative freedom only.

Nevertheless, careful as he is to set limits to freedom, Schleiermacher did not wish to appear to deny its presence in any way, lest the descriptive distinction between the God-relationship and the world-relationship be thereby obliterated. The utter denial of freedom is the course that true pantheism must take—a course wholly unjustified by the phenomena of self-consciousness, in Schleiermacher's view—for however limited the freedom of the self may be, it must nonetheless be recognized as real. In this way, Schleiermacher believed, he had set himself apart decisively enough from both the Spinozists and Fichteans.[21]

While, then, relative freedom and relative dependence (or being, relatively determined by an other) imply each other,[22] the feeling of absolute dependence specifies the immediate consciousness that *includes* the relative freedom and dependence which inform all personal existence. The decisive point of Schleiermacher's argument here is that absolute dependence does not contradict relative freedom or supersede relative dependence but merely opposes them both in their mutual entailment and hence also presupposes them, in the sense that all opposites presuppose each other. The world and God, therefore, cannot be confused, or the one reduced to the other, save through an equally confused self-consciousness. For even if the world, as the totality of all objects, is conceived as a unity, our own selves included, nevertheless the resultant sense of being one with the world does not expunge the feeling of relative freedom and dependence, for the only unity imaginable here is still a unity of separate parts out of which the reciprocal moments of freedom and determination may and do arise.[23] On the other hand, the feeling of absolute dependence that Schleiermacher calls the

[21] Gl., §32, 2. Schleiermacher consoled himself that the same critic charged him simultaneously with being a Spinozist and a Fichtean. Send., p. 26 (599).

[22] Gl., §4, 2.

[23] Gl., §32, 2.

God-consciousness does not permit the imagining of such divisibility in its "whence," since it includes no corresponding freedom or reciprocity.[24] This God-consciousness is not aroused by the presence to the self of any discrete object that is involved in a nexus of defining relations. As a level of consciousness it can only be designated as a felt relation of dependence that accompanies or pervades the total self-consciousness, working out from the immediate self-consciousness into the self in the totality of its connections to and within the world. Within the limits prescribed by the religious self-consciousness, therefore, God and the world are related but distinct realities; they can neither be identified nor can the knowledge of the relation to one be had apart from the knowledge of the relation to the other.

In summarization of the argument as we have presented it so far, we may say that Schleiermacher conceived of religion as the basal form of self-consciousness in which being-in-relation appears as the fundamental phenomenon, and this being-in-relation is again three-fold involving a species of relation to the self, a complex of relations to the world, and another, encompassing and opposing relation to a "whence," which furnishes the original meaning of

[24] A ready objection arises to this construction of the self in its world- and God-relations. Is it not possible that the world is the object of both types of relation, the relation of absolute dependence as well as the relations of relative dependence and relative freedom? Could not the "whence" of absolute dependence refer to the world in its ultimate unity, where the organic interconnectedness of all being is finally exhibited and understood, while relative dependence and freedom correspond to parts of the world considered simply as a multiplicity of beings? Schleiermacher's reply to this question is contained essentially in his *Dialektik*. The term *world* as used in the first sense, for the ultimate organic unity of all being, stands for a transcendental, regulative idea that is a product of thought alone but never can be known. The feeling of absolute dependence does not, therefore, point to the world in this sense, that is, to a regulative idea of thinking. Immediate self-consciousness is posited only in relation to that which is present in its own simple or non-synthetic identity. The unity of the world and the oneness of God are two different things; the former is the goal of all striving toward knowledge, though no instance of knowing realizes it; the latter is the presupposition of all thought but is present to the thinker only in his immediate self-consciousness. *Cf.* Dial. (O), pp. 303f.

the term *God*. This summary statement of course includes only the barest beginnings of Schleiermacher's developed phenomenology of the religious self-consciousness, for we have not even touched upon the specifically Christian determination of this self-consciousness, nor followed *The Christian Faith* into its account of the doctrine of creation as it devolves out of the three-fold relatedness of self-consciousness. Nevertheless, it is already sufficiently clear not only that Schleiermacher's whole theological enterprise in *The Christian Faith* rests upon both the distinctness of and the connection between these types of relation to being, but also that he sought to establish the case for this multiple relatedness quite independently of any explicitly metaphysical considerations.

By the nature of the case, Schleiermacher believed, as soon as this articulation of feeling is reduced to philosophical categories, the level of meaning has been transposed to a new plane upon which the realities ingredient in the religious self-consciousness as such can never be projected without the appearance of a certain concomitant distortion.[25] To be sure, as we have seen, he recognized that the theologian cannot avoid assuming the responsibility of precisely this kind of transposition, since the essential purpose of theological reflection is the conceptual representation of the religious consciousness. There is a sense in which the theologian really can do no more than discard those philosophical concepts that are most unsatisfactory and then strive to qualify those that are least unsatisfactory with enough care to make them serviceable, though none can ever be directly identified with the reality it is employed to express. Schleiermacher rejected out of hand, therefore, all formulas that blur the distinction between God and the world as unfit for the dialectical task.[26] Even so, in his terms the business of refuting pantheism or monism cannot be left wholly to the alterna-

[25] *Cf.* the discussion of the philosophical formulas for the relation of God and the world in Dial. (O), pp. 297ff.

[26] Gl., §28, 1.

tive philosophical formulas that are in fact adopted, for they can only express more or less faithfully the contents of the religious consciousness. It is the contents themselves that must be the final authority. Schleiermacher's defense against the criticism of pantheism, therefore, stands or falls with the reality of the distinctions that he discovers and describes as present in self-consciousness, for, as we have seen in a preceding chapter, he insisted that the meaning of every theological assertion, no matter how dialectical or speculative its appearance may be, must be capable of recapitulation from the standpoint of the religious consciousness alone, and not from any other.[27]

Still, granting to Schleiermacher the persuasiveness or at least the feasibility of his exposition and vindication of properly religious and theological meaning, as over against crypto-philosophical connotations, the present-day reader can scarcely deny that the appearance of immanentism in Schleiermacher's thought remains. *The Christian Faith* lacks an adequate expression of the transcendence of God. It is, of course, true that Christian thinking has always encountered the utmost difficulty in articulating the infinite-finite or, better, the creator-creature relation. The long history of theology shows a constant correction of one school or generation by the next on this score, so that the intention of theology as a whole is clear enough. But in practice, the individual theologian errs in this respect in one or another of two broad directions. He tends either to absorb the relation and one of its terms into the remaining term or else to emphasize the discontinuity between God and the creature so as to make all real relation impossible. The latter propensity arises in the interests of securing the absoluteness and aseity of God by endowing him with a perfection that requires no relation to other being. But it results in so construing the priority of God as to make any and every relation, even a relation that is avowedly extrinsic to his deity, so problematical as to be inconceivable. Obvi-

[27] Gl., §16, postscript.

ously, the Christian beliefs in God both as creator and as redeemer are attenuated by such a radical doctrine of transcendence. The classical doctrine of the impassibility of God has always encouraged theologians to run this risk; and more recently the crisis theology of the twenties and thirties, which took as its motto Søren Kierkegaard's "infinite qualitative difference" between eternity and time, which is exemplified in the earlier writing of Karl Barth, embodies this disposition. The first mentioned danger, that of appearing to close the distance between God and the creature, becomes acute when the theologian begins his thinking by assuming the relation between God and the world, adopting the assumption not because he believes relation is constitutive of God's being, but because it is constitutive of the creature's and because it is only on the basis of such a relationship to God that God can be known at all. However, even though relation between God and man is only the necessary presupposition of man's knowledge of God and not of God's being as God, the distinction between those two "necessities" is easily forgotten or overlooked. Schleiermacher manifestly ran this last mentioned kind of theological danger, though he has for company a considerable number of the formative theologians of Christian history. With Augustine and Calvin, whom he cited as his particular mentors in theology,[28] and, we may add, with Jonathan Edwards who represents on American soil the same theological tradition and spirit, Schleiermacher conceived the central religious reality to be the situation of the creature who finds himself as a being whose ex-

[28] These two men are cited as authorities more frequently than any other authors in *The Christian Faith. Cf.* Redeker, Vol. II, p. 564. So far as the history of ideas is concerned, the link between Jonathan Edwards and Schleiermacher is supplied by Augustinianism and Calvin on the theological side and on the philosophical side by Platonism and the Earl of Shaftesbury, who influenced Schleiermacher and affected Edwards through Francis Hutcheson's *An Inquiry into the Original of our Ideas of Beauty and Virtue. Cf.* LS[2], pp. 173ff. and *Jonathan Edwards: Representative Selections,* ed. C. H. Faust and T. H. Johnson, New York (1935), p. lxxxii, note 211.

istence at every level is implicated in a God-relationship. Schleiermacher did not set himself the task of asking and answering the question, "How is this relation possible?" Instead, he accepted this relationship as given, believing that his work was to reflect upon the problem of appropriating the God-relation and also the other relations that inform and qualify personal existence. The appropriation of these relationships individually and in their proper order requires that the self achieve clarity of consciousness about them and about their respective import. The fact, however, that Schleiermacher began with relationship as given, instead of attempting to establish it in a speculative fashion, did not mean that he was oblivious to the danger of monism. He sought to guard against it, as we have already seen.

It was in the religious context so understood that Schleiermacher carried on his theological reflection. Undoubtedly, even the most sympathetic reader of *The Christian Faith* can scarcely suppress a sense of the incongruity between Augustine's "Our hearts are restless until they find rest in Thee," or the stately opening sentences of *The Institutes of the Christian Religion*, or Edwards' vivid and affecting passages on the new sense of the heart for the excellency of God, on the one hand, and the dense, dry language of the fifth proposition of *The Christian Faith*, on the other, where the author first stipulates the relation between the God-consciousness and the world-consciousness. Nevertheless, even the most polemical interpreter of Schleiermacher's theological thinking cannot overlook the fact that his statement of the religious situation is not essentially different from that with which the Augustinian-Reformed tradition has long since made the Western world familiar. Religion as a universal, human phenomenon symbolizing the inextricable relatedness of personal existence led Schleiermacher to take his stand in the tradition that is constrained to begin its thinking with a God who is already in relation to man and with a human nature already in relation to God, because personal existence is given in and through that relation. It is this fact that is at once the first certitude and the greatest disturbance in human selfhood.

Schleiermacher's development of the religious consciousness as the disclosure of the relational character of human nature shows that his use of religion is shaped by his interest in the conformation of personal existence. To read Schleiermacher as one who sought to isolate in human nature a religious a priori is, therefore, to misread him. Religion is not the name for a faculty or category of the mind which, in distinction from scientific and ethical judgments, yields knowledge of God.[29] Religion stands for man in his position as the being on whom God and the world converge. Religious consciousness designates the human self-consciousness that must learn to bear the weight of these relations by finding or receiving a form in which these converging realities are reconciled into their proper order. The antithesis between religion and revelation, which dominates so much of post-Hegelian theology, is lacking in *The Christian Faith* simply because religion stands for man in the totality of

29 Schleiermacher's conception of religion and the religious consciousness can be likened to that of Rudolf Otto only improperly. Otto posits a particular, intuitional sense of God as numinous being and so finds the seed of religion in a peculiar a priori for the irrational manifestation of deity. Subsequently, Otto experiences difficulty in relating this irrational *mysterium* to the moral and rational ideas of God. The difficulty is rooted in his original psychology. Schleiermacher places the self in the entirety of its being as dependent on God. Feeling of absolute dependence is not the name of a special faculty. Again, where Otto is concerned with the various colorations of the sense for the numinous, in the feelings of awe, creatureliness, attraction, etc., Schleiermacher is intent upon the existence-relationship(s) in which the self's identity is determined and integrated. Hence, the term, a priori, at least within Otto's meaning, as designating within the soul a specific point of contact with the Absolute, cannot be transferred to *The Christian Faith*. Therefore, despite the fact that Otto is one of Schleiermacher's interpreters and conceives his own approach to be an improvement upon Schleiermacher's, the *Idea of the Holy* should not be taken as a clue to the meaning of the feeling of absolute dependence and the associated idea of the religious self-consciousness.

his being and not simply or primarily for man the knower.[30] Within the framework of Schleiermacher's conception of religion, it would make little sense to speak of revelation as the power or event which expropriates religion and supplants it in consciousness, for religion is not the name of a particular, albeit false, knowledge of God; it is the name for the multiple relatedness of personal existence, which manifests itself in consciousness through feeling. To depict revelation as expunging religion in this sense would be equivalent to showing revelation or the revealer as the destroyer of self-consciousness and identity, an alternative that Schleiermacher certainly could never have chosen. Therefore, instead of antithesis, as between religion and revelation, there can at most be a tension evident in *The Christian Faith*, and the tension is between the various provisional forms of equilibrium the self achieves in its position between God and the world and the ultimate ordering of the God- and world-relationships, to which Schleiermacher gave the name of redemption. Revelation, to be sure, does not lie wholly

[30] A silent assumption of the attack on natural theology by recent Protestant theology is that knowledge is a form of power. This assumption no doubt reflects the extent to which technological science has become the norm of all our conceptions of knowing. In any case, a natural or innate knowledge of God seems to represent some form of human power over, or claim upon, God, according to this way of thinking, and this in part accounts for the vehemence with which crisis theology rejected the notion of a seed of religion present in all men, an innate idea of God, obscured and vitiated, but still abiding in human nature. For Schleiermacher, however, religion does not stand for any sort of "original knowledge" of God. He is prepared to admit the possibility of such "original knowledge" (Gl., §4, 4), but he excludes it from the province of religion. In *The Christian Faith* religion stands for the whole man as a mirror (to borrow one of Calvin's favorite analogies) of the bearing of the creator upon creation. Religion does not stand for the ready access that man has to God, nor for the means whereby the rational creature may reverse the order of being and advance toward God on terms not first provided by the creator. Religion is coterminous with the life-unity of the self, with its identity as given in the "whence" that it cannot reduce to any finite term. Only if the individual could dispose at will of his own existence and identity (*Sosein*), could he have at his disposal his relation to God. But this is precisely the point that Schleiermacher's analysis controverts. Religion is a feeling of *absolute* dependence.

outside the sphere of Schleiermacher's interest, but just as the religious consciousness of *The Christian Faith* is a more inclusive phenomenon than any faculty for the conceptual knowledge of God, so redemption is a broader and deeper reality than the idea of revelation present in so much present-day theology. In this connection, it is instructive to recall that Schleiermacher expressly rejected the notion of a natural religion,[31] for the notion of natural religion is heavily weighted on the side of noesis, and it flourished particularly in eighteenth-century England, where it assumed the form of a doctrine of an unvarying, universal knowledge of a supreme being and moral governor. In *The Christian Faith,* however, the author insists that religion is always historically differentiated, and he does so because here religion symbolizes the effort of the entire self-consciousness to achieve the inner order to which it is prompted by its feelings of involvement in multiple dependencies and an ultimate dependence. Such personal, religious striving bespeaks the fact that what is needed in the world is not an idea of God but a causative power to order the self in its dependencies. For Schleiermacher to have abandoned the mundane plane of religion, therefore, would have been tantamount to deserting the historical, finite world within which redemption is required and wrought, and where the theologian responsible to the preaching church must carry on his work.

§2 THE MISERY OF SIN

According to Schleiermacher man is a religious being, and the word *religion* is the name for the situation in which men by nature find themselves. Men are bound in a network of relative dependencies and in an absolute dependence. Moreover, it is only because man is a religious being in this sense that redemption is relevant to him. And since revelation is meaningless apart from redemption, it

[31] Gl., §6, postscript.

is similarly the case that revelation is relevant to man only because he is a religious being. Hence, for Schleiermacher, religion is the presupposition of his analysis of redemption and revelation.

It is equally true, however, that redemption is the presupposition of Schleiermacher's understanding of religion and of man as a religious being. This fact becomes clear in *The Christian Faith's* presentation of sin and again in Schleiermacher's treatment of Adam and original righteousness, and we shall attend to these two themes in this and the following section.

In the discussion of sin, the theme of the quest of order on the part of the individual self-consciousness, as it exists in its network of relations and dependencies, emerges again, as it did in the characterization of religion. In fact, it is only in the analysis of sin and the correlative sense of blessedness that Schleiermacher's delineation of man as a religious being becomes concrete, for there is no religion without an inchoate consciousness of sin or, as we shall see, without the remembered foretaste of joy. Indeed, Schleiermacher saw in the religious consciousness a prefiguration of redemption, although, to be sure, this prefiguration has a special sense in *The Christian Faith*, which is part of the larger issue we must now consider.

Here again the Augustinian-Reformed tradition in which Schleiermacher set himself offers certain helps to the interpretation of his work, although, on this score the book is perhaps in less need of exegetical supplements than elsewhere. With Augustine and Calvin, Schleiermacher held not only the conviction that man's religiousness is a statement of his relatedness to Being and beings, but he shared with them also the perception of this relatedness as involvement in a dynamic order. This order is an order of Power and powers within Power, and insofar as these relations bear upon human nature and existence, they must be personally and historically appropriated. If, as Calvin admonishes his reader, "true and substantial wisdom" has two parts, the knowledge of God and of ourselves, then these knowledges become "steady and certain," when "revealed to our minds and confirmed to our hearts." Such wisdom or faith is the transformed fruit of the seed of religion. The seed cannot bring it forth of itself. Again, if man is a citizen of two cities, and if his proper citizenship lies in sojourning within the earthly as a native of the heavenly, then this is a citizenship confirmed only when it is proved through the suffering, of which the earthly incarnate Christ is the pattern and mediator. On the level of his theological psychology, Schleiermacher stands somewhere between the author of *The Institutes of the Christian Religion* and the author of *The City of God*. He is less introspective and discerning than Augustine but more willing to enter into detail than the ever practical Calvin. He recalls the former by his technique of psychological analysis but carries on the tradition of the latter in his direct and appreciative emphasis on human existence in the world. In broad agreement with them both, he teaches that the soul is suspended, as it were, from the point of convergence of distinct relations that belong together by their very nature in a particular order. Yet, the constitution of the self is such that it is capable either of reproducing afresh in itself the true order of these relations or of distorting that order and thereby denying the structure of being in and through which it lives. That is to say, according to Schleiermacher and his chosen masters, the order of being becomes historical in man. It becomes internal, moral and, therefore, problematical, creating the precondition of personal disorder and confusion.

Upon this possibility of personal disorder and upon the reality of human freedom, Augustine and Calvin built their doctrines of sin. Augustine employed his metaphysical-theological psychology to picture the corruptness of Adam and all humanity in Adam as a declination from true life before God through the disorderedness of man's loves for God and himself and through his concomitant ignorance of the true ratio between infinite and finite. Calvin used the metaphors of the dark "labyrinth" and the "factory of idols" to contrast the created purpose of the soul, to be the mirror of the divine government and glory, with the actual condition in which all men wander since Adam's fall by reason of their "brutish forgetfulness of God." Schleiermacher, in his turn, also recognized the universal problem of religion, and so of human nature, to be the confusion reigning in human consciousness, where the order of being that sustains personal existence is distorted and perverted.

When Schleiermacher described this confusion in the external forms it creates, he spoke of it as fetishism and polytheism, for both of these types of religion blur the distinction between the self's relation to God and its relation to the world, and they mistakenly connect the feeling of absolute dependence with some discrete, intra-worldly object.[32] But when he described this condition as apprehended from within and experienced as a confusion and inhibition of that maturity for which the self struggles vainly, he gave it the name of sin.[33] The sinfulness of sin's confusion lies in its fetishistic, polytheistic substitution of the rhythm of life within the world for the order and stability that arise beyond the world-relationship, within the God-relationship. The reader may understand Schleiermacher as saying here that sin is the striving to secure in the temporal alone what can only be given by eternity. Defined in the earlier language of *The Christmas Eve*, sin is the deification of "becoming," or, in words appropriate to *The Christian Faith*, one can state it as the succumbing of the feeling of absolute dependence to the temporal cycle of pleasure and pain, and hence it is the yielding of the self's identity to the vacillation of the pleasant and unpleasant moments of its involvement in the world through its sensible self-consciousness. However, aside from the much greater precision of expression that is present in *The Christian Faith*, there is little fundamental difference between the view of sin contained

[32] Gl., §8; also §5, 1.
[33] Gl., §66.

in the earlier work and that which the reader encounters in the magnum opus. In both instances psychological categories dominate the entire discussion, while political, social and purely mythical metaphors are conspicuously absent.[34] Therefore, the reader necessarily misses the characterizations of sin as disobedience of God and as infidelity, not to speak of the mythical representation of sin as bondage to Satan, which are so typical of the Calvin whom Schleiermacher otherwise espoused and defended. The consequence of this limitation in the language of *The Christian Faith*—a limitation that is part and parcel of the "scientific" thrust of the whole enterprise—is an obvious impoverishment of the theology and piety Schleiermacher received from his spiritual precursors. But the confusion and conflict with which he is directly concerned is still recognizably the same confusion and conflict of the self with itself that his predecessors more fully acknowledged and described. His text is the seventh chapter of Romans, "in my members another law at war with the law of my mind," and he conceives of sin as the failure "to take command of one's self."[35] Clearly, such an approach, with its virtual exclusion of political, familial and social analogies for the perversion of the soul's relation to God, does not mean that Schleiermacher completely lacked an understanding of the dynamism of sin. Sin is not simply fate or flaw in human nature,[36] but the weight of his interpretation falls upon the defectiveness of sinful human existence and activity rather than upon the assertive, catastrophic moments of the will's rebellion. The

[34] While Schleiermacher does call sin a "turning away from God," the metaphor of rebellion or disobedience is not significantly present, and its absence is undoubtedly coupled with the unimportance of the rôle that divine law plays in his theology (*cf.* Gl. §68, 3) and with the omission, from his view of the divine economy of creation and redemption, of any serious consideration of Israel and its Scriptures.

[35] Gl., §67, 2.

[36] For a discussion of the possibility of reading Schleiermacher as having reduced sin to proportions consonant with an evolutionary naturalism or monism, see below, Ch. V, pp. 214ff. and §3.

many equally original moments of such failure and fresh instants of culpability are always present in the background of self-consciousness, to be sure, but the focus of his doctrine of sin lies on the inner sense of disproportion between the spirit and the flesh. In a word, it is the pain of sin that stands at the forefront of these pages in *The Christian Faith*. The confusion that manifests itself in the identification of God with the elements of the world-consciousness becomes the source of misery, when it appears in its true nature as the offspring of the conflict between the two kinds of feeling that seek to govern the tenor of the self's existence and identity, the feeling of absolute dependence, on the one hand, and the feelings of the reciprocally related moments of world-consciousness, on the other.

However, to describe sin as misery and pain is to imply that sin is the privation of blessedness, and the reality of human sinfulness emerges, therefore, insofar as its opposite is also effectively present in personal existence. This is the reason that the substantive discussion of the doctrine of sin falls within the second of the two major divisions of *The Christian Faith*, the division over which Schleiermacher wrote: "Unfolding of the facts of the religious self-consciousness as they are determined by the antithesis [of sin and grace]." The author's use of the word *antithesis* is meant by him to be taken seriously. For wherever and whenever the God-consciousness is present, not only is there manifest the confusion of sin but also a blessedness corresponding to the relative strength and clarity in self-consciousness of the feeling of absolute dependence. And so, wherever and whenever personal existence enters into the world of self-awareness, there is the seed, at least, of true joy.[37]

By rendering sin as pain and placing it in the psychic antithesis or co-inherence of misery and joy, Schleiermacher is simply being consistent with the whole program of which *The Christian Faith* is the execution, namely, the presenting of this faith in the

[37] Gl., §87, 1.

form of a description of Christian religious affections. But he is also doing more than that. He thereby emphasizes the fact all-important to him, that the diagnosis and representation of sin as internal confusion and conflict presuppose and belong to the wider view of religion as the expression of the personal quest of order; and the order sought is not one which is supernatural, in the sense that it is wholly alien to "natural" human life, but it is, rather, an order inhering in the very constitution of the self, an order that discloses itself in an affective fashion and is related to the pain of the sinner's confusion much as truth is related to the mind's awareness of its own ignorance. Human misery here is the misery that feeds upon the remembered foretaste of blessedness.

Nevertheless, fundamental as this idea of sin in practice is for the entire structure of Schleiermacher's book, it remains relatively abstract, for the paragraphs of *The Christian Faith* are strangely and inconsistently scant in the observations they offer of concrete psychological detail, despite their self-limitation to the human religious consciousness. Therefore the reader, who would understand what this misery and joyful serenity or blessedness are, profits if he brings to this book the characterizations of mood with which Schleiermacher filled his earliest writings, particularly the dialogue entitled *The Christmas Eve*. For it is obvious that sin conceived as misery and consequently as the privation of blessedness demands something more than purely formal statements about the perfection of the self-conscious personal existence that it thwarts. In the Christmas dialogue, Schleiermacher offered such concrete psychological material. There he presented the joy and serenity evoked by the celebration of Christ's coming into the world of men as the highest pitch of the Christian affections. As we may recall from our earlier examination of the work,[38] this highest affective state of the self is the mood or "attunement" of the soul that integrates the individual moments of personal history, be they pleasurable or

[38] *Cf.* above, Ch. I.

painful, into the unity of a life that includes and transcends the antitheses of temporal experience. This highest state, a living equilibrium of the soul, is neither a stiff posture nor a particular pleasure-response in the sensible- or world-consciousness. It is not "a joy over this or that," as Kierkegaard remarked in his *Journals*, "but the soul's mighty song 'with tongue and mouth, from the bottom of the heart.'" Jonathan Edwards is of help again in interpreting *The Christian Faith* here with his distinction between an affection, which is an abiding tempering of the soul, and a passion, which is abrupt, disruptive and volatile. The blessedness of which Schleiermacher writes is the former. It is enduring and pervasive, not unlike what Edwards called a "new principle of the heart." As such, the highest affective state of the soul opposes rather than contradicts temporal pleasure and pain, and is the expression of the ease with which the God-consciousness assumes its rightful rôle in relation to the sensible world-consciousness, accepting but never annulling the pleasant and the unpleasant moment alike.[39] Yet, because Schleiermacher has set himself to describe in *The Christian Faith* only the religious self-consciousness that actually exists and struggles in history, and because, therefore, he must eschew all pretension to an inwardly experienced serenity that would befit only the consummation of historical effort and travail, he cannot present this blessedness in its perfection. Thus, this highest living equilibrium of the soul is never without its own co-inhering pain, manifesting the impotence, the tardiness and the vacillation of the God-consciousness in the exercise of its sovereignty of the self. And so the feeling of absolute dependence preserves in the total religious self-consciousness a "living seed of sin ever ready to burst forth . . . an abiding consciousness of sin, now preceding the sin itself as a warning presentiment, now accompanying it as an inward reproof, or following it as penitence."[40] But, it is important

[39] Gl., §5, 4.
[40] Gl., §66, 1.

always to remember, the pain of sin is not the same as the pain that stands in antithesis to pleasure and that with pleasure informs every moment of time. For the task of the religious self-consciousness is to remain constant in its government of every temporal moment alike, whether the moment be filled chiefly with pain or pleasure. In a word, growth toward blessedness is growth not away from the world but rather into a deep and lasting awareness of the distinction between these two different orders of suffering and two different orders of heightened life.[41]

If then religion is the disclosure of the identity of the self existing between God and the world, we see especially clearly in the treatment of sin and human misery a confirmation of this interpretation. Religion, sin and blessedness are not three wholly different phenomena. They are not external to each other; each is a part in the others, each names the whole of which the others are parts. Religion is one with the internal prompting of the self to discover its final equilibrium, and it prompts not merely an abstract question about the soul's true order of existence but also prompts the question through the native movements of the soul itself. Piety is the symbolization, in the affective content of self-consciousness, of the self's restless pursuit of its place in the scheme of things. This pursuit can never be satisfied by a speculative grasp of the whole but only by an endowment of the personal tranquility and sense of order that is true joy and the absence of which is the original vitiation of our humanity.

§3 ADAM

With his theological predecessors, Schleiermacher predicated his thinking on the conviction that men are fettered in an inner

[41] The failure to subordinate the states created in the soul by its relations to the world and, concomitantly, the identification of religious blessedness with worldly happiness or "beauty of the soul" constitutes what Schleiermacher calls aesthetic religion. *Cf.* Gl., §9.

confusion and disorder of which man himself is the originator. But he departs widely from previous theology in his radical simplification of the place and rôle of Adam in the divine plan for history. For Adam, according to *The Christian Faith,* is not an individual who plunged the whole of mankind into sin and guilt and consequent confusion. To adhere to that customary view would be nothing less than subscription to the grotesque theory that attributes to a single person the power to alter the nature of the human race, and Schleiermacher's understanding of God and of man would not permit him to use that notion. By inference, we can see that to Schleiermacher's mind the proponent of the orthodox doctrine of the inherence of all men in Adam must assume responsibility for turning Adam into a monster and for transposing the culpability of sin from the individual members of mankind to a figure standing outside the race and outside history.[42] The alternative Schleiermacher chose at this point is another example of the scientific criticism of theological concepts that he exercised throughout his systematic theology.[43] To avoid the contradiction implicit in the myth of Adam as the real, sole determiner of human misery, he offered a redefinition of original human perfection that allows for the presence of sin in the human race, even at the time of its creation. In its simplest terms, original perfection now stands for the human "predisposition to God-consciousness" and for the concomitant human disposition to communicate this God-consciousness and thereby to appropriate it thoroughly into a fully developed, personal self-consciousness.[44] Hence, instead of positing perfection as a fully developed and static human condition present

[42] Gl., §72. Kierkegaard's discussion of Adam, the race and original sin, in *The Concept of Dread,* forms a certain parallel to, and may be partly dependent on, Schleiermacher's treatment in *The Christian Faith.* For the relation of SK's idea of sin to Schleiermacher's, see Torsten Bohlin, *Kierkegaards dogmatische Anschauung,* trans. I. Meyer-Lüne, Gütersloh (1927), pp. 93ff., especially p. 132, n. 1.

[43] *Cf.* above, Ch. III, §4.

[44] Gl., §60.

in the first individual, with Irenaeus and other fathers of the church Schleiermacher locates perfection in a latent power or potentiality of human nature, but then he attributes this perfection of predisposition to all men equally. At the same time, he also locates sin in all men equally, refusing to speculate on its origins or to give its beginnings a mythical clothing. Rather, he insists that it likewise is fully original in each and all. The logic that *The Christian Faith* pursues here is identical with what we have already observed in its treatment of the pain of sin. Just as, when we have regard to the affective content of sin, we cannot speak of it as misery apart from the recognition of at least a remembered foretaste of joy, so also, when we employ moral or political language and conceive of sin now not as misery but as failure to take command of one's self, we cannot think it apart from the idea of an original righteousness. Sin, in this sense, names the departure of the soul from a normative state of adherence to God. But the tension between righteousness and sin must be a tension within human nature and not a tension between a mythical and monstrous individual standing outside the human race (the orthodox Adam) and ordinary men. Therefore righteousness and sin are co-original, and it is because they are coeval as two predispositions of the soul that no active righteousness can triumphantly issue forth *of itself* in history.[45]

There can be no doubt that to speak as Schleiermacher does of sin and perfection as coeval in created human nature gives to his thinking on God and man that appearance of divine arbitrariness and determinism which have long been criticized as reprehensible in the theologies of other men. It is not, however, the novel treatment of Adam that is responsible for this appearance, for whether Adam be taken as a single figure or as symbolic of the race, the enigma of sin's entrance into the world through human nature remains qualitatively the same. The real difficulty here rather lies in the problem of reconciling the goodness of God and, by exten-

[45] Gl., §72, 6.

sion, of his creation with the possibility and actuality of moral evil, and on this score Schleiermacher, as we shall see in some detail below, shares with his Calvinist fellows and forebears the ancient dilemma of affirming both the almightiness and goodness of God, on the one hand, and human accountability for human misery, on the other.

However, on the point immediately at hand the constitution and identity of adamic humanity, Schleiermacher's reasoning is not only wholly typical of the style and direction of *The Christian Faith*, but it is also uniquely decisive. It requires, as we have now seen, that he take the name *Adam* from the first pair in the garden of Eden and give it to every individual, or, if not the actual name itself, then that for which it stands in the lexicon of the Christian theologian. The mystery of the entrance of sin alongside the equally mysterious presence of the underivable goodness of existence is not confined to one moment in history but is timeless in the sense that it belongs to each experienced moment, and though each individual inherits from his fathers and his contemporaries the guilt that they have brought into the world, yet this intra-human bond of transmission and inheritance does not expunge the fact of "an absolutely common guilt for all."[46] For this reason, Schleiermacher spoke not simply of "the first Adam" but of "the first Adams" as well, meaning thereby each and every man.

We meet here in this movement of thought a most striking and significant fact, the import of which, though not immediately apparent, perhaps, we nevertheless recognize when we ask how this original perfection of predisposition toward God-consciousness is discernible. As a predisposition only, rather than as a fully developed personal consciousness, such perfection of righteousness and serenity is stultified by the presence of original sin, the presence, that is to say, of the oblivion of God in the disorder and confusion of the self's feelings of multiple dependence. Yet the consciousness

[46] *Ibid. Cf.* also "Erwählung," p. 451.

of sin, without which sin itself does not exist for the individual,[47] requires the perception of that righteousness and inclination toward the creator from which sin is the turning away. But if *The Christian Faith*, as we have seen, would discard from the armory of our imagination the mythical Adam of paradise as the mirror of human perfection, what access have the Adams of history, barred from Eden and encumbered with their own inner confusion, to the righteousness that causes men to feel their sin as sin? Can each such Adam espy such righteousness in his own latent, stultified predisposition to a regnant God-consciousness? Schleiermacher's answer to this question is clear. The power to recognize sin as sin and to recognize the order and conformation of the existence for which he was created comes to the individual not from "Adam" but from Christ. Therefore, Schleiermacher declared in another place, we can easily dispense with the practice of gazing into the perpetual obscurity of the mythical progenitor of the race, when we have Christ in his "everlasting brightness."[48] And, in fact, if we adhere in our reasoning to the logic of *The Christian Faith*, we not only *may* dispense with this mythical Adam as the mirror of true righteousness, but we *must* do so, for while each man's self-consciousness belongs indefeasibly to himself, the power that raises it toward the equilibrium of blessedness comes not from the storehouse of the imagination alone but from the ever renewed historical communication of life and light that originates in the preaching of Jesus of Nazareth.

So Jesus of Nazareth and his work of redemption are bound up with the whole view of the religious identity of human nature in *The Christian Faith*. The religious consciousness does not mani-

[47] Schleiermacher evidently did not wish to affirm that sin is simply consciousness of sin, so that there can be no sin for which there is only a later dawning of consciousness and hence of remorse. But he does say that without consciousness of sin, sin does not exist as sin. Compare Gl., §66, 1 with Gl., §68, 2.

[48] "Erwählung," p. 452.

fest itself apart from the consciousness of sin, and sin similarly is recognizable only in the sphere of the work of the redeemer. There is, to be sure, no *necessary* connection between these "facts" or elements of experience, but on the other hand there is a *historical* relation between them, in a sense that bears further exploration.

Chapter Five

THE MEASURE OF CHRIST

§1 CHRISTO-MORPHIC THEOLOGY

In *The Christian Faith* Schleiermacher regards the datum of humanity under the aspect of the form of Christ. His procedure is —if the reader will permit a metaphor now grown archaic—to consider human religious self-consciousness as the sphere and to present the figure of Christ not as the celestial but as the historical "intelligence" that seeks to bring this anarchic inner world under the government of its motions. We suggest this metaphor for the sake of interpreting such language as one finds in proposition 11, where Schleiermacher states that "Christianity is a monotheistic faith, belonging to the teleological type of religion, and is essentially distinguished from other such faiths by the fact that in it everything is related to the redemption accomplished by Jesus of Nazareth." To be sure, other portions of the work bear in a significant fashion upon this procedure, but §11 is important because it comes before the reader's eyes at so early a point in the book's argument. More than that, it is an especially important text because in it Schleiermacher himself raises the question that we have anticipated in the previous chapter.[1] The question entailed in §11, as

[1] *Cf.* above, Ch. IV, §1, pp. 175ff.

well as in the work at large, is about the kind of relation that obtains between Christianity and religion, and the language that the author there employs is in effect an answer to that question.

We have seen that the problem of religion is also the problem of human nature, on Schleiermacher's terms, and that the delineation of religion is also the delineation of human self-consciousness in its felt relations to God, the world and the self. Inasmuch, therefore, as the matter of religion is human nature itself, the task of stating the relation of Christianity to religion in general may also be viewed as the task of stating the relation of Christianity to human nature. And, again, inasmuch as Schleiermacher believes that every man is an "Adam" in his own right, the problem of relating Christianity to religion is also the problem of relating Christ to "Adam"; it is the problem of relating the author of Christianity to the man whose religion Christianity becomes. Consequently, when we reflect on Schleiermacher's idea of the connection between Christianity and human religiousness, we are simultaneously reflecting on the position of Christ with respect to "Adam," and when we ask how "Adam" stands with respect to Christ, we are asking how the view of human religion in *The Christian Faith* is affected by its author's understanding of Christianity. Whether we inquire, then, about Christ and "Adam" or about Christianity and religion, we are inquiring about the same relation.

The answer that we have put forth in reply to this double-sided question is that the relation is, in a specialized sense, one between form and matter. Christ exercises a forming, re-forming, informing influence upon the "matter" of human nature and human religion. In effect, what we are dealing with, in considering this particular turn in Schleiermacher's thinking, is his highly characteristic Christo-centrism, to borrow an idiom from the theological vocabulary of our own day. A word of caution is required here, however. The reader will not find Schleiermacher justifying all that he says about God and man by his doctrine of Christ. Christology is not the archimedean point by means of which *The Christian Faith* moves all the other doctrines of theology before the reader's view. It is not the absolute center about which everything else revolves. So far as the doctrinal, objective content of his thinking is concerned, Schleiermacher's theology like that of Calvin and others before him has more than one center and does not pretend to exhibit the artificial simplicity of the circle.[2] In *The Christian Faith* the redeemer is only one among a plurality of objects of theological knowledge, but at the same time he is paramount and central as the agent who reforms and shapes anew the Christian's relations to God, the world and himself. It is particularly in the context of his doctrines of human nature and of the created order that Schleiermacher stresses this forming influence of Christ upon human self-consciousness and human nature. For the sake of distinguishing Schleiermacher's manner of theological reflection, therefore, from the attitude and method that style themselves as Christo-centric in the above-mentioned material and objective senses, we may call it Christo-morphic. His theology is Christomorphic in two senses. First of all, it asserts that Jesus of Nazareth objectively exhibits what human nature ideally is, although Schleiermacher does not on this account counsel Christians to imitate Jesus in any naïve way, as we shall see subsequently. In this sense, then, the redeemer is the measure of human nature. And, in the second place, the redeemer is the historical person whose pres-

[2] Schleiermacher makes no attempt, for example, to derive a knowledge of God from the disclosure of God exclusively circumscribed by the figure of Jesus. His doctrine of God has more than one source, and while this fact may be adjudged a weakness by Barthian critics, it nevertheless places Schleiermacher in a substantial theological tradition. In this tradition, Christ is the reformer of man's knowledge of God and of himself. Christ is not the sole objective center of that knowledge, for neither God nor man can be "extracted," as it were, from Jesus Christ. But in the presence of Jesus Christ, God and man emerge anew in human understanding and existence. On this score, Schleiermacher is closer to, and more faithful to, Calvin than is Barth. Schleiermacher's weakness is that he does not give to Christ, in his thinking about God, nearly the same power of reforming the mode of thought that he allows him, in his thinking about man.

ence mediated through Scriptures, preaching and the Holy Spirit becomes the abiding occasion for the reorganization and clarifying of the Christian's consciousness of his absolute dependence, of his identity in the world, and of his appropriate actions toward and responses to others. Thus, *The Christian Faith* presents the redeemer as the one in whom "Adam" is finally formed. The inchoate self-consciousness of unredeemed man, suffering in the darkness of its own disorder, receives a new impetus toward light and order from the life that is in Christ, and it is only by beholding itself in the moments when it receives light from this other life that it can recognize the origin, the nature and the goal of the personal existence that has struggled in confusion hitherto to form itself. This rôle of Christ is, as we have noticed before, taken from Schleiermacher's best loved Scripture, the Fourth Gospel and especially its prologue, according to which that life is light which comes to men from God.[3]

The evidences of this view of Christ as the measure of man and the informer of adamic self-consciousness are both small and large and are to be found throughout *The Christian Faith*. One of them we have already encountered in the discussion of sin and Adam, in which we have seen that Christ affords the norm by which we recognize in ourselves the original righteousness that sin obscures. Now, in marking still other instances of this evidence, we can come to a better understanding of the trend of the whole work

[3] For Schleiermacher's christology of the Word, in which life and light are one, see his homilies on the Gospel of John, especially that one preached "Sonntage Misericordias Domini, 1823." SW II/8, pp. 5ff., and also above, Chapter III, pp. 146f. As is well known, Schleiermacher had a special regard for the Fourth Gospel. He defended its priority in time over the Synoptics, and, more importantly for our understanding of his theology, wrote to his friend, Lücke, that he had wished so to construct *The Christian Faith* that the reader might clearly see at every point that John 1:14 ("And the Word became flesh and dwelt among us, full of grace and truth; we have beheld his glory, glory as of the only Son from the Father.") is the base text of the entire dogmatics, "just as it should be for the whole execution of his vocation on the part of the clergyman." *Cf.* Send., p. 34 (611).

as well as to a better appreciation of the difficulties Schleiermacher faced, in following out his intentions, and that face those, perhaps, who continue to be engaged in the enterprise of writing Christian systematic theology. But in order to estimate the significance of these other evidences of Christo-morphism, we shall have to turn, first of all, to a closer examination of the understanding of redemption and the redeemer, upon which *The Christian Faith* is founded.

§2 THE SECOND ADAM

Schleiermacher conceives of Jesus Christ as the second or last Adam, and his conception of the redeeming work of Christ lends itself most readily to description as "person-forming" work. Christ creates persons. He does not create them *ex nihilo*; but he creates persons in the sense that through his communication of his own life in deed and word and in the subsequent preaching of the church he brings into focus in other selves the feeling of absolute dependence, the consciousness of sin and of the overcoming power of God, and the consciousness of the good-pleasure of God. By stepping into relation with men and mankind he brings them into complete existence as human beings and as particular men who have particular identities. Therefore, from the perspective of the man who finds himself drawn into this relationship to Christ, the specific fact that the preaching of Christ has aroused faith in his own heart must be recognized as part of the divine ordaining act that chose Jesus of Nazareth to be the person in whom the creative power of God became uniquely united with human nature and henceforth efficacious in the world. Indeed, since there is no distinction permissible within the will of God, according to Schleiermacher, the decree to create the world and to appoint Jesus of Nazareth as the inaugurator of the kingdom of spiritual men is one decree, and, Schleiermacher concludes, therefore we can say "that Christ even as a human person was ever coming to be simultaneously with the world itself."[4] This particular "person-forming action" upon human nature and of human nature is the place and the time in which the final forming of the believer's personhood was also begun, in the eternal decree of God.[5] So the Christ of *The Christian Faith* is the head of the race, "the first born of all creation" (Colossians 1:15), and the beginning and beginner (*archēgos*) of our salvation (Hebrews 2:10). He is the one in whom the God-consciousness enters the race as regnant and in whom the consciousness of kind (*Gattungsbewusstsein*) becomes as broad as the race itself, enabling him to communicate to all the dwelling of God with man. Through him men are raised to life from the dead mass of spiritual passivity and confusion.[6]

The work of Christ is preeminently the forming of human nature into its ordained inner proportions; and, the regeneration of man by the hearing of the Word and the gift of the Spirit is, correspondingly, a being conformed to the image of Christ. For these reasons we have coined the term *Christo-morphism* to describe the prevalent thrust of Schleiermacher's theological thinking about the redeemer, redemption and the redeemed. But it would be an in-

[4] Gl., §97, 2.

[5] Gl., §120, 2: "personbildende Handlung der menschlichen Natur."

[6] "Erwählung," pp. 485ff. A comparison of the christology of *The Christian Faith* and of the essay on election with Schleiermacher's address, "Ueber den Begriff des grossen Mannes" (SW III/3, pp. 73ff.), is helpful to the understanding of the former, because it contradicts the interpretation of Schleiermacher's theology that presents Jesus as the highest product of the evolution of human nature. Only *that* man may be called great, Schleiermacher writes, through whom the mass of people ceases to be a mass, through whom it is aroused to set itself apart and acquire a sense of identity in the place of "a dreaming life of slumber." But the great man's influence is always limited to the realm nature has appointed for him; "he has a determinate home" (pp. 80, 82). "Should one be conceived in whom lies the power to awaken a new life in the whole human race of all zones and times and to befriend the whole in one all-encompassing organization, he would be a man transcending all human proportions and at the same time would be one who reduced all human greatness to nothing. This mystery, however, which lives in the faith of millions—a faith ever again renewing and purifying itself—we can only mention here in order to exclude it from our consideration" (p. 81).

justice to *The Christian Faith* and the underlying intention of its author, were we not to proceed cautiously in the use of the term as an interpretative device, lest we foster the supposition that the idea of the redeemer is an a priori of the religious consciousness.

Certainly such apriorism would be wholly inconsistent with the style of thinking and reflecting that we have traced in our analysis of Schleiermacher's ethics and of his approach to the matter of theology, for we have learned that consciousness for Schleiermacher is consciousness only insofar as it is related to being external to the reason and spirit of the subject. It was on this premise that he issued his principle for the system of the sciences, namely, that each discipline must have its empirical, descriptive arm as a counterbalance to its constructive and speculative responsibilities, and for the same reason he rejected the idea of a highest science embracing all others and standing above both ethics and physics, the historical and the natural sciences. Likewise, in keeping with his methodological tenets, he disallowed the philosophical contention for the existence of pure innate ideas, and insisted that all thinking begins in response to its social context and historical antecedents, and issues in a position that reflects the historical, natural limitations of the thinker as well as his inward and finite individuality. But it is not the canon of consistency alone that warns the interpreter of *The Christian Faith* to proceed with wariness at this juncture. Schleiermacher speaks his mind directly enough on this score, both in *The Christian Faith* itself and in related theological enterprises, so that there can be no question of his distaste for and dissatisfaction with a speculative theory of redemption and the redeemer, and of his desire to avoid the appearance of gnosticism and docetism.

One piece of evidence for this bent of Schleiermacher's mind was foreshadowed in the discourses of Ernst and Eduard in *The Christmas Eve*, and occurs again in *The Christian Faith*. It is the argument to the historicity of Christ on the ground that the religious self-consciousness vitiated by sin could not of itself produce the impression of a sinless redeemer. This is an argument that is essentially negative, and it was directed in all probability against the position that Immanuel Kant propounded in his work, *Religion within the Limits of Reason Alone*. What is at stake in this argument is not the question concerning the existence of the man, Jesus of Nazareth; that problem had not confronted Schleiermacher, and it is, in any case, not the fundamental historical problem facing Christianity, even in an age of historical skepticism. Rather the point against which *The Christian Faith* lodges its weight is the demand that the sinlessness of Jesus be proved, that Jesus of Nazareth be demonstrated to be the Christ. In answer to this demand, Schleiermacher replied that such proof cannot be given. However, what theology can and must do is to describe how Christian faith originated and how it is experienced in the present. And this description entails the attribution to Jesus of a sinless nature and the communication of his perfection (the regnant God-consciousness) to the fellowship of believers. The objection that arises against this attribution to Jesus of sinlessness and the power of communicating the God-consciousness to others is that faith itself made Jesus the redeemer, that the human longing for sinless perfection simply seized upon the exceptional moral figure of Jesus, once history offered him to human eyes, and made of him the embodiment of that perfection.[7] Schleiermacher's criticism and rebuttal of this objection rest upon the fact that it allows for far too tenuous and arbitrary a connection between faith and the author and pioneer of faith, Jesus Christ himself. We cannot say that faith made Jesus the redeemer, Schleiermacher explains, for in such faith "the arbitrary decision of the believer would have become more marked on every transference of it, since it would not have been supported by the original impression made by His person; and consequently the certainty would have become less. Gradually the thought would more and more have gained ground that another might come, to whom that conception might be transferred with better right. So

[7] Gl., §88, 2.

that in this way there could only arise a decreasing faith in Jesus, and thus an increasing un-belief."[8] Hence the element of arbitrary choice on the part of men concerning the one in whom they will rest their faith makes this objection inoperative in Schleiermacher's mind; it does not perceive that faith is elicited by the persuasiveness of its object, and even if we recognize as we must that both the biblical picture of Christ and the New Testament as a whole are themselves the original expression of the Christian community's faith, still we must acknowledge that the New Testament witness itself declares that it was Christ who chose his disciples, "that the very recognition of that perfection was [Christ's] own work."[9] And this conception of Christ as the redeemer who raises his disciples to the level on which they may understand him and receive his words, so that they are not slaves but friends, is, as we have had occasion to note before, a conviction fundamental to Schleiermacher.[10] Hence, Christ completes the creation of faith; faith does not create Christ.

Consequently, while Schleiermacher speaks of Christ as the exemplar (*Vorbild*) of perfected human nature, he does not fear that he has given his case away to those who contend that an exemplar stands on a continuum with those for whom he is the example and need not, therefore, define an absolute perfection but only a relatively greater perfection than the human condition of those who recognize their own misery and guilt. To be sure, Christ is in a fashion an example to men. But the exemplary does not contain within itself the power of salvation, the power that transforms and delivers the sin-confused self-consciousness. The exemplary status of Christ is at best a medium for the communication of that power. The power itself originates beyond the limits of human nature, beyond the self-consciousness of the individual, and beyond

[8] *Ibid.*
[9] *Ibid.*
[10] *Cf.* above, Ch. I, pp. 45ff.

his consciousness of the content of the race of men (*Gattungsbewusstsein*).[11] Such power can emanate only from the absolute man as an historical individual, only from him who is the expression of human nature in that relationship to God for the sake of which God has ordained the order of being. Schleiermacher designates this latter quality of the redeemer as his *Urbildlichkeit*, and he argues that the Christian does not derive his conception of such power from his own imagination, vitiated as it is by the corporate sinfulness of the race, but from the historical individual who is the last Adam, Jesus of Nazareth.[12]

[11] *Cf.* Gl., §93, especially paragraph 3. In paragraph 2 of the text under this proposition the Edinburgh E. T. incorrectly reads: "the more the individual subordinates his personal consciousness to the God-consciousness." It should read: "the more the individual subordinates his personal consciousness to the consciousness of kind" (*Gattungsbewusstsein*, not *Gottesbewusstsein*).

[12] Gl., §93, 2 and 3. The rendering of the German *Urbildlichkeit* by the English term *ideality* paves the way for misunderstanding of the text in these paragraphs, unless the reader keeps in mind that the ideality connoted by *Urbildlichkeit* is closer to the objective, normative *eidos*, or form, of Platonic philosophy than to the a priori ideas of reason in Kantian philosophy. David Friedrich Strauss' remark that just as Kant made the existence of God a postulate of practical reason, so Schleiermacher made the "dogma of Christ" a postulate of Christian experience is accurate up to a point (*cf.* above, Ch. I, p. 64, fn. 86). Where Kant made the interests of the free moral agent determinative for the faith of rational man, Schleiermacher made the experience of grace and sin determinative for the faith of the rational-feeling individual. However, the parallelism between the two men does not lie at the point on which Strauss evidently meant the emphasis to fall, the act of postulating. Strictly speaking, there is no postulation in Schleiermacher's reasoning about the redeemer, for his purpose is to move between the experience of sin and grace, on the one hand, and the New Testament picture of Christ, on the other. The experience of sin and grace combats skepticism about the historical existence of the Christ depicted in the New Testament but it does not postulate his existence and his character. Kant's postulation of the existence of a just creator covers a movement from the recognition of the felt interests of the moral subject to a transcendent plane from which all experience and knowledge are barred. The true parallelism between Schleiermacher and Kant appears here in the comparison of the rôle of interest in Kant's philosophy with the rôle of feeling in Schleiermacher's thought. An interest belongs to that class of subjective phenomena which cannot be said to have a strictly rational status but nevertheless irresistibly affect reason's reasoning. Hence, we have in *The Critique of Practical Reason* a trace of the anthropological and epistemological path that Schleiermacher later followed.

Yet if we are to assess fairly the vulnerability of Schleiermacher to the charge of apriorism with respect to his doctrine of Christ, we must also take account of a second strand in his thinking, which in *The Christian Faith* is subordinated to the critical treatment of the theories that seek to dispense with the historical figure of the redeemer. This second strand is Schleiermacher's interest in the specific and concrete character of Jesus. It is not enough simply to parry the thrusts directed at the historicity of the redeemer and to assert that Jesus as redeemer did in fact live and die in a certain time and place. The singularity and idiosyncratic character of his life must also receive their due, for Jesus did not accomplish a colorless redemption; his own personality as well as personhood entered into what he did. His work and his identity are inseparable; he lived and acted as a genuine historical agent.

Now quite apparently there is no portrait of Jesus in *The Christian Faith*. We must infer that its author did not regard a system of Christian doctrine as the proper place in which to present one. But Schleiermacher did occupy himself with the problem of writing a life of Jesus, and he did believe that the principles forged or discovered in an inquiry into the possibility of reconstructing the life of Jesus are intimately related to the principles of systematic and dogmatic theology. Indeed, christology and historical inquiry into the life of Jesus stand in the same kind of reciprocal relation that obtains between exegetical theology in general and systematic theology.[13] Consequently, the theological idea of Christ constantly requires criticism in the light of historical investigation of the sources of a life of Jesus.

This relation between the life of Jesus and christology expresses one of the most important senses in which Christian faith is dependent upon historical fact. The theologian must always approach the fact of Jesus of Nazareth with as much objectivity as he can command, employing all available material and critical tools.

[13] *Cf.* above, Ch. III, §2, pp. 149ff.

Therefore, Schleiermacher believed, the theologian is constantly risking his faith in scientific research, yet any shunning of such investigation betrays a lack of faith.[14] A distinction must be made, however, between a life of Jesus that is only a chronology (*Chronik*) and a description of the life of Jesus that is a history (*Geschichte*).[15] A chronology is a description of the external moments in the life of the subject, of moments which have first of all to be separated from each other by the author and then connected again in a narrative account. It is what R. G. Collingwood in our century has dubbed "scissors and paste" history. The disparate and conflicting views of Jesus within the New Testament itself, which Schleiermacher recognized, would make a chronology difficult if not impossible. A history, on the other hand, is the endeavor to grasp and describe the life-unity of the subject. Such a history is what Schleiermacher believed to be of importance for faith and theology, for it is only on the basis of a history in this sense that the theologian enables himself to discriminate within the New Testament materials themselves that which is genuinely Christian from that which is false interpretation of Jesus. To be sure, all of the Gospels as well as the reports concerning Jesus in the other parts of the New Testament are interpreted accounts; they are informed by the response of the writers to Jesus' communication of himself, but it is still necessary to attempt a sifting out of that which is an adequate or authentic interpretation of what Jesus displayed through deed and word about himself from the spurious or what

[14] Leben Jesu, pp. 15(S), 20f. The bulk of text in this volume consists of material taken from student notebooks arranged under paragraph or lecture headings from Schleiermacher's own notes. I have not found that the material is at variance with the principles or particulars encountered in the important books that came from Schleiermacher's own hand or that are extant in fine critical editions, such as *The Christian Faith* itself, the *Brief Outline of the Study of Theology,* the introduction to the works of Plato, the *Sendschreiben an Lücke* or the edited lectures on hermeneutics, ethics, and aesthetics, and the various essays cited in these pages. Where I cite Schleiermacher's own notes, I append the symbol, (S).

[15] *Ibid.,* p. 1(S).

has come to be called the heretical. Heretical views of Christ are present in the New Testament, views such as the one later called the Ebionite heresy,[16] and a criterion is necessary for the business of perceiving them. Such a criterion can be furnished only by what Schleiermacher calls a history.

The task of a history of Jesus is, then, to discern the life-unity of Jesus, to discern his sense of identity by an intensive and comparative study of the documents in the New Testament. Schleiermacher was of the opinion that this life-unity is accessible to the methods of historical investigation and interpretation as he had laid them down in his own hermeneutics. He did not pretend that the biblical historian can claim proof for his findings, since all matters of historical fact elude the quest of demonstrative certainty. But he did believe that the central witness of the New Testament to the identity of Jesus stands in faithful conformity to Jesus' own teaching concerning himself. What is today called the messianic self-consciousness and what Schleiermacher called Jesus' God-consciousness formed part of Jesus' own conception of himself and was not simply attributed to him by his disciples. To adopt the alternative of attributing the idea of Jesus' unique relationship to God to the mistaken or gratuitous inventiveness of the earliest community surrounding him and founded by him is, of course, to say that Christianity is an error, and requires that we abandon it as false. To Schleiermacher's mind, this alternative also necessarily involves the concomitant conviction that Jesus consciously deceived his followers. He adamantly maintained that one cannot separate a fully naturalistic view of Christ and the admission that Jesus permitted himself such deception.[17] Nor, for the same reasons, can we sup-

[16] *Ibid.*, pp. 24f.

[17] *Ibid.*, pp. 79(S),84f. Schleiermacher argues that if one still wishes to maintain the naturalistic interpretation of Jesus without subscribing to the hypothesis that Jesus consciously intended to deceive, then one must hold that *all* of the reports we have concerning Christ are unreliable or uncertain, "so that we should not be able to use them in order to construct a definite picture of

pose that Jesus employed the term *Son of God* merely because it was current in the language. Depending to a large extent upon the Fourth Gospel and affinitive elements in the theology of Paul and *Hebrews*, Schleiermacher finds in the New Testament that the christology Jesus himself held is one in which Son of God contains the idea of the "grown son who knows the full will of his Father and is wholly in accord with it; this is the notion that is present in

---

him; the original narrators must have imported their own views into the utterances of Christ throughout, and then it is not possible to pursue the object [of investigation] historically. In every narrative, even in those which intend to be only reports, the judgment of the narrator speaks out with it, for it is *his* conception; but if we agree that nothing of the discourse of Christ is communicated without also being falsified through the erroneous and exaggerated estimate of his person which arose against his own will, then naturally nothing remains; but this itself is of the highest improbability. If we suppose that Christ did not intend to deceive his disciples, then neither can we believe that he would not always have corrected them, had they clung to convictions about him against his will—convictions that would not have been in accord with his own—and then a false view of him would not have been able to creep into the reports about him" (italics mine). Schleiermacher did not take into account here the notion of the so-called primitive myth-making mentality which does not consciously falsify but nevertheless produces reports that are erroneous from the standpoint of the modern scientific consciousness. D. F. Strauss in his *Life of Jesus* shortly thereafter did employ this notion and so avoided the hypothesis that Jesus intentionally deceived his followers while at the same time maintaining that none of the reports about him is reliable, and hence the historical Jesus is inaccessible. Yet it is not clear that Strauss effectively disposed of Schleiermacher's method of argument. Apart from the fact that the problem of myth in historical knowledge has yet to receive a comprehensive theological elucidation, and apart from the fact that it is not self-evident that myth wholly "falsifies," the pertinence of Strauss' procedure to Schleiermacher's is an open question. For Schleiermacher's case rests upon the conviction that there is continuity between Jesus' self-consciousness and the apostolic accounts of him. No one today will contest the presence of myth in the New Testament. The issues Schleiermacher poses are whether there is continuity between Jesus' presentation of himself to his followers and his followers' declarations about him in their preaching and narratives, and, furthermore, whether there is efficacy (power of salvation and giving of the Spirit of God) in this chain of preaching. The "new quest of the historical Jesus," although it is encumbered by a less sophisticated idea of history, appears to be returning to Schleiermacher's thesis, and this is not difficult to understand, since Bultmann's own principles of hermeneutics derive ultimately from Schleiermacher's, mediated by Dilthey, as well as from Heidegger who also is indebted to Dilthey.

the *Letter to the Hebrews,* and it is the same as the expression Christ uttered concerning the unity between himself and the Father."[18] Alongside Jesus' sense of his own high dignity, and intrinsic to this sense, is his clear consciousness of his vocation to found a new community, the community of life and the Spirit. The very unity between the Father and the Son on which the Gospel of John dwells at such length indicates as much, for when the Fourth Evangelist reports that "as the Father hath life in himself; so hath he given to the Son to have life in himself," Schleiermacher interprets "to have life in oneself" as meaning "the life that is power to impart life."[19] The whole development of Jesus' self-consciousness, in which the God-consciousness or the dwelling of God within him must also be understood, therefore, is also a development of his power to communicate his life or self-consciousness.[20] Hence, both Jesus' sayings about himself and his teaching that the kingdom of heaven is at hand are twin foci of his work and message, and the proclamation that the kingdom is at hand "at the same time contains a demand to assent to it, that is, to the founding of a community . . . and [that] explicitly in immediate connection with the person of Christ as the founder and the center. Accordingly, we see here that the principal points to which everything else is only an addition are the teaching of Christ about his own person and his vocation."[21] Schleiermacher further concludes, in this vein, that the title *Son of Man* means "like other men" in the sense that Jesus possesses a "co-consciousness" (*Mitbewusstsein*) of the differences, internal as well as external, of other men.[22] This is the perfectly developed consciousness-of-kind (*Gattungsbewusstsein*) and sympathy, which *The Christian Faith* predicates of Christ, and it is in the instrumentality for the work of redemption.

[18] *Ibid.,* p. 293. *Cf.* Heb. 3:5f.; Gal. 4:3f.; John 5:25ff.
[19] *Ibid.*
[20] *Ibid.,* pp. 130(S),135f.
[21] *Ibid.,* p. 262; also p. 259(S).
[22] *Ibid.,* p. 294; also p. 134.

It is clear, therefore, that Schleiermacher sought to avoid the dangers of apriorism in his presentation of the person of the redeemer. To be sure, he could not pretend that the fact of Jesus is demonstrable; his conception of history and historical method was too well developed for that. Nor could he maintain that the divinity of Christ is perceptible or intelligible outside the sphere of Christ's work; his idea of Christian dogma and theology as the expression of the Christian religious self-consciousness prevented him from doing that. But he was able to give cogent grounds for believing that it is unreasonable to attempt to derive the figure of Christ from the religious imagination. And, on the positive side, he endeavored to keep his theological doctrine of Christ in correlation with his critical reading of the New Testament.

Consequently, the christology of *The Christian Faith* and that of the lectures on the life of Jesus are identical in all important features. Accordingly, just as *The Christian Faith* rejects the ancient christological formula of the two natures of Christ,[23] Schleiermacher also discards the venerable exegetical device that attributes certain scriptural sayings and deeds of Jesus to his divinity and others to his humanity. If we must take the titles *Son of God* and *Son of Man* as representing the *one* Christ rather than two different principles in him,[24] for the same reasons we must also affirm at the level of systematic theology that the redeemer is like all other men in his human identity. The indwelling of God in Jesus is, to be sure, such that he differs as much from the first man as from all others;[25] he is an absolutely new creation, whom neither the first Adam nor the other Adams of history can approach. But the being of God in Christ cannot be rendered by the doctrine of a divine nature conjoined to a human nature. It is rather "the constant potency of his God-consciousness" that distinguishes Jesus from all

[23] Gl., §96, §97.
[24] Leben Jesu, pp. 287ff.(S).
[25] Gl., §94, 1.

other men and that constitutes "the veritable existence of God in him."[26] Thus Jesus of Nazareth is the archetypal man. His ideality (*Urbildlichkeit*) expresses the special presence of the creative power of God in him. The creative power of God, however, does not merely manifest itself in Christ; it becomes productive in him and through him, ramifying outward from him through his communicating and imparting of himself to others, in alliance with the Spirit.

Hence, it is neither the naked power of God that Christ communicates, nor is it merely himself as teacher of new doctrine about God that Christ proffers to others. What he gives are the power of God in the embodiment of his own ideal humanity and himself as the source from which men may receive that same power. These two aspects of Jesus, which Schleiermacher calls his *Urbildlichkeit* and his *Vorbildlichkeit*, cannot be separated. By virtue of the former he is the redeemer; by virtue of the latter he communicates redemption. Therefore, while the *Vorbildlichkeit* or exemplary status of Jesus does not signify his life-giving power as the redeemer appointed eternally by God, it does signify his solidarity with the human race, apart from which there could be no communication of redemption. To say that Jesus is an exemplar is not to reduce him to the dimensions of "the great man" whose influence upon his fellows has set, natural limits; rather it is to affirm that Jesus as redeemer is fully a man of his times. He is a first-century Jew among first-century Jews in Galilee and Judea. For Schleiermacher believed that Jesus' unique dignity must not prevent one from thinking of him as standing "under the potency of the times and of his peoples' character."[27] Otherwise, as the redeemer he could not have exercised a dominating influence upon his own time and people, and without the means of affecting his own times and generation he cannot affect others. "Any activity of Christ that we would

[26] *Ibid.* A being that has a nature is by definition a limited being. The term *nature* is not applicable to God, therefore, and cannot be used to describe the special relation of the redeemer to God.

[27] Leben Jesu, p. 12. *Cf.* Gl., §93, 3 and 4.

want to think of as being wholly deprived of that [historical determination] would have been something absolutely alien to the men about him; but such [an activity] as that can never be more than an object of attention."[28] It could not be assimilated. The fact that Jesus naturally expressed himself in Aramaic, for example, does not mean that Aramaic itself was sufficient to bring forth the God-consciousness in others, but Aramaic nevertheless is a part of the specific humanity that enabled the redeemer to be an exemplar, first to his countrymen, and then, through the translation of Aramaic into other tongues, to other men.

Apart from this intrinsic relation of his historical personality to his environing nature and history and society, Jesus would stand as a surd. There would be nothing in his outward appearance that could enable the individual, intent upon understanding the life of Jesus, to gain access to his inner life-unity and self-consciousness. There would be nothing, moreover, that could enable the Christian of a later generation to envision how Jesus might have acted and comported himself in that later time. Yet such "translation" is essential to the meaning of Jesus for Christian faith. Translation of this order, necessary as it is, has no license to modernize Jesus; but it is indispensable to faith in the redeemer that we be able to transpose his inner disposition into our own circumstances. It comes to this, Schleiermacher believes, "to carry over to ourselves his character in its relations to his circumstances without superimposing our relations upon him."[29] An abstract Christ would not be able to perform this function. Only the concrete can at the same time have universal meaning. Schleiermacher calls this probing for the inner unity in its specific relations to the outer circumstances of Jesus' life the endeavor to place oneself in position to "construe" Jesus' way of acting or to "calculate" his character. The endeavor to construe or calculate the identity of Christ must always be firmly grounded in the material that is afforded us by the historical docu-

[28] *Ibid.*, p. 13.
[29] *Ibid.*, p. 16. *Cf.* p. 15(S).

ments, for otherwise the intrusion of phantasy is certain. But, in any case, the endeavor itself cannot be interpreted as our striving to achieve some kind of mastery over him by having a factual knowledge of him at our disposal. On the contrary, just as knowledge of other persons always requires a degree of openness toward them, knowledge of Christ presupposes above all that his influence has begun to exercise itself upon us.[30]

In this fashion, Schleiermacher's christology contains a double reference. It points to the past figure of the redeemer, Jesus of Nazareth, as the historical occasion for the rise of Christian faith, upon which Christian faith forever remains dependent. At the same time, it points to the Christ whose own identity has become a living part of the consciousness of his followers. Through his communication of himself and of the life in him, and through the responding efforts of Christians to transpose his disposition into their own personal circumstances and existence, Christ becomes the reformer of the religious self-consciousness. The historical redeemer stands as the author of Christian faith and as the medium through which the man informed by his faith apprehends his relation to God, to the world and to himself. This summarizes the initial sense in which the theology of *The Christian Faith* is Christo-morphic. It is a theology that attempts to articulate the contents of the consciousness of the man whose personal existence is qualified through and through by the relation to Christ.

§3 CHRIST AND RELIGION

Among other evidences of Christo-morphism in *The Christian Faith* is the rejection of the eighteenth-century notion of a natural religion.[31] The philosophical reasons for this rejection have already appeared in our account of Schleiermacher's ethics. There we saw

[30] *Ibid.*, p. 17.
[31] Gl., §6, postscript.

him affirming that the general and the particular ought never to be construed by the observer as standing outside of each other, with the differentia of the particular individual entity being represented as merely accidental accretions, which are best thought away in order to grasp the entity's essence. Such a procedure would be in flat contradiction of the principle of organic inherence of part and whole, a principle which was rooted in Schleiermacher's nature. Where history is concerned, and the subject matter is, accordingly, man as agent, the universal is rather to be sought out as present fully and in a unique way in each of its particular embodiments. Each member of the human race is a compendium of the whole but such a compendium as is not to be found elsewhere, and the road to the comprehension of the whole lies through the thorough critical comparison and intensive understanding of individuals. By reason of this fact, the idea of man, whether it be of man philosophizing or man struggling to order his relations to God and the world, is always qualified by the historical identity of the individual in and through which it is grasped. As Schleiermacher repeatedly contended, both in his ethics and in his philosophy of thinking, the universal is thought historically; both the effort to understand and the object of the act of understanding are conditioned by the time(s), the place(s) and the ethos of the subject-object relation. (The reader need only recall Schleiermacher's theory of language for an exemplification of this point.) A complete knowledge of the class of men would constitute a knowledge of all the embodiments of the human race. Only God can enjoy such a knowledge. The investigator whose reasoning and judging is discursive can approximate it only from afar. For him actual understanding rises out of the dialectic between the idea of the universal, so far as it can be formulated, and the understanding of individuals, to the degree that they are comprehended in all of their relationships. So, knowledge of the general emerges through and is conditioned by intensive understanding of the particular.

The theological parallel of this principle figures prominently in *The Christian Faith* and, when interpreted, clarifies its special Christo-morphic tendency. This tendency manifests itself in the treatment of the connection between Christianity and other positive religions as well as in the handling of the relation between Christianity and religiousness as such and vice versa.

Schleiermacher's idea of historical consciousness would have forbidden him to state the relation of Christianity to the other religions from the standpoint of an idea of universal religion. Whatever may be universally present in all religions, so far as it is knowable, can be grasped only through an understanding of the full historical identity of the particular religious faith that gives concrete form to the inquirer's own self-consciousness. Self-knowledge is requisite to knowledge of the other, just as knowledge of the other is requisite to knowledge of the self. The writings from the *Speeches* of 1799 onward show a consistent adherence to this maxim. Therefore, instead of attempting to survey religion and the religions solely from above, the inquirer must seek out the relations in which other religions stand to his own by examining them as they appear in the historical unity of his own religious self-consciousness. Hence, inquiry into the religions cannot proceed by stripping away the layers of individualization in search of the generic, for, however much a specific religious self-consciousness may approach the proportions of piety as it is recognizable everywhere, the identity of the former is always stamped with the particular character of the mediator of its appearance. Schleiermacher was clear, for example, about the pervasiveness of the Christian identity of the Christian church. Though this church is still involved in the slow historical process of becoming itself or being made itself, nevertheless, the process is one of being ever more deeply molded both inwardly and outwardly by the identity of the church's founder. And, as the founder, Jesus of Nazareth does not simply add new and special maxims to a minimal, universally selfsame religiousness already present in the members. Christ in his own specific identity is the mediator, first directly and then through his followers, of the Christian religious self-consciousness in its totality.[32] Thus the Christian, insofar as he is formed by his relation to the redeemer, does not think of his Christian identity as consisting of one stratum resting upon other strata of an older, more universal order; rather, he thinks of his Christian identity as forming and reforming itself dynamically in his self-consciousness as it strives to realize its own unity and integrity.

If the principles adduced so far are correct, then it follows that the man who finds himself Christianly determined and formed must renounce the practice of drawing absolute distinctions of truth and falsity between the various religions; for it is only in the light of what positively informs his own religious consciousness that he is able to recognize piety elsewhere. "The whole delineation that we are here introducing," Schleiermacher admonishes the reader, "is based . . . upon the maxim that error never exists in and for itself but always along with some truth, and that we have never fully understood it until we have discovered its connection with truth and the true thing to which it is attached."[33] Hence, the Christian, even though he may be certain of the superiority of Christianity or of the indefeasibility of his attachment to it, will have to reason analogically, and perceive in other religions that which, though imperfect, is nevertheless like his own. The alternative to recognizing analogies is to use the word *religion* equivocally for phenomena that are held to be wholly dissimilar. Or else, one must be prepared to deny that his misery, which is recalled and intensified in the Christian while it is being overcome by the redeemer, has any resemblance to what is suffered by the struggling humanity of other kinds of worshippers. The recognition of like-

[32] Gl., §10, 2. Schleiermacher similarly maintains that other religions, at least of the higher kind, are also organic wholes. Gl., §33, 3.

[33] Gl., §7, 3.

ness, however, does not entail the conclusion that the imperfect is the seed from which the perfect exfoliates, according to an inner natural law. Schleiermacher never assented to an evolutionary view of religious development. But he was prepared to recognize continuities and, like Augustine and Calvin, to interpret the worship of idols as the worship of men moved by a fear not wholly unleavened by true piety and reverence, just as the Christian who is moved by a fuller though still imperfect reverence and love does not deny the persistence of an unbaptized fear in his heart, without thereby impugning the reality of the love of God.[34]

Not even the religion that flows from the work of the redeemer, Christ, can claim an absolute difference between itself and other religions. One could make such a claim only if one could present Christianity as entirely contradicting the nature of human religion and human nature itself. And to accomplish this, one would have to transpose Christianity into a series of divinely delivered doctrinal statements, after the fashion of the rationalism that Schleiermacher set out to combat. Christian "truth" of such an order—a truth that would show all other religions to be false—could be only the knowledge that God has of himself through himself. But the historical unity of the human religious self-consciousness is not capable of enjoying the knowledge that God has of himself through himself. And Christianity, above all, ought to make no such pretension, for it is the acknowledgment of God disclosing himself in relation: in relation to the minds and hearts of persons through the relation of the total, historical, personal existence of Jesus of Nazareth.[35] This relational character of revelation constitutes one of the most important senses in which Christianity is a historical faith. If it is to remain faithful to its historical character, then it can achieve universality only by rejecting universality of the abstract sort and recognizing in other religions and human reli-

[34] *Cf.* Gl., §8, postscript 1.
[35] Gl., §10, postscript.

giousness adumbrations, however truncated, immature and vitiated, of the relation to God that informs the Christian religious self-consciousness. Hence, other religions will have to be ranged on a scale defined by the relative clarity with which they embody the ordered self-consciousness whose joy and steadfastness are fully displayed in the redeeming life of Jesus of Nazareth, to whom everything in Christian faith is related.

In this fashion, Schleiermacher's view of religion and the religions displays the Christo-morphic tendency of his theological thinking. He does not represent Christianity as being dependent upon human religiousness or other particular religions, as though the former evolved out of the latter according to an immanent law. Nor does he attempt to argue that true religion appears in Christianity alone. Instead he regards other religions and religiousness as such through his own Christianity-determined consciousness and organizes the data of religion around the central fact of the communication of redemption by the redeemer, Jesus of Nazareth.[36] There are accordingly two criteria or principles by which other religions may be classified in relation to Christianity. The first criterion is the relative clarity with which the religion in question exhibits the distinction between the feeling of absolute dependence upon God and the feeling of partial dependence and partial freedom with respect to the world of finite entities and forces. The more clearly these two grades of feeling are distinguished within self-consciousness, the more nearly does the religion in question approach to the acknowledgment of one God that lies at the heart of Christianity. The second criterion is the relative efficacy with which the feeling of absolute dependence instills in the individual person, not only a consciousness of the dependence of all finite being upon God but also a sense of individual purpose, a sense of participating in the divine goal of history. Both of these criteria are drawn directly from Christian faith itself which, shaped as it is

[36] *Cf.* Gl., §7, §8, §9 and §11.

both inwardly and outwardly by the person of the redeemer, recognizes but one creator and unceasingly shapes the individual toward one direction of life, membership in the spiritual kingdom of which Christ is the inaugurator. Schleiermacher's definition of the Christian religion concisely states these two criteria. "Christianity is a monotheistic faith, belonging to the teleological type of religion, and is essentially distinguished from other such faiths by the fact that in it everything is related to the redemption accomplished by Jesus of Nazareth."[37] All of the other chief manifestations of religion are ranged around this center and defined by the degree to which they approximate its form. But on the grounds that have here been set forth it is clearly useless to argue the priority of the "center" over the "circumference" or of the "form" over the "matter" of the religious self-consciousness. Whichever may be conceptualized and expounded first, the other is all the while present. They are given together and, though they are bound together by no kind of logical necessity, neither is meaningful for theology apart from the other.

To be sure, his appreciation of the historical character of thinking and inquiry could not, and did not, prevent Schleiermacher from "transcending" Christianity (or any other positive religion for that matter), in the logical sense of subsuming it under the category of piety, in order that the peculiarity of its form and content might be better grasped conceptually through comparison. In a well known proposition in his *Brief Outline of the Study of Theology* he affirmed the necessity of such a procedure, as he did again in §6 of the first edition of *The Christian Faith*.[38] Critical comparison, as we have learned from his lectures on philosophical ethics, is fundamental to his entire style of thinking, which is distinguished at every point by insistence on the unending dialectic between direct, intuitive mental apprehension and the critical,

[37] Gl., §11.

[38] KD², §33. See also Schleiermacher's own comment on the misunderstanding of §6 in the first edition of *The Christian Faith*. Redeker, Vol. 2, p. 500.

comparative labor of judgment. But such subsuming of the particular under the universal does not imply the deduction of the former from the latter, for that which is historically given can never be demonstrated as necessary; it can only be accepted in its contingency and, after the fact of its appearance, compared with kindred phenomena. This double-sided or dialectical character of inquiry permitted Schleiermacher to carry on, and encourage others to carry on, a comparative study of Christianity and other religions, while at the same time he felt no jeopardy to his own or to the inquirer's faith. For, on the one hand, the more such a double method is employed, the more familiar the investigator must become with the inner individuality of his own religion; and, on the other hand, Schleiermacher conceived faith in any case to be not the result of rational argument or systematic reflection alone but rather the summary name for a total formation of the entire self-consciousness, as our earlier study of his idea of theology has indicated. Therefore, commitment to one's own religion does not and should not preclude the scrutiny of its relations to other instances and forms of piety. At least, it could not for the Schleiermacher who held to these principles of inquiry and reflection and who belonged to the faculty of a university all the time that he preached in his own church.

It was for these reasons that Schleiermacher felt himself both able and obliged to prefix to his theology an introductory series of paragraphs, which he designated as material "borrowed" from ethics and the philosophy of religion, borrowed, that is to say, from his own principles of inquiry into historical agents and particularly into the forms of religious association of such agents. He described this introduction as the "definition of the place" of Christianity and, therefore, also of the place within the spectrum of historical and religious phenomena where theological reflection takes its rise.[39] It is, of course, true that Schleiermacher gives the first characterization of Christianity in the introduction to *The Christian*

[39] Send., p. 55 (636).

Faith alongside his general account of religion. But the actual Christian determination of the feeling of absolute dependence is given fully only in the body of the work, in the dogmatic theology proper, and the import of the author's distinction between the "place" and the specific elucidation of the Christian religious self-consciousness hinges upon his position that no historical phenomenon—including, of course, Christianity—can be demonstrated a priori[40] but that it can be related after the fact to the general principles and categories of ethics or history.[41] Accordingly, the significance of adducing feeling in the introduction as the provenance of religion lies in Schleiermacher's desire to attest to the relation of Christianity to that which is recognizable as the core of human existence. He does this not in order to present Christianity as an inference from the general form of human existence but to exhibit the radical position it holds in human nature. In this sense, the introductory discussion of religion, of the types of religion, and of the specific form and content of Christian faith, with all the propositions borrowed from ethics and the philosophy of religion, is just as much after the fact of Christianity as are theological thinking and all dogmatics.[42]

The comparison "from above" of one religion with another, therefore, is not a way of inquiry that is self-sustaining but is, rather, one moment in a larger method that requires the investigator to approach and examine his material from a point within a particular historical religion as well. In *The Christian Faith*

[40] Gl., §2, 2; §33; also Send., p. 55 (636).

[41] *Cf.* above, Ch. II, §3 for the relation of ethics to the positive sciences.

[42] The reader of *The Christian Faith* should note that while the introduction to that work, §1–§31 in the 2nd edition, is prefatory to the dogmatic body of the work, it is not the case that the whole of the introduction is extratheological. Only §1–§10 are designated as borrowed from other sciences, specifically "ethics" and its sub-science, "the philosophy of religion," though Schleiermacher could well have added that he borrowed from hermeneutics as well. §11–§31, on the other hand, are either taken from apologetics, an intratheological discipline (KD², §39), or have to do with the relation of dogmatics to the church and with dogmatics' own principle of order.

Schleiermacher is not concerned to do more than suggest what such a critical comparison might entail. (In effect, he simply indicates the science responsible for such comparison, and he clearly distinguishes between the use he means to make of it for his theology and the fashion in which ethics would order and conduct itself for its own ends.[43]) Nor does he give his interest seriously to anything more than a sketch of the way in which the macrocosm of religions appears to the Christianly-determined religious self-consciousness.[44] For despite the fact that he is freely borrowing from other disciplines, everything that Schleiermacher says in these introductory pages is said "relative to [Christian] Dogmatics" and subserves the purposes of his theological thinking.[45] Hence it is that these borrowings from other sciences neither justify the theological task upon which Schleiermacher is engaged nor are intended in any way to prove the "truth or necessity of Christianity." The function of these borrowings is simply to show how the theologian who is explicating the contents of the Christian religion relates the substance of Christianity to the world of religion and to the disciplines that treat and analyze that world. The integrity of Christianity itself, however, can be shown only by Christian life and explained only by Christian theology.

§4 CHRIST AND CREATION

The Christo-morphic turn in Schleiermacher's theological thinking is discernible even more tellingly in another part of *The Christian Faith,* where the issue is the relation of the doctrine of creation to the doctrine of redemption. Like the problem of the connection between Christian faith and religion, the sense in which the doctrine of creation is prior to the doctrines of the redeemer and redemption is a peculiar difficulty for much of present-

[43] Gl., §2, especially paragraph 3 and postscript 1.
[44] Gl., §11–§14.
[45] Gl., §11, 5.

day theology, because in our times theologians have become sensitive to the possibility of seeming to separate these doctrines and so encouraging the supposition that creation and redemption can be discussed independently of each other. The ultimate consequence of such a separation, it is feared, would be the growth of the further assumptions that the doctrine of God the creator is only synthetically related to the doctrine of redemption in Christ and that in practice it can be expounded quite sufficiently on its own terms without any reference to sin and salvation. As Karl Barth has shown in his *Church Dogmatics*, theology has become protective of the *Christ*-ian focus of the first article of the creed, in which the Christian church has confessed for centuries its faith in "God the Father almighty, maker of heaven and earth." The problem now, stated in its simplest form, is how to allow the first article to stand in its place without weakening or limiting the importance of the second article, which confesses the events of redemption through Christ.

Schleiermacher, as we have already mentioned in Chapter III, labored over this puzzle, although on the surface the text of *The Christian Faith* betrays little of such preliminary meditation on method, for the arrangement of doctrines in the body of the book is traditional enough, moving from creation and nature to Christ and redemption and then to fulfillment. However, it is often a mistake simply to assume that the order of exposition in any technical treatise directly reflects the hierarchy of importance and of meaning (and, therefore, the order of being) as it appears to a mind occupied in clarifying and interpreting the multiple facets of experience. Certainly we must be cautious in interpreting so dialectical a spirit as Schleiermacher. In actual fact, he was himself much in doubt concerning the more satisfactory way of unfolding and systematizing the Christian's religious self-consciousness, as he acknowledged in his open letter to Lücke.[46] There was much that commended to him the plan of commencing his doctrinal exposi-

[46] Send., p. 30 (605).

tion with the person and work of Christ, and he felt that the arrangement he finally did adopt left correspondingly much to be desired.

Schleiermacher's uncertainty about the proper sequence of materials in *The Christian Faith* is in some ways as informative for our understanding of his thinking as is the actual order on which he settled. The uncertainty was the by-product of his conception of the particular kind of identity and unity that possess the religious self-consciousness, and it reminds us once more of the importance of these concepts of identity and unity in Schleiermacher's theology. He knew that self-consciousness does not display an unambiguous chronological structure with the prior and posterior clearly distinguished and seriate. One corollary of the lecture on ethics, especially pertinent here, is that the self in appropriating its identity in dialogical relation to the community also appropriates its own history through the agency of the presence of other selves. In the formation of selfhood, the past is not simply the presupposition of the present, but the present forms the basis on which the past is assimilated in self-consciousness. We may also recall at this point Schleiermacher's observation in his psychology of the fact that the consciousness of being an "I" always presupposes a "thou," since memory cannot reach back to the absolute origins of the individual; and, therefore, beyond the point at which memory falters, the individual is dependent on the descriptions of himself furnished by others.[47] To be sure, this experience does not mean that the I is derived from the thou, but the ability to say "I" is given through a thou or community of persons.[48] Schleiermacher scarcely brings these considerations to the fore, even in the introductory paragraphs of *The Christian Faith* that are "borrowed from ethics," but his brief allusions to the rise of the religious self-consciousness obviously involve these principles.[49]

[47] *Cf.* above, Ch. II, p. 116.
[48] SW III/6, *Psychologie,* pp. 14-20.
[49] *Cf.,* e.g., Gl., §6; §10, 2.

These principles manifest themselves visibly in Schleiermacher's debate with himself on the proper order of the exposition of classical Christian doctrines. To be conscious of oneself as a Christian is a form of consciousness that can scarcely be segregated from one's consciousness of having been created and posited in existence in a particular way. These are distinguishable phenomena of the inner world, but they co-inhere in the same organic unity of consciousness. But if this is the actual state of affairs, Schleiermacher seems to have asked himself, then what is the theological merit of treating the doctrine of creation, which corresponds to the feeling of being determined in such-and-such-a-way in such-and-such-a-world,[50] before the doctrine of redemption, which arises from that complex of phenomena of consciousness Schleiermacher described as the "antithesis of sin and grace"? In a word, what is the merit of presenting the doctrine of God the creator before the doctrine of God the re-creator, when it is the latter doctrine that expresses our fuller, more personal sense of identity and direction? An omnipotence that has set all things in motion but whose goal one does not know, or an omniscience whose care for the objects of its knowing remains enigmatic—these are empty and lifeless notions. But the case is entirely different, Schleiermacher declared, if we apprehend that omnipotence in and through our awareness of the new creation inaugurated by Jesus Christ, or if that otherwise enigmatic omniscience manifests itself to us as the "good-pleasure" of God, which is indeed good in our own experience.[51] An exposition that explicated this latter logic, Schleiermacher supposed, would have rendered much more clearly the connection of each doctrine of theology to the center of all Christian thinking: "And the Word was made flesh and dwelt among us."[52]

However, a number of reasons persuaded him to sacrifice the

[50] Gl., §4, 4 and §34.
[51] Send., p. 32 (608).
[52] Send., p. 34 (611).

advantages inherent in this last mentioned order for the more conventional scheme of creation and redemption in *The Christian Faith*. Quite candidly he admitted to a disinclination toward "anti-climax"; and a treatment of creation and preservation that followed the work of Christ would almost necessarily have been brief, Schleiermacher said. But, more importantly, he resisted any curtailment or other apparent diminution of the status of creation-faith, because of his fear that the prodigious growth of natural science, with its ever increasing prospect of becoming a queen science, would destroy all faith in God as creator, unless the doctrine were so restated as to show that it involved no conflict with such science.[53] Schleiermacher, of course, did not propose to build his theology of creation on the foundations of any materials taken from natural science. That kind of apologetical procedure, which has become so familiar more recently, is wholly foreign to his conception of theology, though he could no more entirely free his mind of the unconscious influence of current natural science than can any man. Nevertheless, his restatement intends to be a restatement of the original import of the creation-faith of the Christian church and as such seeks to formulate principles that are prior to any and every specific procedure in the natural sciences and that can be considered as conflicting only with alien theologies but not with the immediate premises and results of research. Schleiermacher believed that unless such a task were undertaken, the alternative would be retreat into a biblical literalism that is inimical to natural science and dangerously isolated from contemporary culture. "Shall the knots of history come asunder in this way:" he asked, "Christianity with barbarism and science with unbelief?"[54]

An additional discouragement to the reversal of the usual order of the exposition of creation and redemption arose out of Schleiermacher's foreseeing in such a procedure the possibility of

[53] Send., pp. 36f. (612ff.).

[54] Send., p. 37 (614).

fostering a resemblance in his theology to the speculative, gnostic kind of Christianity that he so despised. Placing Christ and his work of redemption before the doctrine of God the creator would give to the book an esoteric cast and perhaps raise the suspicion that *The Christian Faith* might be an ecclesiastically disguised piece of idealistic philosophy, which, as D. F. Strauss later expressed it, sees in Jesus Christ not one who is the saviour of mankind but rather an individual who is significant only insofar as he is the occasion for others to grasp the eternal ideas that man and God are one, that divinity is the truth of humanity, and humanity the actuality of the divine nature.[55] With a little of the irony that his wit easily commanded, Schleiermacher confessed to Lücke that he willingly gave up the chance to appear as one of the privileged few who possessed the "precious jewel" of the "idea" of God and man and who enjoyed therefore a secure basis for their faith, in distinction from the thousands of ordinary Christians.[56] Consequently, Schleiermacher rejected the redemption-creation sequence, and returned to the traditional order. An additional positive advantage of this conventional procedure lay in the fact that by beginning his theology with the doctrine of creation he made the distinction between God and man his point of departure; and by refusing to penetrate behind the feeling of absolute dependence into the mysteries of God's "self-alienation" or God's yearning for an "other" or God's decision to duplicate outside of himself the "otherness" within himself, Schleiermacher avoided the pitfall of neo-gnosticism that has plagued theology from Hegel to Barth.

When, consequently, Schleiermacher wrote in §29 that he would present first the "facts of the [Christian] religious self-consciousness . . . as they are presupposed by the antithesis expressed in the concept of redemption, and secondly, as they are determined

[55] *Cf.* D. F. Strauss' remarks on the higher religion of the idealist in his *Life of Jesus,* "Concluding Dissertation."

[56] Send., pp. 38f. (615ff.).

by that antithesis," he used the word *presupposed* at the peril of misleading the reader from a right understanding of the genuinely new and instructive in *The Christian Faith's* account of the theological content of Christianity. The paragraphs that elucidate this proposition attempt to put up such a warning, but in actual fact the corresponding proposition of the first edition (§33) is still clearer as a statement of its author's mind. For obviously, the Schleiermacher who could entertain the deliberations we have mentioned above did not and could not have treated creation simply as presupposition of redemption, especially since he recognized that the creating power receives, in our minds, its character and its telos from redemption, and since he conducted himself throughout his inquiries as one who always respected the historical nature of the unity of the mind. But it is his actual treatment of the doctrine of creation that most directly corrects the misleading connotations of the word *presupposition*. For it is what another generation used to call the "evangelical" meaning of the creation-faith of the church that Schleiermacher consistently and exclusively emphasizes.

With the instrument we have called his "ecclesiastical" criticism, he cut away from the deposit of the church's long discussion of *creatio ex nihilo* every detail he judged superfluous, oftentimes in a fashion that still appears abrupt to present-day readers. Wherever a speculative rather than authentically religious motive seemed to have intruded with its contributions, Schleiermacher pruned and rooted out.[57] For example, he believed that creation, as a theological symbol, has nothing to do with the question concerning the difference between God's willing of himself and willing of the world or with conjectures about the possibility of the created order having been arranged otherwise than the actual system of existing beings.[58] In fact, much of the text in this part of *The Christian*

[57] *Cf.* the discussion above of the relation of theology and philosophy, Ch. III, pp. 169ff.

[58] Gl., §54.

Faith is devoted to the excision of puzzles, paradoxes and antinomies hallowed by tradition but rejected by Schleiermacher, not because they have no meaning at all but because they have no practical theological meaning.[59] The basic meaning of the creation-faith that Christian theology must express and clarify is simply affirmation that all being is in the hands of God and that there is no causality which is not in reality the vehicle of God's single wisdom-will. No temporal moment, be it one of pleasure or pain, be it one that enables or limits the self, is incapable of being the occasion for the steady presence of the consciousness of God. Hence Schleiermacher holds the brief statement of the old Roman symbol still to be the most adequate formula of such faith, and he cites it before all others: "I believe in God almighty."[60] The content therefore that theological reflection finds in the confession of God as creator is not replete with the ontological detail of a *Summa Theologica,* in which the universal and particular, actuality and potentiality, form and existence, are ranked in a hierarchy of being, but it is a content mirroring the absolutely sovereign activity of God as he is present in the Christian religious self-consciousness with its feelings of simple dependence and relative freedom and dependence in the world. "God," we remember Schleiermacher as saying, "means to us that . . . to which we attribute our being-in-such-and-such-a-way."[61] And the doctrine of creation is the delineation of the clarified and stabilized self-consciousness of the man who acknowledges that his own existence expresses an impenetrable, indecomposable, divinely willed concourse of being. Such faith and such a doctrine are born not out of the judgment that this is the best of all possible worlds (a vacuous judgment to Schleiermacher's mind)[62] but out

[59] However, this development is clearly anticipated by Calvin in the *Institutes.*

[60] Gl., §37.

[61] Gl., §4, 4.

[62] "Erwählung," p. 470.

of assent to the fiat that is immediately apprehended in the feeling of absolute dependence. Creation-faith is misconstrued, therefore, if it is interpreted as confidence in the *principle* of order. It is rather an attitude of resignation, assent and confidence in the *particular* order that converges on one's own being, specifies one's identity before God, and gives one a sense of being a part of the original plan of creation. As *The Christian Faith* expounds it, the doctrine of creation has a consistently personal bearing. This bearing appears with special clarity in Schleiermacher's dialectical reduction of the affirmations both of creation *ex nihilo* and of conservation of the world to the same primal fact of the religious consciousness: the consciousness of an undivided, simple personal dependence that reflects a divine activity which cannot be separated into discrete moments of origination and conservation of the creature but manifests itself as an indivisible causality. The identification of the producing and disposing powers of God as one power disallows the subordination of the part to the whole of creation, of the individual to the race. Thus the individual and particular are not mere vehicles through which the genus perpetuates itself. Instead, the doctrine of creation is interpreted to symbolize the confidence that each man and all men together are rooted equally directly in the divine vision of mankind.[63]

This "evangelical" exposition of the doctrine of creation revolves upon the principle that the presence of the power of God is more manifest in the sense of the interconnectedness of all finite beings than in the belief in so-called supernatural phenomena.[64] It emphasizes personal acceptance of the order of creation as a whole, and it rests directly on the confidence that the divine will for the whole order is also good for the individual. It identifies the exercise of the universal creating, ordering power of God with the kingdom of God. Creation-faith is for Schleiermacher nothing short of assent

[63] Gl., §54, 2.
[64] Gl., §46, §47 and §49.

to the present government of God. It is, moreover, confidence in and assent to the disposing power that has placed the individual person in existence in such-and-such-a-way in such-and-such-a-world.

Confidence and trust of this magnitude, however, do not lie within the resources of "adamic" human nature. Adam and his brothers can well conceive of omnipotence, but the ability to assent to this omnipotence and confide in it presupposes the appropriation of the mind of Christ. And this is the reason why Schleiermacher's doctrine of creation is Christo-morphic in its tenor. The impulse to express a doctrine of creation, in Christian faith, arises from faith in the creating and disposing God and from confidence in his good-pleasure. But this disposition, in turn, arises only in the religious self-consciousness that has been informed by the presence of Christ. Hence, the Christian doctrine of creation, as Schleiermacher understands it, is essentially an expression of a new attitude toward God as the one to whom we attribute our being-in-such-and-such-a-way, a new attitude crystallized in the God-consciousness of the redeemer and communicated to men through his life and preaching.

Schleiermacher did not go the length of maintaining that the *doctrine* of creation depends on the *doctrine* of Christ. To reason in that fashion would be to lapse into the rationalistic Christianity that Schleiermacher repudiated. But he did perceive that the religious consciousness expressed by the first article of the Apostles' Creed is a consciousness decisively molded by the redemption wrought by Jesus of Nazareth. All of the reservations that led him to hesitate in giving priority to the doctrine of creation in his exposition in *The Christian Faith* clearly attest to this. Consequently, he realized that the matter of the doctrine of creation does not stand in a simple external relation to the matter of the doctrine of the redeemer and redemption. Creation-faith is and is not the presupposition of the doctrine of redemption. It is the presupposition of redemption, because it is the feeling of being absolutely dependent, of having our being-in-such-and-such-a-way, that the redeemer reforms and informs. It is not the presupposition of redemption, because it is much more than that; genuine creation-faith is dependent on the redemption wrought by Christ, because the feeling of absolute dependence is fully formed only in and through the agency of Christ, the Spirit and the church. Hence, the conception of God as creator and governor is a conception that is more appropriately descriptive of a fully formed Christian religious consciousness than of a minimally developed religious consciousness. For the doctrine of creation is the religious expression of the person who has come, by virtue of the redeemer, to a full acknowledgment of and consent to the omnipotent power of God in himself and in the world. The work of the redeemer is to communicate his own consciousness of God steadfastly regnant both in time of pleasure and of pain. In appropriating this communication, the Christian is brought to his own true relation to God, to himself and to the world, and God's work of creating human nature is completed in the Christian by the work of Christ. Patently basing his reasoning on the association of ideas and images in I Corinthians 15:45-49, where Paul speaks of the first man, the natural man, the man of earth, and the second man or spiritual man, Schleiermacher declares that the real content signified by the title *redeemer* can be more properly rendered by the phrase, *the one who completes the creation of man.*[65] For just as the "appearance of the first man constituted at the same time the physical life of the human race; the appearance of the second Adam constituted for this nature a new spiritual life, which communicates and develops itself through spiritual fructification . . . and if the work of creation has only been completed through the second and equally original communication [of the Spirit] in the second Adam, yet both moments originate in one, undivided, eternal divine decree and form . . . one and the

[65] Gl., §89, 1.

same system of nature, even though it is one we cannot attain to ourselves."[66]

We may then say of Schleiermacher's theology that in it the doctrines of creation and redemption stand in a peculiar tension. Each possesses its own integrity; neither finds its justification entirely in the other. Each expresses a distinguishable content of the Christian religious consciousness. But inasmuch as everything in Christian faith "is related to the redemption accomplished by Jesus of Nazareth," the consciousness of creation is informed and reformed by the relation to Christ, and from the perspective of this relation to Christ the awareness of utter dependence is in itself incomplete apart from the life and presence of the second Adam. This is the sense in which the doctrine of creation is Christomorphic.

Schleiermacher himself, however, has summed up the matter in another way, by saying that even if creation and redemption appear in the Christian consciousness as equally original works, nevertheless "both moments originate in one divine decree." We must, consequently, turn finally to his doctrine of election and predestination for a better understanding of his theological thinking. It is in this doctrine, he writes, that we have "faith speaking about what is fundamental to the conception of history and to true self-scrutiny."[67]

§5 GOD'S GOOD-PLEASURE

The doctrine of the eternal decree that elects men in and through Jesus Christ is the most encompassing single statement of the principle of the interconnection of the doctrinal contents of *The Christian Faith*. The twin biblical ideas of decree and election are present in a virtual way from the very start of the doctrinal

[66] Gl., §94, 3. Slightly changed from the E.T.
[67] Gl., §120, 2.

body of the work (§33). They emerge onto the surface at the point where Schleiermacher turns to the person and work of Christ (§86, §87) and from that juncture onward become increasingly clear in the importance they possess for the whole theology of *The Christian Faith*, until the movement of thought they symbolize culminates in §116 - §120.

The virtual though unexpressed presence of the idea of the electing decree of God is indicated, in the paragraphs dealing with the created order, by such characteristics of Schleiermacher's thinking as his refusal to allow either the distinction between the operating and coöperating wills of God or any other kind of differentiation within the divine causality.[68] This insistence upon the unity of God's will has many consequences. So far as the question of the origin of evil is concerned, God cannot be associated with what appears to be evil in a manner unlike his association with that which seems good.[69] But of more importance for the matter at hand is the fact this position means that any and all speculation concerning the possibility of the self existing in some other world than the actual world impinging on its consciousness is idle and vain.[70] The inseparability of the self in its particular *Sosein* from the actual world is a corollary of the fundamental assurance of faith that the individual is as firmly rooted in the will of God as is the entire order of being, even though the finite mind is not capable of grasping the whole of being in any kind of intellectual intuition or synthetic judgment. To postulate such divisibility between the self and its world would introduce an unjustifiable speculative element

[68] Gl., §48, especially 3. *Cf.* also "Erwählung," pp. 440ff. "Therefore I can do nothing else but praise Calvin, because he would not permit the distinction between the divine predestination and divine permission, so generally heard in the language of common life and edification, to obtain in the realm of more scientific doctrine" (p. 447).

[69] This disallowal of all differentiation within the divine will entails the consequence that evil must be regarded as a defect of being, as a "partial non-ens." Gl., §48, 3.

[70] Gl., §54, 2.

into the religious consciousness and its undivided feeling of absolute dependence.[71]

In connection with the appearance, the status or dignity, and the work of the redeemer, the architectonic function of the doctrine of election becomes explicit in such declarations as that Jesus Christ is the redeemer to the extent that he is the one in whom the completion of the creating work of God is communicated, and, again, that to "believe that Jesus is the Christ, and to believe that the kingdom of God (that is the new corporate life which was to be created by God) had come, [are] the same thing,"[72] for that of which the Christian is conscious in a paramount fashion when he confronts Christ is the fact that all that he has suffered as the misery of sin was foreordained in relation to Christ and all that Christ brings into human life appears as the inauguration of the perfected order of life for which adamic humanity yearned.

And, finally, in unfolding the contents of the doctrine of election itself, in §120, Schleiermacher explains: "Christ therefore was determined as He was, only because, and in so far as, everything as a whole was determined in a certain way; and conversely, everything as a whole was only so determined, because, and in so far as, Christ was determined in a certain way. To say this is obviously to take our stand upon the divine good-pleasure, and to say that the determination in both cases is what it is simply through the divine good-pleasure."[73] "Indeed," Schleiermacher adds, "faith in Christ is itself nothing else than sharing in this divine good-pleasure which abides on Christ and the salvation grounded in him."[74]

These quotations and references show well enough that the doctrine of the divine election of each man according to the ir-

[71] One consequence of this position is the statement that prayer and answer to prayer take place solely according to the "original divine plan" for the created order. Gl., §47, 1.

[72] Gl., §87, 3.

[73] Gl., §120, 3.

[74] *Ibid.*

reducible, impenetrable good-pleasure of God is an intrinsic and basic element in the conceptual articulation and expression of the contents of the God-consciousness that is mediated and nurtured by Jesus Christ, according to the theology of *The Christian Faith*. And there are many other instances that could just as easily be adduced to strengthen or repeat the same point, but the intention of the analysis here being carried out only requires us to pay particular attention to the fact that the doctrine of election is not, as it were, an independent and possibly otiose fragment of the classical Christian theological tradition barely surviving in Schleiermacher's thinking. On the contrary, the doctrines of election, eternal divine decree and predestination are inexpugnably and pervasively present and active in the whole of the Christian view of man before God and in the world set forth in *The Christian Faith*. For support of this judgment, we may recall Edward's speech, the last of the three homilies on the meaning of Christmas in *The Christmas Eve*, in which Schleiermacher declares through Edward's voice that Christ is the presupposition of the celebrants' understanding of man, that in respect to Christ "everything before him was intimation, was related to him, and was good and divine only on account of him," so that in Christ the Christmas eve participants rejoice over that which preceded him, over the new humanity that belongs to them collectively on account of him, and over all the persons who are yet to be born into the church that is on its way to becoming inclusive of the whole world.[75] This speech by Edward representing the Schleiermacher of 1805 who had just entered upon his career of teaching theology suggests the relatively early crystallizing of his theological persuasion around the Augustinian, Calvinistic tenets of divine predestination and election. But of even more importance for the interpretation of his mature convictions is the major article of the year 1819, published just before the first edition of *The Christian Faith*, entitled "Concerning the Doctrine of Election,

[75] *Cf.* above, Ch. I, §5, p. 66.

with special reference to aphorisms of Dr. Bretschneider,"[76] in which Schleiermacher begins by confessing that ever since he had occupied himself with theology he had been astonished over the objections brought against the foremost exponents of the doctrine of election, Augustine and Calvin, to the effect that the espousal of divine election contradicted both the clear witness of Scriptures and sound reason.[77] The doctrine of election, Schleiermacher states, is not only the conviction defended by men whose perspicacity in theological matters has never been surpassed by their critics; it is also, as Calvin explicitly declares, a doctrine of the Scripture-reading church, and it is as little speculative in its nature as are the doctrines of the justice and the almightiness of God.[78] Indeed, the doctrine of election is so intimately connected with the biblical and Christian evangelical arché of all believing in, trusting in and thinking about God as the creator, preserver, redeemer and perfecter of the creature, that to discard it or reject it as either unbiblical or speculative is to open the way to the weakening of the doctrines of sin and the absolute prevenience of the grace of God. And in *The Christian Faith* Schleiermacher firmly designates such Pelagianism as one of the limiting heresies into which theological thinking cannot stray without sacrificing its specifically Christian character.[79] Wherever faith in God begins to stir in the human heart, wherever and whenever an access of the Spirit of God is apprehended, the individual who is the subject of such experience must acknowledge that there and then God has taken the initiative and God alone is at work. If, Schleiermacher reasons, one clings to the supposition that the stirrings of faith in the soul are prepared for by the "natural moral feelings" of humanity, one must still ask whether these seemingly natural moral feelings, which are inter-

[76] "Ueber die Lehre von der Erwählung, besonders in Beziehung auf Herrn Dr. Bretschnieders Aphorismen," SW I/2, pp. 393-484.

[77] *Ibid.*, p. 395.

[78] *Ibid.*, p. 422.

[79] Gl., §22. *Cf.* also "Erwählung," pp. 449f.

preted as the first manifestations of love to God and which may be mediated to us through the common mind and culture of the society and generation in which we live, are not in fact stirrings brought forth by the Spirit which "bloweth where it listeth." Schleiermacher himself fully subscribes to the dictum of Calvin that the spiritual does not exist in human nature and that faith does not arise, except through regeneration.[80] Whoever wonders, therefore, why faith has taken root in himself at this particular time rather than at another, or why this man and not that man has been moved by the Spirit in a fashion he is not able to resist, can finally appeal only to the gracious electing activity of God (*Gnadenwahl*).[81]

Despite his ardent defense of Augustine and Calvin as fully biblical thinkers in their espousal of the predestinating decree of God, Schleiermacher was aware of the fact that election, taken by itself, could easily appear as a doctrine exemplifying independent speculation concerning the Godhead. He took particular care therefore to dispel such a misinterpretation both of the doctrine as it had been articulated by these masters of the classical tradition and of the genesis of the doctrine in his own conception of theology. The idea of a divine decree is not, Schleiermacher admitted, a direct expression of the Christian religious or immediate self-consciousness. Apparently he regarded it as one of those terms and concepts that Christian thought borrows from the language of other provinces of the human spirit, in this case that of politics, and appropriates to its own uses. But granted the fact that a doctrinal "proposition indicative of a divine decree is not as such an expression of the immediate self-consciousness," nevertheless the term and concept can be used to designate the content of the Christian religious self-consciousness, provided this content first of all rightly

[80] *Cf.* "Erwählung," the footnote on p. 407 citing Calvin's *Institutes*, Bk. II, ch. 3, 1: "Nihil autem habemus spiritus nisi per regenerationem."

[81] *Cf. ibid.*, p. 402 for the term *Gnadenwahl*. It has become the cardinal rubric in Karl Barth's *Church Dogmatics* (*cf.* Vol. II, part 2).

reflects that which has been brought into the world through redemption.[82] The reader may interpret fairly Schleiermacher's intention here, if he regards the ideas of decree and election as more or less pictorial representations, as theological ideograms or psychograms, as it were, of the stabilized condition of the self-consciousness of the man whose relationships to God, to the world and to himself have been informed by and conformed to the figure of Jesus Christ.

To be sure, such an interpretation presupposes that the doctrine of election stands in the closest possible connection with the redeemer himself. And this, indeed, is the precise connection that Schleiermacher sought not so much to establish but to elucidate as the very structure of the Christian religious self-consciousness. In addition to what we have already noted about the manner in which the doctrine of election becomes openly influential in *The Christian Faith* where the person and work of Christ occupy the center of attention, there is the further significant statement by Schleiermacher, made in his lectures on the life of Jesus, that trust in the good-pleasure of God belongs to the very core of Jesus' teaching about God and about his own person and office. This pivotal teaching concerning the good-pleasure of God is not exemplified in the well-known saying about the sun God causes to shine upon the fields of the righteous and unrighteous alike (Matthew 5:45) but in Jesus' utterance about *himself*, that those who come to him are given him by the Father (John 6:37, 44). In such teaching we have the seed of the doctrine of predestination developed later by Paul, by Peter and by the *Letter to the Hebrews*.[83] Hence, Schleiermacher looks upon the good-pleasure of God as an expression of faith that is intrinsic both to Jesus' understanding of his own relationship to God and to his teaching about his work and relation to others. He views the doctrine of election as an articula-

[82] Gl., §90, 2.

[83] Leben Jesu, pp. 295ff.(S). Note the Christo-centrism here.

tion of faith arising naturally in the apostles' reflections on their relationship to Christ. It is the doctrinal affirmation of faith apprehending that the self, by no merit of its own but solely by the ordination of the creating and redeeming God, shares in the divine good-pleasure that rests upon Jesus of Nazareth. It is the ultimate theological statement of the evangelical principle of justification by grace alone through faith.

It is not surprising therefore that Schleiermacher cites with approval the famous admonition of Calvin that the elect of God do not have the certitude of their election either in themselves or in God imagined apart from the Son, but "Christ is the mirror in which we contemplated our election."[84] In Schleiermacher's language this sentiment of Calvin's is translated to say that in Christ we behold the good-pleasure of God, and in our experience of the grace of God mediated to us through the preaching of Christ we recognize our share in that good-pleasure. From the religious point of view, or, more precisely, from the point of view that takes man as a religious being seriously, this is the circumstance in which genuine human freedom fully appears; and since freedom is the mark and even the condition of personhood, it is also the circumstance in which the individual is crowned with true personal existence.[85] Outside of faith the will of God wears the aspect of arbitrary tyranny, and the fact that an individual self is what it is seems to be grounded in a wholly capricious divine activity. The tradition shaped chiefly by Augustine and formulated again by Calvin describes the individual to whom the will of God is only arbitrary and irrational as the fallen man who is not able to love God. Therefore only insofar as sin is being decisively overcome in the self by the new life and inner order communicated to the sinner by God through Christ, is the self enabled to affirm the will of God as the good-pleasure of God, enabled to love God, and

[84] "Erwählung," p. 422, 2nd note.
[85] *Ibid.*, p. 456.

thereby endowed with freedom and the full measure of humanity. In this latter circumstance, to ask why the self is what it is, is to ask not about the capriciousness of God but about his good-pleasure that has communicated the Spirit through the preaching of his Word and opened the ear of the self to hear. Accordingly, Schleiermacher describes the sinful man, the man in whose self-consciousness grace and sin do not yet form an antithesis, as less than fully a person, while that man is fully a person who has been reborn through the grace whose source is Christ.[86] He is free; he possesses a God-consciousness that by the virtue of the divine life in Christ is becoming regnant in his total self-consciousness.

We cannot say that eternal divine election denotes in Schleiermacher's total theology a simple theorem. It does not have respect simply to the doctrine of God, and least of all is it a proposition concerning the being of God in himself or concerning distinctions internal to the Godhead, for God is known only in relation to the creature. Nor does the doctrine pertain simply to the individual and rest upon inner psychological experiences of happiness or well-being in the sensible self-consciousness. Neither does it have an exclusively christological reference, although the faith that reposes its confidence in the decree or good-pleasure of God derives from Christ. The doctrine of election is rather a theological formula that provides a summary statement of the complex situation of the self in its determining and defining relations to God, to the world and the families and societies of man, and to itself as these relations are simultaneously ordered anew, clarified, and interpreted by Jesus of Nazareth. Without it the corpus of Christian theology remains partially inchoate and open to the influences of Pelagianism, on the one hand, and of Manicheanism, on the other. For where everything that is and occurs is not ascribed to the all-encompassing wisdom-will of God, the temptation is ever present to conceive of man as less than utterly dependent on God and as possessing a

[86] *Ibid.*, pp. 458f.

measure of autonomy over against the prevenience of the grace of God, or to conceive of the order of being as partly determined by a Satanic power or other force alien to the dominion of God. But with the aid of the doctrine of election Christian faith is able to express the confidence that, more than any other element, distinguishes it from other kinds of faith—the confidence that history and the self belong to the good, not the good evolved by the immanent law of history itself but the good of the divine good-pleasure.

The criticism of *The Christian Faith,* that charges Schleiermacher with presenting in his magnum opus an evolutionary view of history and a redeemer who is only the highest product of that evolution, falls short of its mark, because it does not reckon with Schleiermacher's use of the Christian doctrine of election and the confidence in the divine good-pleasure that the doctrine expresses. The good-pleasure of God is a way of characterizing the love of God for that which he has created and preserves; it is not the judgment of history on what history has produced.

Moreover it guards against the misunderstanding of God's love as being directed upon individuals in isolation from the order of being in general. For Schleiermacher, that which stands highest in the order of created being and nearest, therefore, to God is the spiritual life in man that embodies a stable and regnant consciousness of God in any and every pleasure- and pain-filled moment of time. But such spiritual life is precisely the life that apprehends *God's* good-pleasure and embraces its own ordained share in it. This fully-conscious spiritual life is the new order, the kingdom of God, that Jesus Christ and the preaching of Christ bring into existence.

Schleiermacher's use of the biblical notion of the divine good-pleasure and his statement of the doctrine of election carry his theological thinking to its highest reach. Here the relations of religion, Christ and theology are shown in his thought in their simplest and most profound form. The good-pleasure of God is, first of all, an especially apt phrase for Schleiermacher's theology, because it conveys the fact that the stuff with which the theologian is dealing, even the Christian theologian, is human religion. The paramount role that the divine good-pleasure plays here, as the substance of the doctrine of election, reminds us that theology is the daughter of religion. God does not work on men to impart doctrines to them. He works on men to give them a new mind, a new life.

In the second place, the content for which good-pleasure stands is obviously an affective content. It signifies the Christian religious self-consciousness that does not fear the power of sin and inner confusion but feels itself graciously enabled to enjoy the consciousness of absolute dependence on God. But, as the phrase itself indicates, this blessedness that good-pleasure signifies is an affection that points beyond itself; the pleasure in which the Christian man finds his true existence and freedom is not a pleasure that wells up from his own being; his blessedness is, rather, a reflection of the good-pleasure that is first and last the good-pleasure of God. This participation in the divine good-pleasure is the mode in which the Christian appropriates his appointed place and time in God's government of history.

Yet, this good-pleasure of God is also the gift of Christ. It is, like everything else in Christian faith, related to the redemption wrought by Jesus of Nazareth. But, in an especial way, it, more than any other element in the Christian religious self-consciousness, symbolizes the presence of Christ, for God's good-pleasure arises in the Christian man through the agency of the quickening Word. The sense of absolute dependence upon a "whence" and the feeling of being determined in part by a world of objects and persons are not the work of Christ. The work of Christ consists of bringing these relations to God and to the world into their proper order and harmony, the order and harmony decreed for each by God. The work of Christ is to give the shape of his own spiritual life to others, to cause them to come of age, as it were, and make them brothers of the last Adam as they had been brothers of the first. Hence, the divine good-pleasure testifies not only to the humble religious condition of our humanity; it testifies as well to the absolute sovereignty of God and to the unceasing informing and reforming presence of Christ—in Scriptures, in preaching and the Spirit, and in the kingdom of God in the world.

INDEX

INDEX